Todd Lammle's CCNA® IOS® Command Survival Guide

Todd Lammle

Wiley Publishing, Inc.

Acquisitions Editor: Jeff Kellum
Development Editor: Lisa Thibault
Technical Editor: Patrick J. Conlan
Production Editor: Eric Charbonneau
Copy Editor: Kim Wimpsett
Production Manager: Tim Tate
Vice President and Executive Group Publisher: Richard Swadley
Vice President and Executive Publisher: Joseph B. Wikert
Vice President and Publisher: Neil Edde
Compositor: Craig Johnson, Happenstance Type-O-Rama
Proofreader: Amy McCarthy
Indexer: Ted Laux
Anniversary Logo Design: Richard Pacifico
Cover Designer: Ryan Sneed

Published by Wiley Publishing, Inc., Indianapolis, Indiana

Published simultaneously in Canada

ISBN: 978-0-4701-7560-6

For general information on our other products and services or to obtain technical support, please contact our Customer Care Department within the U.S. at (800) 762-2974, outside the U.S. at (317) 572-3993 or fax (317) 572-4002.

Wiley also publishes its books in a variety of electronic formats. Some content that appears in print may not be available in electronic books.

Library of Congress Cataloging-in-Publication Data is available from the publisher.

10 9 8 7 6 5 4 3

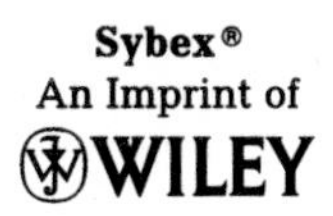

Dear Reader

Thank you for choosing *Todd Lammle's CCNA IOS Command Survival Guide*. This book is part of a family of premium quality Sybex books, all written by outstanding authors who combine practical experience with a gift for teaching.

Sybex was founded in 1976. More than thirty years later, we're still committed to producing consistently exceptional books. With each of our titles we're working hard to set a new standard for the industry. From the paper we print on, to the authors we work with, our goal is to bring you the best books available.

I hope you see all that reflected in these pages. I'd be very interested to hear your comments and get your feedback on how we're doing. Feel free to let me know what you think about this or any other Sybex book by sending me an email at `nedde@wiley.com`, or if you think you've found a technical error in this book, please visit `http://sybex.custhelp.com`. Customer feedback is critical to our efforts at Sybex.

Best regards,

Neil Edde
Vice President and Publisher
Sybex, an Imprint of Wiley

Acknowledgments

Kudos to Jeff Kellum for coming up with the idea for this book. This was one of my favorite books I have written.

Thanks to Lisa Thibault for her patience and gentle but effective direction and also thanks to Eric Charbonneau for helping me organize and keep my thoughts going in one direction—which is no easy task! Also, thanks to Pat Conlan for his technical expertise. Finally, thanks to copy editor Kim Wimpsett, proofreader Amy McCarthy, and compositor Craig Johnson; all of who helped to create this fantastic title.

About the Author

Todd Lammle, CCSI, CCNA/CCNP/CCSP, MCSE, CEH/CHFI, FCC RF Licensed, is the authority on Cisco Certification internetworking. He is a world renowned author, speaker, trainer and consultant. Todd has over 25 years of experience working with LAN's, WAN's and large licensed and unlicensed Wireless networks. He is president of GlobalNet Training and Consulting, Inc., a network integration and training firm based in Dallas. You can reach Todd through his forum at `www.lammle.com`.

Contents at a Glance

Contents

Introduction

I know it's kind of wrong to say this type of stuff about your own stuff, but I'm just going to do it—this is a really good book! It might even be the most interesting book I've written so far. A big reason for this is that its scope allowed me to go above and beyond covering the usual CCNA study guide material and really detail the commands I used in the guide, plus a lot of additional commands that just happen to be some of my personal favorites.

Do remember that, although very cool indeed, this volume isn't intended to be a one-stop shop for passing the CCNA exams. Think of it and use it as a supplement to other study material—like, well, my Sybex CCNA study guide! But seriously, I want you to know that this book will complement anything no matter what you have stashed in your personal arsenal to pass the exams—it's that good, and yes, I said it myself. By the way, know that lots of other people (who I didn't pay) think so too!

How to Use This Book

If you want a solid foundation for the serious and I hope successful goal of effectively preparing for the Cisco Certified Network Associate (CCNA) suite of exams—including the ICND1, ICND2, and the CCNA composite 640-802—then this is your baby! I've spent hundreds of hours putting together this book with the sole objective of helping you to pass the whole group of CCNA exams while actually learning learn how to configure Cisco routers, switches, and tons of other things too.

So, yes, this book is loaded with lots of valuable information, and you will get the most out of all that and your studying time if you understand how I put the book together.

To maximize your benefit from this book, I recommend the following study method:

1. My recommendation is to read the full Sybex *CCNA Study Guide Sixth Edition* and then just start reading this book from Chapter 1 and don't stop until your all the way through Chapter 12. This study method will really help you concentrate on the command needed to cover the many CCNA objectives.
2. Study each chapter carefully, making sure you fully understand the command covered in each chapter. Pay extra-close attention to any chapter that includes material covered you struggled with when reading the full study guide.
3. `Check out www.lammle.com` for more Cisco exam prep questions and updates to this book and other Cisco books I have written. The questions found at `www.lammle.com` will be updated at least monthly, if not weekly or even daily! Before you take your test, be sure and visit my website for questions, videos, audios, and other useful information.
4. Make sure you download any new PDF files found at `www.lammle.com` or `www.sybex.com/go/IOS` so you have the latest technical information covered by the latest CCNA objectives.

To learn every bit of the material covered in this book, you'll have to apply yourself regularly and with discipline. Try to set aside the same time period every day to study, and select a comfortable and quiet place to do so. If you work hard, you will be surprised at how quickly you learn this material.

What Does This Book Cover?

This book covers everything you need to know in order to understand the CCNA exam objective commands. However, taking the time to study and practice with routers or a router simulator is the real key to success.

You will learn the following information in this book:

- Chapter 1 introduces you to the Cisco Internetwork Operating System (IOS) and command-line interface (CLI). In this chapter you will learn how to turn on a router and configure the basics of the IOS, including setting passwords, banners, and more. IP configuration using the Secure Device Manager (SDM) will be discussed in Chapter 12.
- Chapter 2 provides you with the management skills needed to run a Cisco IOS network. Backing up and restoring the IOS, as well as router configuration, are covered, as are the troubleshooting command tools necessary to keep a network up and running. Chapter 12 will provide you the SDM configuration covered in this chapter.
- Chapter 3 teaches you about IP routing. This is an important chapter, because you will learn how to build a network, add IP addresses, and route data between routers. You will also learn about static, default, and dynamic routing using RIP and RIPv2 (with a small touch of IGRP).
- Chapter 4 dives into more complex dynamic routing with Enhanced IGRP and OSPF routing.
- Chapter 5 gives you a background on layer-2 switching and how switches perform address learning and make forwarding and filtering decisions. Network loops and how to avoid them with the Spanning Tree Protocol (STP) will be discussed, as well as the 802.1w STP version.
- Chapter 6 covers virtual LANs and how you can use them in your internetwork. This chapter also covers the nitty-gritty of VLANs and the different concepts and protocols used with VLANs, as well as troubleshooting.
- Chapter 7 covers security and access lists, which are created on routers to filter the network. IP standard, extended, and named access lists are covered in detail.
- Chapter 8 covers Network Address Translation (NAT). New information and all the configuration commands, troubleshooting, and verification commands needed to understand the NAT CCNA objectives are covered in this chapter.
- Chapter 9 covers wireless technologies. This is an introductory chapter regarding wireless technologies as Cisco views wireless. Make sure you understand your basic wireless technologies such as access points and clients as well as the difference between 802.11a, b, and g. This chapter is more technology based than configuration based to cover the current CCNA objectives.

- Chapter 10 covers IPv6. This is a very fun chapter and has some great information. IPv6 is not the big, bad scary monster that most people think it is. IPv6 is an objective on this new exam, so study this chapter carefully. This chapter is more technology based then configuration based to cover the current CCNA objectives. Keep an eye out at `www.lammle.com` for up-to-the-minute updates.
- Chapter 11 concentrates on Cisco wide area network (WAN) protocols. This chapter covers HDLC, PPP, and Frame Relay in depth. You must be proficient in all these protocols to be successful on the CCNA exam.
- Chapter 12 covers SDM for basic router configures that we covered in Chapters 1, 2, 3, and 4.

For up-to-the minute updates covering additions or modifications to the CCNA certification exams, as well as additional study tools and review questions, be sure to visit the Todd Lammle forum and website at `www.lammle.com` or `www.sybex.com/go/ccnafastpass`.

Cisco Certified Network Associate (CCNA)

The CCNA certification was the first in the new line of Cisco certifications and was the precursor to all current Cisco certifications. Now you can become a Cisco Certified Network Associate for the meager cost of this book and either one test at $150 or two tests at $125 each—although the CCNA exams are extremely hard and cover a lot of material, so you have to really know your stuff! Taking a Cisco class or spending months with hands-on experience is not out of the norm.

Once you have your CCNA, you don't have to stop there—you can choose to continue with your studies and achieve a higher certification, called the Cisco Certified Network Professional (CCNP). Someone with a CCNP has all the skills and knowledge he or she needs to attempt the routing and switching CCIE lab. Just becoming a CCNA can land you that job you've dreamed about.

Why Become a CCNA?

Cisco, not unlike Microsoft and Novell (Linux), has created the certification process to give administrators a set of skills and to equip prospective employers with a way to measure skills or match certain criteria. Becoming a CCNA can be the initial step of a successful journey toward a new, highly rewarding, sustainable career.

The CCNA program was created to provide a solid introduction not only to the Cisco Internetwork Operating System (IOS) and Cisco hardware but also to internetworking in general, making it helpful to you in areas that are not exclusively Cisco's. At this point in the certification process, it's not unrealistic that network managers—even those without Cisco equipment—require Cisco certifications for their job applicants.

If you make it through the CCNA and are still interested in Cisco and internetworking, you're headed down a path to certain success.

What Skills Do You Need to Become a CCNA?

To meet the CCNA certification skill level, you must be able to understand or do the following:

- A CCNA certified professional can install, configure, and operate LAN, WAN, and wireless access services securely, as well as troubleshoot and configure small to medium networks (500 nodes or fewer) for performance.
- This knowledge includes, but is not limited to, use of these protocols: IP, IPv6, EIGRP, RIP, RIPv2, OSPF, serial connections, Frame Relay, cable, DSL, PPPoE, LAN switching, VLANs, Ethernet, security, and access lists.

How Do You Become a CCNA?

The way to become a CCNA is to pass one little test (CCNA Composite exam 640-802). Then—poof!—you're a CCNA. (Don't you wish it were that easy?) True, it can be just one test, but you still have to possess enough knowledge to understand what the test writers are saying.

However, Cisco has a two-step process that you can take in order to become a CCNA that may or may not be easier than taking one longer exam (this book is based on the one-step 640-802 method; however, this book has all the information you need to pass all three exams.

The two-step method involves passing the following:

- Exam 640-822: Interconnecting Cisco Networking Devices 1(ICND1)
- Exam 640-816: Introduction to Cisco Networking Devices 2 (ICND2)

I can't stress this enough: It's critical that you have some hands-on experience with Cisco routers. If you can get ahold of some 1841 or 2800 series routers, you're set. But if you can't, I've worked hard to provide hundreds of configuration examples throughout this book to help network administrators (or people who want to become network administrators) learn what they need to know to pass the CCNA exam.

Since the new 640-802 exam is so hard, Cisco wants to reward you for taking the two-test approach. Or so it seems anyway. If you take the ICND1 exam, you actually receive a certification called the Cisco Certified Entry Networking Technician (CCENT). This is one step toward your CCNA. To achieve your CCNA, you must still pass your ICND2 exam.

Again, this book is written to help you study for all three exams.

For Cisco-authorized hands-on training with CCSI Todd Lammle, please see www.globalnettraining.com. Each student will get hands-on experience by configuring at least three routers and two switches—no sharing of equipment!

Where Do You Take the Exams?

You may take any of the CCNA exams at any of the Pearson VUE authorized centers (`www.vue.com`) or call (877) 404-EXAM (3926).

To register for a Cisco Certified Network Associate exam, follow these steps:

1. Determine the number of the exam you want to take.
2. Register with the nearest Pearson VUE testing center. At this point, you will be asked to pay in advance for the exam. At the time of this writing, the exam for the 640-802 is $150 and must be taken within one year of payment. You can schedule exams up to six weeks in advance or as late as the same day you want to take it—but if you fail a Cisco exam, you must wait five days before you will be allowed to retake the exam. If something comes up and you need to cancel or reschedule your exam appointment, contact Pearson VUE at least 24 hours in advance.
3. When you schedule the exam, you'll get instructions regarding all appointment and cancellation procedures, the ID requirements, and information about the testing-center location.

Tips for Taking Your CCNA Exams

The CCNA Composite exam test contains about 55 questions and must be completed in 75 to 90 minutes or less. This information can change per exam. You must get a score of about 80 to 85 percent to pass this exam, but again, each exam can be different.

Many questions on the exam have answer choices that at first glance look identical—especially the syntax questions! Remember to read through the choices carefully because close doesn't cut it. If you get commands in the wrong order or forget one measly character, you'll get the question wrong. So, to practice, do the hands-on exercises at the end of this book's chapters over and over again until they feel natural to you.

Also, never forget that the right answer is the Cisco answer. In many cases, more than one appropriate answer is presented, but the *correct* answer is the one that Cisco recommends. On the exam, you're always instructed to pick one, two, or three, never "choose all that apply." The latest CCNA exams may include the following test formats:

- Multiple-choice single answer
- Multiple-choice multiple answer
- Drag-and-drop
- Fill-in-the-blank
- Router simulations

In addition to multiple choice and fill-in response questions, Cisco Career Certifications exams may include performance simulation exam items. They do allow partial command responses. For example, `show config`, `sho config`, or `sh conf` would be acceptable. `Router#show ip protocol` or `router#show ip prot` would be acceptable.

Here are some general tips for exam success:

- Arrive early at the exam center so you can relax and review your study materials.
- Read the questions *carefully*. Don't jump to conclusions. Make sure you're clear about *exactly* what each question asks.
- When answering multiple-choice questions that you're not sure about, use the process of elimination to get rid of the obviously incorrect answers first. Doing this greatly improves your odds if you need to make an educated guess.
- You can no longer move forward and backward through the Cisco exams, so double-check your answer before clicking Next since you can't change your mind.

After you complete an exam, you'll get immediate, online notification of your pass or fail status, a printed Examination Score Report that indicates your pass or fail status, and your exam results by section. (The test administrator will give you the printed score report.) Test scores are automatically forwarded to Cisco within five working days after you take the test, so you don't need to send your score to them. If you pass the exam, you'll receive confirmation from Cisco, typically within two to four weeks, sometimes longer.

This book covers everything CCNA related. For up-to-date information on Todd Lammle Cisco Authorized CCNA CCNP, CCSP, CCVP, and CCIE boot camps, please see `www.lammle.com` or `www.globalnettraining.com`.

How to Contact the Author

You can reach Todd Lammle through GlobalNet Training Solutions, Inc., (`www.globalnettraining.com`), his training and systems Integration Company in Dallas, Texas—or through his forum at `www.lammle.com`.

Chapter 1

Basic IOS Commands

This book starts by introducing you to the Cisco Internetwork Operating System (IOS). The IOS is what runs Cisco routers as well as some Cisco switches, and it's what allows you to configure the devices. You use the command-line interface (CLI) to configure a router, and that is what I'll show you in this chapter.

The Cisco router IOS software is responsible for the following important tasks:

- Carrying network protocols and functions
- Connecting high-speed traffic between devices
- Adding security to control access and stop unauthorized network use
- Providing scalability for ease of network growth and redundancy
- Supplying network reliability for connecting to network resources

You can access the Cisco IOS through the console port of a router, from a modem into the auxiliary (or aux) port, or even through Telnet and Secure Shell (SSH). Access to the IOS command line is called an *exec session.*

Once you have attached your console cable (this is a rolled cable, sometimes referred to as a *rollover cable*) to the router and have started your terminal software, you will be ready to power on the router. Assuming that this is a new router, it will have no configuration and thus will need to have, well, everything set up. In this chapter, first I'll cover the power-on process of the router, and then I'll introduce the setup script.

For up-to-the minute updates for this chapter, please see `www.lammle.com`

Booting the Router

The following messages appear when you first boot or reload a router:

```
System Bootstrap, Version 12.4(13r)T, RELEASE SOFTWARE (fc1)
Technical Support: http://www.cisco.com/techsupport
Copyright (c) 2006 by cisco Systems, Inc.
Initializing memory for ECC
c2811 platform with 262144 Kbytes of main memory
Main memory is configured to 64 bit mode with ECC enabled
Upgrade ROMMON initialized
```

```
program load complete, entry point: 0x8000f000, size: 0xcb80
program load complete, entry point: 0x8000f000, size: 0xcb80
program load complete, entry point: 0x8000f000, size: 0x14b45f8
Self decompressing the image :
   ########################################################################
   ############################################## [OK]
 [some output cut]

Cisco IOS Software, 2800 Software (C2800NM-ADVSECURITYK9-M), Version
   12.4(12), RELEASE SOFTWARE (fc1)
Technical Support: http://www.cisco.com/techsupport
Copyright (c) 1986-2006 by Cisco Systems, Inc.
Compiled Fri 17-Nov-06 12:02 by prod_rel_team
Image text-base: 0x40093160, data-base: 0x41AA0000

[some output cut]

Cisco 2811 (revision 49.46) with 249856K/12288K bytes of memory.
Processor board ID FTX1049A1AB
2 FastEthernet interfaces
4 Serial(sync/async) interfaces
1 Virtual Private Network (VPN) Module
DRAM configuration is 64 bits wide with parity enabled.
239K bytes of non-volatile configuration memory.
62720K bytes of ATA CompactFlash (Read/Write)
```

Notice the following in the previous messages:

- The type of router (2811) and the amount of memory (262,144KB)
- The version of software the router is running (12.4, 13)
- The interfaces on the router (two Fast Ethernet and four serial)

Figure 1.1 shows a picture of an 1841 router, which is what is called an *integrated services router* (ISR), just like the 2811 router output shown earlier.

FIGURE 1.1 A Cisco 1841 router

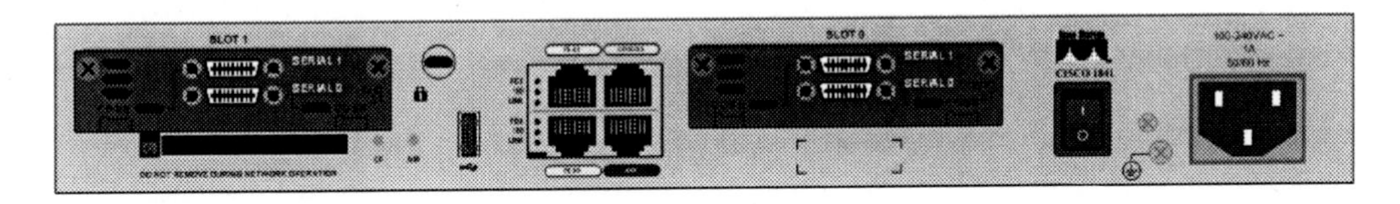

An 1841 router holds most of the same interfaces as a 2800 router, but it's smaller and less expensive.

Setup Mode

If the router has no initial configuration, you will be prompted to use setup mode to establish an initial configuration. You can also enter setup mode at any time from the command line by typing the command **setup** from something called *privileged mode*. Setup mode covers only some global commands and is generally just not helpful. Here is an example:

```
Would you like to enter the initial configuration dialog? [yes/no]: y

At any point you may enter a question mark '?' for help.
Use ctrl-c to abort configuration dialog at any prompt.
Default settings are in square brackets '[]'.

Basic management setup configures only enough connectivity
for management of the system, extended setup will ask you
to configure each interface on the system

Would you like to enter basic management setup? [yes/no]: y
Configuring global parameters:

  Enter host name [Router]:Ctrl+C
Configuration aborted, no changes made.
```

You can exit setup mode at any time by pressing Ctrl+C.

Router Configuration Modes

One key to navigating the CLI is to always be aware of which router configuration mode you are currently in (see Table 1.1). You can tell which configuration mode you are in by watching the CLI prompt.

TABLE 1.1 Router Configuration Modes

Mode	Definition	Example
User EXEC mode	Limited to basic monitoring commands	Router>
Privileged EXEC mode	Provides access to all other router commands	Router#

TABLE 1.1 Router Configuration Modes *(continued)*

Mode	Definition	Example
Global configuration mode	Commands that affect the entire system	`Router(config)#`
Specific configuration modes	Commands that affect interfaces, sub-interfaces, routing processes, or lines only	`Router(config-subif)#`

Once you understand the different modes, you will need to be able to move from one mode to another within the CLI. The commands in Table 1.2 allow you to navigate between the assorted CLI modes.

TABLE 1.2 Moving Between Modes

Command	Meaning
`Router>`**`enable`**	Changes from user EXEC to privileged EXEC mode
`Router#`**`disable`**	Changes to user EXEC from privileged EXEC mode
`Router#`**`config term`**	Changes to global configuration mode from privileged mode
`Router(config)#`**`exit`**	Exits from any configuration mode to privileged mode (Ctrl+Z is also commonly used)
`Router(config)#`**`interface <int>`**	Enters interface configuration mode from global configuration mode
`Router(config)#`**`interface <subint>`**	Enters subinterface configuration mode from global configuration mode
`Router(config)#`**`line <line>`**	Enters line configuration mode from global configuration mode
`Router(config)#`**`router eigrp 1`**	Enters router configuration mode from global configuration mode

Editing and Help Features

One difference between a good and a great CLI engineer is the ability to quickly edit the line being entered into the router. Great CLI engineers can quickly recall previously entered commands and modify them, which is often much quicker than reentering the entire command. Table 1.3 shows some of the editing commands most commonly used.

TABLE 1.3 CLI Editing Commands

Command	Meaning
Ctrl+P or Up arrow	Shows last command entered
Ctrl+N or Down arrow	Shows previous commands entered
`show history`	Shows last 10 commands entered by default
`show terminal`	Shows terminal configurations and history buffer size
`terminal history size`	Changes buffer size (the maximum is 256)
Ctrl+A	Moves your cursor to the beginning of the line
Ctrl+E	Moves your cursor to the end of the line
Esc+B	Moves back one word
Ctrl+B	Moves back one character
Ctrl+F	Moves forward one character
Esc+F	Moves forward one word
Ctrl+D	Deletes a single character
Backspace	Deletes a single character
Ctrl+R	Redisplays a line
Ctrl+U	Erases a line
Ctrl+W	Erases a word
Ctrl+Z	Ends configuration mode and returns to EXEC mode
Tab	Finishes typing a command for you

The CLI also provides extensive online help. Any great CLI engineer will have an excessively worn question-mark key on the keyboard! Table 1.4 shows some examples of using the online help.

TABLE 1.4 Online Help Commands

Command	Meaning
`Router#?`	Shows all available commands
`Router#c?`	Shows all available commands beginning with the letter *c*
`Router#clock ?`	Shows all available options for the `clock` command

Using the Question Mark

The only command is the question mark; however, it does make a difference where you use it. When entering complex IOS commands, it is common to use the question mark repeatedly while entering the command, as in the following example:

```
Router#clock ?
  read-calendar    Read the hardware calendar into the clock
  set              Set the time and date
  update-calendar  Update the hardware calendar from the clock
Router#clock set ?
  hh:mm:ss  Current Time
Router#clock set 11:15:11 ?
  <1-31>  Day of the month
  MONTH   Month of the year
Router#clock set 11:15:11 25 aug ?
  <1993-2035>  Year
Router#clock set 11:15:11 25 aug 2007 ?
  <cr>
Router#clock set 11:15:11 25 aug 2007
*Aug 25 11:15:11.000: %SYS-6-CLOCKUPDATE: System clock has been updated from
18:52:53 UTC Wed Feb 28 2007 to 11:15:11 UTC Sat Aug 25 2007, configured from
console by cisco on console.
```

Using the Pipe

The pipe (|) allows you to wade through all the configurations or other long outputs and get straight to your goods fast. Table 1.5 shows the pipe commands.

TABLE 1.5 Pipe Commands

Command	Meaning
Router#**sh running-config | ?**	Shows the options for the pipe command. These include the ability to begin, include, exclude, and so on.
Router#**sh run | begin interface**	Shows the running configuration, beginning at the interface configurations.
Router#**sh ip route | include 192.168.3.32**	Shows all entries in the IP routing table that include the IP address 192.168.3.32.

Here's an example of using the pipe command to view just interface information on a router:

```
Router#sh run | ?
  append    Append redirected output to URL (URLs supporting append operation
            only)
  begin     Begin with the line that matches
  exclude   Exclude lines that match
  include   Include lines that match
  redirect  Redirect output to URL
  section   Filter a section of output
  tee       Copy output to URL
!
Router#sh run | begin interface
interface FastEthernet0/0
 description Sales VLAN
 ip address 10.10.10.1 255.255.255.248
 duplex auto
 speed auto
!
```

Configuring a Router

In the following sections, I'll introduce the commands used to do basic router configuration. You'll use these commands (or should use them) on every router you configure.

Hostnames

You can set the identity of the router with the `hostname` command. This is only locally significant, which means it has no bearing on how the router performs name lookups or how the router works on the internetwork. Table 1.6 shows the command for setting a router's hostname.

TABLE 1.6 Setting a Router Hostname

Command	Meaning
Router(config)#**hostname** *name*	Sets the hostname of this router

Here's an example of setting a hostname on a router:

```
Router#config t
Router(config)#hostname Todd
Todd(config)#
```

Banners

You can create a banner to give anyone who shows up on the router exactly the information you want them to have. Make sure you're familiar with these four available banner types: exec process creation banner, incoming terminal line banner, login banner, and message of the day banner (all illustrated in Table 1.7).

TABLE 1.7 Setting a Banner

Command	Meaning
Router(config)#**banner motd #**	Enters a banner MOTD message and ends the message with the # character
Router(config)#**banner exec #**	Enters a banner exec message and ends the message with the # character
Router(config)#**banner incoming #**	Enters a banner incoming message and ends the message with the # character
Router(config)#**banner login #**	Enters a banner login message and ends the message with the # character

The following describes the various banners:

MOTD banner The MOTD banner will be displayed whenever anyone attaches to the router, regardless of how they access the router.

Exec banner You can configure a line activation (exec) banner to be displayed when an EXEC process (such as a line activation or incoming connection to a VTY line) is created. By simply starting a user exec session through a console port, you'll activate the exec banner.

Incoming banner You can configure a banner to be displayed on terminals connected to reverse Telnet lines. This banner is useful for providing instructions to users who use reverse Telnet.

Login banner You can configure a login banner to be displayed on all connected terminals. This banner is displayed after the MOTD banner but before the login prompts. The login banner can't be disabled on a per-line basis, so to globally disable it, you have to delete it with the `no banner login` command.

Passwords

You can use five passwords to secure your Cisco routers: console, auxiliary, Telnet (VTY), enable password, and enable secret. However, other commands are necessary to complete the password configurations on a router or switch, as shown in Table 1.8.

TABLE 1.8 Setting Passwords

Command	Meaning
Todd(config)#**enable password todd**	Sets the enable password to Todd.
Todd(config)#**enable secret todd**	Sets the enable secret password to Todd. Supersedes the enable password.
Todd(config)#**line** *line*	Changes to line mode to configure the console, aux, and VTY (Telnet).
Todd(config-line)#**password password**	The line password for aux, console, and VTY (Telnet) are all set in line configuration mode.
Todd(config-line)#**login**	When a line is configured to use a password, the login command must be set to prompt for login.
Todd(config)#**service password-encryption**	Encrypts the passwords in the clear-text configuration file (both running-config and startup-config).

Setting Passwords

Here's an example of setting all your passwords and then encrypting them in the plain configuration file:

```
Todd#config t
Todd(config)#line aux ?
  <0-0>  First Line number
Todd(config)#line aux 0
Todd(config-line)#password aux
Todd(config-line)#login
Todd(config-line)#line con 0
Todd(config-line)#password console
Todd(config-line)#login
Todd(config-line)#exit
Todd(config)#line vty 0 ?
  <1-1180>  Last Line number
  <cr>
Todd(config)#line vty 0 1180
Todd(config-line)#password telnet
Todd(config-line)#login
Todd(config)#enable password todd
Todd(config)#enable secret globalnet
Todd(config)#service password-encryption
Todd(config)#do show run
Building configuration...
[outut cut]
!
enable secret 5 $1$S0a2$rLcwXpbme3zIrl2.TS1kX.
enable password 7 010709005F
!
[output cut]
!
line con 0
 exec-timeout 1 40
 password 7 050809013243420C
 logging synchronous
 login
line aux 0
 password 7 03054E13
 login
line vty 0 4
 password 7 105A0C150B1206
```

```
 login
line vty 5 1180
 password 7 0010160A0A5E1F
 login
!
 [output cut]
Todd(config)#no service password-encryption
```

Some other console helpful commands include the following. This sets the console timeout in second and minutes from 0-35791:

```
Todd(config-line)#exec-timeout ?
```

This redisplays interrupted console input:

```
Todd(config-line)#logging synchronous
```

Here's an example of setting the exec-timeout and logging synchronous commands:

```
Todd)#config t
Todd(config)#line con 0
Todd(config-line)#exec-timeout ?
  <0-35791>  Timeout in minutes
Todd(config-line)#exec-timeout 0 ?
  <0-2147483>  Timeout in seconds
  <cr>
Todd(config-line)#exec-timeout 0 100
Todd(config-line)#logging synchronous
```

Setting Up Secure Shell (SSH)

Instead of Telnet, you can use *Secure Shell*, which creates a more secure session than the Telnet application that uses an unencrypted data stream. SSH uses encrypted keys to send data so that your username and password are not sent in the clear. Table 1.9 lists the commands.

TABLE 1.9 SSH Commands

Command	Meaning
`ip domain-name Lammle.com`	Sets your domain name. You must set this.
`crypto key generate rsa general-keys modulus`	Sets the size of the key up to 2048.
`ip ssh time-out`	Sets the idle timeout up to 120 seconds.

TABLE 1.9 SSH Commands *(continued)*

Command	Meaning
`ip ssh authentication-retries`	Sets the max failed attempts up to 120.
`line vty first-line last_line`	Chooses your VTY lines to configure.
`transport input ssh telnet`	Tells the router to use SSH and then Telnet. You do not need the **telnet** command at the end of the line, but if you don't use it, only SSH will work on the router.

Here's an example of how you set up SSH on a router:

1. Set your hostname:

```
Router(config)#hostname Todd
```

2. Set the domain name (both the hostname and domain name are required for the encryption keys to be generated):

```
Todd(config)#ip domain-name Lammle.com
```

3. Generate the encryption keys for securing the session:

```
Todd(config)#crypto key generate rsa general-keys modulus ?
  <360-2048>  size of the key modulus [360-2048]
Todd(config)#crypto key generate rsa general-keys modulus 1024
The name for the keys will be: Todd.Lammle.com
% The key modulus size is 1024 bits
% Generating 1024 bit RSA keys, keys will be non-exportable...[OK]
*June 24 19:25:30.035: %SSH-5-ENABLED: SSH 1.99 has been enabled
```

4. Set the maximum idle timer for an SSH session:

```
Todd(config)#ip ssh time-out ?
  <1-120>  SSH time-out interval (secs)
Todd(config)#ip ssh time-out 60
```

5. Set the maximum failed attempts for an SSH connection:

```
Todd(config)#ip ssh authentication-retries ?
  <0-5>  Number of authentication retries
Todd(config)#ip ssh authentication-retries 2
```

6. Connect to the VTY lines of the router:

```
Todd(config)#line vty 0 1180
```

7. Last, configure SSH and then Telnet as access protocols:

```
Todd(config-line)#transport input ssh telnet
```

If you do not use the keyword `telnet` at the end of the command string, then only SSH will work on the router. I suggest that you use just SSH if at all possible. Telnet is just too insecure for today's networks.

Router Interfaces

Interface configuration is one of the most important router configurations, because without interfaces, a router is pretty much a completely useless object. Plus, interface configurations must be totally precise to enable communication with other devices. Network layer addresses, media type, bandwidth, and other administrator commands are all used to configure an interface. Table 1.10 shows the commands.

TABLE 1.10 Router Interface Commands

Command	Meaning
Todd(config)#**interface fastethernet** *slot/port*	Enters interface configuration mode from global configuration mode.
Todd(config)#**interface serial** *slot/port*	Same as the previous command, except for serial interface 0/0/0 rather than Fast Ethernet interface.
Todd(config-if)#**shutdown**	Shuts down an interface.
Todd(config-if)#**no shutdown**	Enables an interface that is shut down.
Todd(config-if)#**ip address** *address mask*	Configures an interface with an IP address and a subnet mask.
Todd(config-if)#**ip address** *address mask* **secondary**	Adds a secondary IP address to an interface.
Todd(config-if)#**description description**	Adds a description to an interface.
Todd(config-if)#**clock rate rate**	Sets the clock rate of a serial interface in bits per second.
Todd(config-if)#**bandwidth rate**	Sets the bandwidth of an interface in kilobits per second.
Todd#**show interface interface**	Displays the status and configuration of the Fast Ethernet interface.
Todd#**clear counters interface**	Clears the display counters on the serial interface.

TABLE 1.10 Router Interface Commands *(continued)*

Command	Meaning
Todd#**sh ip interface interface**	Displays the layer-3 properties of an interface.
Todd#**sh ip int brief**	Displays the IP interfaces in a summarized table. This is one of the most useful show commands!

Let's take a look at setting both an IP address and a secondary IP address on an interface, and then we'll verify the configuration:

```
Todd(config)#interface fastEthernet 0/0
Todd(config)#interface serial 0/0/0
Todd(config-if)#shutdown
Jul 30 15:31:23.542: %LINK-5-CHANGED: Interface Serial0/0/0, changed state to
administratively down
Jul 30 15:31:24.542: %LINEPROTO-5-UPDOWN: Line protocol on Interface Serial0/0/
0, changed state to down
Todd(config-if)#no shutdown
Jul 30 15:31:27.566: %LINK-3-UPDOWN: Interface Serial0/0/0, changed state to up
Jul 30 15:31:28.566: %LINEPROTO-5-UPDOWN: Line protocol on Interface Serial0/0/0,
changed state to up
Todd(config-if)#ip address 172.16.10.1 255.255.255.0
Todd(config-if)#ip address 172.16.20.1 255.255.255.0 ?
  secondary  Make this IP address a secondary address
  <cr>
Todd(config-if)#ip address 172.16.20.1 255.255.255.0 secondary
Todd(config-if)#description Serial link to Miami
Todd(config-if)#clock rate 1000000
Todd(config-if)#bandwidth 1000
Todd(config-if)#exit
Todd(config)#exit
Todd#show interface s0/0/0
Serial0/0/0 is up, line protocol is up
  Hardware is GT96K Serial
  Description: Serial link to Miami
  Internet address is 172.16.10.1/24
  MTU 1500 bytes, BW 1000 Kbit, DLY 20000 usec,
     reliability 255/255, txload 1/255, rxload 1/255
  Encapsulation HDLC, loopback not set
  Keepalive set (10 sec)
  Last input 00:00:04, output 00:00:08, output hang never
```

```
  Last clearing of "show interface" counters 2d05h
  Input queue: 0/75/0/0 (size/max/drops/flushes); Total output drops: 0
  Queueing strategy: fifo
  Output queue: 0/40 (size/max)
  5 minute input rate 0 bits/sec, 0 packets/sec
  5 minute output rate 0 bits/sec, 0 packets/sec
     34632 packets input, 2479012 bytes, 0 no buffer
     Received 34031 broadcasts, 0 runts, 0 giants, 0 throttles
     0 input errors, 0 CRC, 0 frame, 0 overrun, 0 ignored, 0 abort
     34372 packets output, 2303104 bytes, 0 underruns
     0 output errors, 0 collisions, 5 interface resets
     0 output buffer failures, 0 output buffers swapped out
     112 carrier transitions
     DCD=up  DSR=up  DTR=up  RTS=up  CTS=up

Todd#clear counters s0/0/0
Clear "show interface" counters on this interface [confirm][enter]
Jul 30 15:39:02.818: %CLEAR-5-COUNTERS: Clear counter on interface Serial0/0/0
by console
Todd#sh ip interface s0/0/0
Serial0/0/0 is up, line protocol is up
  Internet address is 172.16.10.1/24
  Broadcast address is 255.255.255.255
  Address determined by setup command
  MTU is 1500 bytes
  Helper address is not set
  Directed broadcast forwarding is disabled
  Secondary address 172.16.20.1/24
  Secondary address 172.16.30.1/24
  Outgoing access list is not set
  Inbound  access list is not set
  Proxy ARP is enabled
  Local Proxy ARP is disabled
  Security level is default
  Split horizon is enabled
  ICMP redirects are always sent
  ICMP unreachables are always sent
  ICMP mask replies are never sent
  IP fast switching is enabled
  IP fast switching on the same interface is enabled
  IP Flow switching is disabled
  IP CEF switching is enabled
  IP CEF Fast switching turbo vector
```

```
  [output cut]
Todd#sh ip int brief
Interface          IP-Address      OK? Method Status          Protocol
FastEthernet0/0    192.168.21.1    YES manual up                up
FastEthernet0/1    unassigned      YES unset  administratively down down
Serial0/0/0        172.16.10.1     YES manual up                up
Serial0/0/1        unassigned      YES unset  administratively down down
Todd#
Viewing, Saving, and Erasing Configurations
```

Once you have gone to all the work of creating a configuration, you will need to know how to save it, and maybe even delete it. Table 1.11 shows the commands used to manipulate configurations.

TABLE 1.11 Commands to Manipulate Configurations

Command	Meaning
Todd#**copy running-config startup-config**	Saves the running configuration to NVRAM
Todd#**show running-config**	Shows the running configuration on the terminal
Todd#**show startup-config**	Shows the start-up configuration (in NVRAM) on the terminal
Todd#**erase startup-config**	Erases the configuration stored in NVRAM

You can manually save the file from DRAM to NVRAM by using the `copy running-config startup-config` command (you can use the shortcut `copy run start` also):

```
Todd#copy running-config startup-config
Destination filename [startup-config]? [press enter]
Building configuration...
[OK]
Todd#
Building configuration...

Todd#show running-config
Building configuration...

Current configuration : 3343 bytes
!
version 12.4
[output cut]
```

The sh start command—one of the shortcuts for the show startup-config command—shows you the configuration that will be used the next time the router is reloaded. It also tells you how much NVRAM is being used to store the startup-config file. Here's an example:

```
Todd#show startup-config
Using 1978 out of 245752 bytes
!
version 12.4
[output cut]

Todd#erase startup-config
Erasing the nvram filesystem will remove all configuration files!
    Continue? [confirm][enter]
[OK]
Erase of nvram: complete
Todd#
*Feb 28 23:51:21.179: %SYS-7-NV_BLOCK_INIT: Initialized the geometry of nvram
Todd#sh startup-config
startup-config is not present
Todd#reload
Proceed with reload? [confirm]System configuration has been modified.
    Save? [yes/no]: n
```

Using the *show* Command

Obviously, show running-config would be the best way to verify your configuration, and show startup-config would be the best way to verify the configuration that will be used the next time the router is reloaded, right?

Table 1.12 shows some basic command you might use every day in a production environment.

TABLE 1.12 Everyday Commands

Command	Meaning
show running config	This shows the configuration that router is using.
show startup-config	This shows the configuration that the router will use when the router is reload.
show interface	This shows the status of all interfaces.

TABLE 1.12 Everyday Commands *(continued)*

Command	Meaning
`show ip interface`	This shows the default IP configuration on all interfaces.
`show ip interface brief`	This command provides a quick overview of the router's interfaces, including the logical address and status.
`show protocols`	This shows the status of layers 1 and 2 of each interface as well as the IP addresses used.
`show controllers`	This shows whether an interface is a DCE or DTE interface.

The `show running-config` command is important and could very well be one of the most used commands on a Cisco router. The `show running-config` command shows the configuration that the router is running. The `show startup-config` shows the backup config, or the configuration that will be used the next time the router is booted.

The `show interface` command is important, and that's what I'll discuss in this section. Here's what it looks like:

```
Router#sh int s0/0/0
Serial0/0 is up, line protocol is down
```

If you see that the line is up but the protocol is down, as shown earlier, you're experiencing a clocking (keepalive) or framing problem—possibly an encapsulation mismatch. Check the keepalives on both ends to make sure that they match, that the clock rate is set (if needed), and that the encapsulation type is the same on both ends. The previous output would be considered a Data Link layer problem.

If you discover that both the line interface and the protocol are down, it's a cable or interface problem. The following output would be considered a physical layer problem:

```
Router#sh int s0/0/0
Serial0/0 is down, line protocol is down
```

If one end is administratively shut down (as shown next), the remote end would present as down and down:

```
Router#sh int s0/0/0
Serial0/0 is administratively down, line protocol is down
```

To enable the interface, use the command `no shutdown` from interface configuration mode:

```
Router#config t
Router(config)#int s0/0/0
Router(config-if)#no shutdown
```

You can get a nice brief overview of the interfaces with the `show interface brief` command:

```
Router#sh ip int brief
Interface          IP-Address      OK? Method Status   Protocol
FastEthernet0/0    unassigned      YES unset  up         up
FastEthernet0/1    unassigned      YES unset  up         up
Serial0/0/0        unassigned      YES unset  up         down
Serial0/0/1        unassigned      YES unset  up         up
Serial0/1/0        unassigned      YES unset  administratively down down
```

```
Todd#sh protocols
Global values:
  Internet Protocol routing is enabled
FastEthernet0/0 is up, line protocol is up
  Internet address is 192.168.21.1/24
FastEthernet0/1 is administratively down, line protocol is down
Serial0/0/0 is up, line protocol is up
  Internet address is 172.16.10.1/24
Serial0/0/1 is administratively down, line protocol is down
Todd#
```

The `show controllers` command displays information about the physical interface itself. It'll also give you the type of serial cable plugged into a serial port. Usually, this will be only a DTE cable that plugs into a type of data service unit (DSU).

```
Router#sh controllers serial 0/0
HD unit 0, idb = 0x1229E4, driver structure at 0x127E70
buffer size 1524 HD unit 0, V.35 DTE cable
cpb = 0xE2, eda = 0x4140, cda = 0x4000
```

```
Router#sh controllers serial 0/1
HD unit 1, idb = 0x12C174, driver structure at 0x131600
buffer size 1524 HD unit 1, V.35 DCE cable
cpb = 0xE3, eda = 0x2940, cda = 0x2800
```

Chapter 2

Managing a Cisco Internetwork

Here in Chapter 2, I'll show you the commands for managing Cisco routers on an internetwork. The Internetwork Operating System (IOS) and configuration files reside in different locations in a Cisco device, so it's really important to understand both where these files are located and how they work.

You'll be learning about the main components of a router, the router boot sequence, and the configuration register, including how to use the configuration register for password recovery. After that, you'll find out how to manage routers by using the `copy` command with a Trivial File Transfer Protocol (TFTP) host when using the Cisco IOS File System (IFS).

I'll wrap up the chapter by exploring the Cisco Discovery Protocol, showing how to resolve hostnames, and presenting some important Cisco IOS troubleshooting techniques.

For up-to-the minute updates for this chapter, please see `www.lammle.com` or `www.sybex.com/go/IOSCommandSurvivalGuide`

Understanding the Internal Components of a Cisco Router

To configure and troubleshoot a Cisco internetwork, you need to know the major components of Cisco routers and understand what each one does. Table 2.1 describes the major Cisco router components.

TABLE 2.1 Cisco Router Components

Component	Description
Bootstrap	Stored in the microcode of the ROM, the bootstrap brings a router up during initialization. It will boot the router and then load the IOS.

TABLE 2.1 Cisco Router Components *(continued)*

Component	Description
Power-on self-test (POST)	Stored in the microcode of the ROM, the POST is used to check the basic functionality of the router hardware and determines which interfaces are present.
ROM monitor	Stored in the microcode of the ROM, the ROM monitor is used for manufacturing, testing, and troubleshooting.
Mini-IOS	Called the *RXBOOT* or *bootloader* by Cisco, the mini-IOS is a small IOS in ROM that can be used to open an interface and load a Cisco IOS into flash memory. The mini-IOS can also perform a few other maintenance operations.
Random-access memory (RAM)	Used to hold packet buffers, ARP cache, routing tables, and the software and data structures that allow the router to function. The running-config file is stored in RAM, and most routers expand the IOS from flash into RAM upon boot.
Read-only memory (ROM)	Used to start and maintain the router. Holds the POST and the bootstrap program, as well as the mini-IOS.
Flash memory	Used to store the Cisco IOS by default. Flash memory is not erased when the router is reloaded. It is electronically erasable programmable read-only memory (EEPROM) created by Intel.
Nonvolatile RAM (NVRAM)	Used to hold the router and switch configuration. NVRAM is not erased when the router or switch is reloaded. Does not store an IOS. The configuration-register file is stored in NVRAM.
Configuration register	Used to control how the router boots up. This value can be found as the last line of the **show version** command output, and by default it is set to 0x2102, which tells the router to load the IOS from flash memory as well as to load the configuration from NVRAM.

Managing the Configuration Register

All Cisco routers have a 16-bit software register that's written into NVRAM. By default, the *configuration register* is set to load the Cisco IOS from *flash memory* and to look for and load the startup-config file from NVRAM.

Checking the Current Configuration Register Value

You can see the current value of the configuration register by using the `show version` command (`sh version` or `show ver` for short), as demonstrated in Table 2.2:

TABLE 2.2 The Show Version Command

Command	Meaning
`show version`	Directs the router where to load the IOS and configuration files from

The only way to view the configuration register is through the show version command:

```
Router#sh version
Cisco IOS Software, 2800 Software (C2800NM-ADVSECURITYK9-M),Version 12.4(12),
RELEASE SOFTWARE (fc1)
[output cut]
Configuration register is 0x2102
```

The last information given from this command is the value of the configuration register. In this example, the value is 0x2102, which is the default setting. The configuration register setting of 0x2102 tells the router to look in NVRAM for the boot sequence.

Changing the Configuration Register

You can change the configuration register value to modify how the router boots and runs. These are the main reasons you would want to change the configuration register:

- To force the system into the ROM monitor mode
- To select a boot source and default boot filename
- To enable or disable the `Break` function
- To control broadcast addresses
- To set the console terminal baud rate
- To load operating software from ROM
- To enable booting from a TFTP server

Table 2.3 shows the two commands we'll use to edit the configuration register:

TABLE 2.3 Configuration Register

Command	Meaning
config-register	Directs the router where to load the IOS and configuration files from
show flash	Displays a list of directories and files in flash memory

Here is an example of how to change the configuration register and then I'll show you how to verify:

```
Router(config)#config-register 0x2101
Router(config)#^Z
Router#sh ver
[output cut]
Configuration register is 0x2102 (will be 0x2101 at next
  reload)
```

Here is the router after setting the configuration register to 0x2101 and reloading:

```
Router(boot)#sh ver
Cisco IOS Software, 2800 Software (C2800NM-ADVSECURITYK9-M), Version 12.4(12),
RELEASE SOFTWARE (fc1)
[output cut]

ROM: System Bootstrap, Version 12.4(13r)T, RELEASE SOFTWARE (fc1)

Router uptime is 3 minutes
System returned to ROM by power-on
System image file is "flash:c2800nm-advsecurityk9-mz.124-12.bin"
[output cut]

Configuration register is 0x2101
```

At this point, if you typed **show flash**, you'd still see the IOS in flash memory ready to go. But in the previous code you told the router to load from ROM, which is why the hostname shows up with (boot) here:

```
Router(boot)#sh flash
-#- --length-- -----date/time------ path
1      21710744 Jan 2 2007 22:41:14 +00:00 c2800nm-advsecurityk9-mz.124-12.bin
2          1823 Dec 5 2006 14:46:26 +00:00 sdmconfig-2811.cfg
```

```
3       4734464 Dec 5 2006 14:47:12 +00:00 sdm.tar
4        833024 Dec 5 2006 14:47:38 +00:00 es.tar
5       1052160 Dec 5 2006 14:48:10 +00:00 common.tar
6          1038 Dec 5 2006 14:48:32 +00:00 home.shtml
7        102400 Dec 5 2006 14:48:54 +00:00 home.tar
8        491213 Dec 5 2006 14:49:22 +00:00 128MB.sdf
9       1684577 Dec 5 2006 14:50:04 +00:00 securedesktop-ios-3.1.1.27-k9.pkg
10       398305 Dec 5 2006 14:50:34 +00:00 sslclient-win-1.1.0.154.pkg

32989184 bytes available (31027200 bytes used)
```

If you want to set the configuration register back to the default, just type this:

```
Router(boot)#config t
Router(boot)(config)#config-register 0x2102
Router(boot)(config)#^Z
Router(boot)#reload
```

Recovering Passwords

If you're locked out of a router because you forgot the password, you can change the configuration register to help you get back on your feet.

To recover a password, you need to turn on bit 6. Doing this will tell the router to ignore the NVRAM contents. The configuration register value to turn on bit 6 is 0x2142.

Here are the main steps to password recovery:

1. Boot the router and interrupt the boot sequence by performing a break, which will take the router into ROM monitor mode.
2. Change the configuration register to turn on bit 6 (with the value 0x2142).
3. Reload the router.
4. Enter privileged mode.
5. Copy the startup-config file to running-config.
6. Change the password.
7. Reset the configuration register to the default value.
8. Save the router configuration.
9. Reload the router (optional).

Table 2.4 shows our password recovery commands:

TABLE 2.4 Configuration Register Commands

Command	Meaning
Ctrl+Break	Key combination used to interrupt router boot sequence
`confreg`	Rommon command for modifying the configuration register
`config-register`	Directs the router where to load the IOS and configuration files from
`copy start run`	Copies the startup-config file to RAM and names it running-config
`config t`	Takes you to global config
`enable secret` *password*	Sets the enable password
`reload`	Reboots the router

Interrupting the Router Boot Sequence

Your first step is to boot the router and perform a break. This is usually done by pressing the Ctrl+Break key combination when using HyperTerminal while the router first reboots.

After you've performed a break, you should see something like this for a 2600 series router (it is pretty much the same output for the ISR series):

```
System Bootstrap, Version 11.3(2)XA4, RELEASE SOFTWARE (fc1)
Copyright (c) 1999 by cisco Systems, Inc.
TAC:Home:SW:IOS:Specials for info
PC = 0xfff0a530, Vector = 0x500, SP = 0x680127b0
C2600 platform with 32768 Kbytes of main memory
PC = 0xfff0a530, Vector = 0x500, SP = 0x80004374
monitor: command "boot" aborted due to user interrupt
rommon 1 >
```

Notice the line `monitor: command "boot" aborted due to user interrupt`. At this point, you will be at the `rommon 1>` prompt, which is called *ROM monitor mode*.

Reloading the Router and Entering Privileged Mode

At this point, you need to reset the router like this:

- From the ISR/2600 series router, type **I** (for initialize) or **reset**.
- From the 2500 series router, type **I**.

The router will reload and ask whether you want to use setup mode (because no startup-config is used). Type **no** to enter setup mode, press Enter to go into user mode, and then type **enable** to go into privileged mode.

Viewing and Changing the Configuration

Now you're past the point where you would need to enter the user-mode and privileged-mode passwords in a router. Copy the startup-config file to the running-config file:

```
copy startup-config running-config
```

or use the following shortcut:

```
copy start run
```

The configuration is now running in *random access memory (RAM)*, and you're in privileged mode, meaning you can now view and change the configuration. But you can't view the `enable secret` setting for the password since it is encrypted. To change the password, do this:

```
config t
enable secret todd
```

Cisco ISR/2600 Series Commands

To change the bit value on a Cisco ISR/2600 series router, you just enter the command at the `rommon 1>` prompt:

```
rommon 1 >confreg 0x2142
You must reset or power cycle for new config to take effect
rommon 2 >reset
```

Resetting the Configuration Register and Reloading the Router

After you're finished changing passwords, set the configuration register back to the default value with the `config-register` command:

```
config t
config-register 0x2102
```

Finally, save the new configuration by typing **copy running-config startup-config,** and reload the router. I will discuss in more detail the use of the copy command in a minute.

Using Boot System Commands

There are some boot commands you can play with that will help you manage the way your router boots the Cisco IOS, but let's remember, we're talking about the router's IOS here, *not* the router's configuration! To change the IOS the router loads, use the boot command in Table 2.5:

TABLE 2.5 The Boot Command

Command	Meaning
boot	Allows the modification of where or what the system will boot. The configuration and IOS files can both be changed.

The boot command has a lot of options. Let's take a look at the most important ones:

```
Router>en
Router#config t
Enter configuration commands, one per line.  End with CNTL/Z.
Router(config)#boot ?
  bootstrap  Bootstrap image file
  config     Configuration file
  host       Router-specific config file
  network    Network-wide config file
  system     System image file
```

The boot system command will allow you to tell the router which file to boot from flash memory:

```
Router(config)#boot system ?
  WORD   TFTP filename or URL
  flash  Boot from flash memory
  ftp    Boot from a server via ftp
  mop    Boot from a Decnet MOP server
  rcp    Boot from a server via rcp
  rom    Boot from rom
  tftp   Boot from a tftp server
Router(config)#boot system flash c2800nm-advsecurityk9-mz.124-12.bin
```

Backing Up and Restoring the Cisco IOS

Before you upgrade or restore a Cisco IOS, you really should copy the existing file to a *TFTP host* as a backup just in case the new image crashes and burns.

But before you back up or restore an IOS image, you need to check these things:

- Make sure you can access the network server.
- Ensure that the network server has adequate space for the code image.
- Verify the file naming and path requirement.
- The `copy flash tftp` command must be supplied with the IP address of the workstation if you are copying from the router flash.
- And if you're copying "into" flash, you need to verify there's enough room in flash memory to accommodate the file to be copied.

Verifying Flash Memory

The ISR router shown in Table 2.6 has 64MB of RAM, and roughly half of the memory is in use.

TABLE 2.6 Verifying Flash Commands

Command	Meaning
`show flash`	Used to find the amount of available memory
`show version`	Useful in determining the amount of memory

The show flash and show version are probably two of your most important commands. Let's go through the outputs of each:

```
Router#sh flash
-#- --length-- -----date/time------ path
1     21710744 Jan 2 2007 22:41:14 +00:00 c2800nm-advsecurityk9-mz.124-12.bin
[output cut]
32989184 bytes available (31027200 bytes used)
```

The amount of flash is actually easier to tally using the `show version` command on the ISR routers:

```
Router#show version
[output cut]
Cisco 2811 (revision 49.46) with 249856K/12288K bytes of memory.
Processor board ID FTX1049A1AB
2 FastEthernet interfaces
```

```
4 Serial(sync/async) interfaces
1 Virtual Private Network (VPN) Module
DRAM configuration is 64 bits wide with parity enabled.
239K bytes of non-volatile configuration memory.
62720K bytes of ATA CompactFlash (Read/Write)
```

Backing Up the Cisco IOS

The copy command has become more powerful over the past few years. Let's use it to discuss backing up the IOS of a router. There are various places to back up an IOS, and a TFTP server is a common place.

The copy command shown in Table 2.7 allows us to manage our file systems:

TABLE 2.7 The Copy Command

Command	Meaning
copy	Used to backup or restore a file to or from a device

There are many new options that are part of the copy command in the new ISR routers. The most important of these is the copy flash tftp and copy tftp flash commands. Let's take a look:

```
Router#copy ?
  /erase            Erase destination file system.
  /noverify         Don't verify image signature before reload.
  /verify           Verify image signature before reload.
  archive:          Copy from archive: file system
  cns:              Copy from cns: file system
  flash:            Copy from flash: file system
  ftp:              Copy from ftp: file system
  http:             Copy from http: file system
  https:            Copy from https: file system
  ips-sdf           Copy from current IPS signature configuration
  null:             Copy from null: file system
  nvram:            Copy from nvram: file system
  pram:             Copy from pram: file system
  rcp:              Copy from rcp: file system
  running-config    Copy from current system configuration
  scp:              Copy from scp: file system
  startup-config    Copy from startup configuration
  system:           Copy from system: file system
```

```
  tftp:           Copy from tftp: file system
  xmodem:         Copy from xmodem: file system
  ymodem:         Copy from ymodem: file system

Router#copy flash tftp
Source filename []?c2800nm-advsecurityk9-mz.124-12.bin
Address or name of remote host []?1.1.1.2
Destination filename [c2800nm-advsecurityk9-mz.124-12.bin]?[enter]
!!!!!!!!!!!!!!!!!!!!!!!!!!!!!!!!!!!!!!!!!!!!!!!!!!!!!!!!!!!!!!!!!!!!!!!!!!!!!!!!
!!!!!!!!
21710744 bytes copied in 60.724 secs (357532 bytes/sec)
Router#
```

Restoring or Upgrading the Cisco Router IOS

What happens if you need to restore the Cisco IOS to flash memory to replace an original file that has been damaged or if you want to upgrade the IOS? You can download the file from a TFTP server to flash memory by using the `copy tftp flash` command:

```
Router#copy tftp flash
Address or name of remote host []?1.1.1.2
Source filename []?c2800nm-advsecurityk9-mz.124-12.bin
Destination filename [c2800nm-advsecurityk9-mz.124-12.bin]?[enter]
%Warning:There is a file already existing with this name
Do you want to over write? [confirm][enter]
Accessing tftp://1.1.1.2/c2800nm-advsecurityk9-mz.124-12.bin...
Loading c2800nm-advsecurityk9-mz.124-12.bin from 1.1.1.2 (via FastEthernet0/0):
!!!!!!!!!!!!!!!!!!!!!!!!!!!!!!!!!!!!!!!!!!!!!!!!!!!!!!!!!!!!!!!!!!!!!!!!!!!!!!!!
!!!!!!
[OK - 21710744 bytes]

21710744 bytes copied in 82.880 secs (261954 bytes/sec)
Router#
```

Using the Cisco IOS File System (Cisco IFS)

Cisco has created a file system called Cisco IFS that allows you to work with files and directories just like you would from a Windows DOS prompt.

You use Cisco IFS commands pretty much the same way you use the `copy` command described earlier:

- For backing up the IOS
- For upgrading the IOS
- For viewing text files

Table 2.8 is a list of the most used Cisco IFS commands:

TABLE 2.8 The Cisco IFS Commands

Command	Meaning
`PWD`	Shows the working directory
`show file`	Gives you information about a specified file or file system
`dir`	Lets you view files in a directory (the default directory is `flash:/`)
`copy`	Upgrades, restores, or backs up an IOS
`more`	Displays the contents of a file
`delete`	Deletes a file from a system or directory
`erase/format`	Erases or formats a file system
`CD`	Changes directories
`MKDIR/RMDIR`	Creates and deletes directories

These Cisco IFS commands can get confusing. Let's work through a few of them:

```
Router#pwd
flash:
Router#dir
Directory of flash:/
    1  -rw-    13937472  Dec 20 2006 19:58:18 +00:00  c1841-ipbase-mz.124-1c.bin
    2  -rw-        1821  Dec 20 2006 20:11:24 +00:00  sdmconfig-18xx.cfg
    3  -rw-     4734464  Dec 20 2006 20:12:00 +00:00  sdm.tar
    4  -rw-      833024  Dec 20 2006 20:12:24 +00:00  es.tar
    5  -rw-     1052160  Dec 20 2006 20:12:50 +00:00  common.tar
    6  -rw-        1038  Dec 20 2006 20:13:10 +00:00  home.shtml
    7  -rw-      102400  Dec 20 2006 20:13:30 +00:00  home.tar
    8  -rw-      491213  Dec 20 2006 20:13:56 +00:00  128MB.sdf
    9  -rw-     1684577  Dec 20 2006 20:14:34 +00:00  securedesktop-ios-
3.1.1.27-k9.pkg
   10  -rw-      398305  Dec 20 2006 20:15:04 +00:00  sslclient-win-
1.1.0.154.pkg
```

```
32071680 bytes total (8818688 bytes free)
Router#show file info flash:c1841-ipbase-mz.124-1c.bin
flash:c1841-ipbase-mz.124-1c.bin:
  type is image (elf) []
  file size is 13937472 bytes, run size is 14103140 bytes
  Runnable image, entry point 0x8000F000, run from ram
Router#delete flash:c1841-ipbase-mz.124-1c.bin
Delete filename [c1841-ipbase-mz.124-1c.bin]?[enter]
Delete flash:c1841-ipbase-mz.124-1c.bin? [confirm][enter]
Router#sh flash
-#- --length-- -----date/time------ path
1         1821 Dec 20 2006 20:11:24 +00:00 sdmconfig-18xx.cfg
2      4734464 Dec 20 2006 20:12:00 +00:00 sdm.tar
3       833024 Dec 20 2006 20:12:24 +00:00 es.tar
4      1052160 Dec 20 2006 20:12:50 +00:00 common.tar
5         1038 Dec 20 2006 20:13:10 +00:00 home.shtml
6       102400 Dec 20 2006 20:13:30 +00:00 home.tar
7       491213 Dec 20 2006 20:13:56 +00:00 128MB.sdf
8      1684577 Dec 20 2006 20:14:34 +00:00 securedesktop-ios-3.1.1.27-k9.pkg
9       398305 Dec 20 2006 20:15:04 +00:00 sslclient-win-1.1.0.154.pkg
22757376 bytes available (9314304 bytes used)
R1#sh file info flash:c1841-ipbase-mz.124-1c.bin
%Error opening flash:c1841-ipbase-mz.124-1c.bin (File not found)
Router#
Router#copy tftp://1.1.1.2//c1841-advipservicesk9-mz.124-12.bin/ flash:/ c1841-
advipservicesk9-mz.124-12.bin
Source filename [/c1841-advipservicesk9-mz.124-12.bin/]?[enter]
Destination filename [c1841-advipservicesk9-mz.124-12.bin]?[enter]
Loading /c1841-advipservicesk9-mz.124-12.bin/ from 1.1.1.2 (via FastEthernet0/
0): !!!!!!!!!!!!!!!!!!!!!!!!!!!!!!!!!!!!!!!!
[output cut]
!!!!!!!!!!!!!!!!!!!!!!!!!!!!!!!!!!!!!!!!!!!!!!!!!!!!!!
[OK - 22103052 bytes]
22103052 bytes copied in 72.008 secs (306953 bytes/sec)
Router#sh flash
-#- --length-- -----date/time------ path
1         1821 Dec 20 2006 20:11:24 +00:00 sdmconfig-18xx.cfg
2      4734464 Dec 20 2006 20:12:00 +00:00 sdm.tar
3       833024 Dec 20 2006 20:12:24 +00:00 es.tar
4      1052160 Dec 20 2006 20:12:50 +00:00 common.tar
```

```
5          1038 Dec 20 2006 20:13:10 +00:00 home.shtml
6        102400 Dec 20 2006 20:13:30 +00:00 home.tar
7        491213 Dec 20 2006 20:13:56 +00:00 128MB.sdf
8       1684577 Dec 20 2006 20:14:34 +00:00 securedesktop-ios-3.1.1.27-k9.pkg
9        398305 Dec 20 2006 20:15:04 +00:00 sslclient-win-1.1.0.154.pkg
10    22103052 Mar 10 2007 19:40:50 +00:00 c1841-advipservicesk9-mz.124-12.bin
651264 bytes available (31420416 bytes used)
Router#
Router#sh file information flash:c1841-advipservicesk9-mz.124-12.bin
flash:c1841-advipservicesk9-mz.124-12.bin:
  type is image (elf) []
  file size is 22103052 bytes, run size is 22268736 bytes
  Runnable image, entry point 0x8000F000, run from ram
```

Backing Up and Restoring the Cisco Configuration

Any changes you make to the router configuration are stored in the running-config file. And if you don't enter a `copy run start` command after you make a change to running-config, that change will go "poof!" if the router reboots or gets powered down. So, you probably want to make another backup of the configuration information just in case the router or switch completely dies on you. Even if your machine is healthy and happy, the backup is good to have for reference and documentation reasons.

In the following sections, I'll describe how to copy the configuration of a router to a TFTP server and how to restore that configuration.

Backing Up the Cisco Router Configuration

The file commands you'll need are listed in Table 2.9:

TABLE 2.9 Verifying and Backing up your configuraiton

Command	Meaning
`show running-config`	Displays the running configuration file from RAM
`show startup-config`	Displays the start-up configuration file from NVRAM

TABLE 2.9 Verifying and Backing up your configuraiton *(continued)*

Command	Meaning
`copy`	Copies configuration and image files
`erase`	Deletes configuration and image files

Verifying the Current Configuration

To verify the configuration in DRAM, use the `show running-config` command (`sh run` for short), like this:

```
Router#show running-config
Building configuration...

Current configuration : 776 bytes
!
version 12.4
```

Verifying the Stored Configuration

Next, you should check the configuration stored in NVRAM. To see this, use the `show startup-config` command (`sh start` for short), like this:

```
Router#show startup-config
Using 776 out of 245752 bytes
!
version 12.4
```

Copying the Current Configuration to NVRAM

You'll then need to copy the current configuration to NVRAM:

```
Router#copy running-config startup-config
Destination filename [startup-config]?[enter]
Building configuration...
[OK]
Router#

Router#copy running-config ?
  archive:        Copy to archive: file system
  flash:          Copy to flash: file system
  ftp:            Copy to ftp: file system
  http:           Copy to http: file system
```

```
https:          Copy to https: file system
ips-sdf         Update (merge with) IPS signature configuration
null:           Copy to null: file system
nvram:          Copy to nvram: file system
rcp:            Copy to rcp: file system
running-config  Update (merge with) current system configuration
scp:            Copy to scp: file system
startup-config  Copy to startup configuration
syslog:         Copy to syslog: file system
system:         Copy to system: file system
tftp:           Copy to tftp: file system
xmodem:         Copy to xmodem: file system
ymodem:         Copy to ymodem: file system
```

Copying the Configuration to a TFTP Server

Once the file is copied to NVRAM, you can make a second backup to a TFTP server by using the `copy running-config tftp` command (`copy run tftp` for short), like this:

```
Router#copy running-config tftp
Address or name of remote host []?1.1.1.2
Destination filename [router-confg]?todd-confg
!!
776 bytes copied in 0.800 secs (970 bytes/sec)
Router#
```

Restoring the Cisco Router Configuration

If you did copy the router's configuration to a TFTP server as a second backup, you can restore the configuration using the `copy tftp running-config` command (`copy tftp run` for short) or the `copy tftp startup-config` command (`copy tftp start` for short), as shown here (the old command that provides this function is `config net`):

```
Router#copy tftp running-config
Address or name of remote host []?1.1.1.2
Source filename []?todd-confg
Destination filename[running-config]?[enter]
Accessing tftp://1.1.1.2/todd-confg...
Loading todd-confg from 1.1.1.2 (via FastEthernet0/0): !
[OK - 776 bytes]
776 bytes copied in 9.212 secs (84 bytes/sec)
Router#
```

```
*Mar  7 17:53:34.071: %SYS-5-CONFIG_I: Configured from tftp://1.1.1.2/todd-
confg by console
Router#
```

Erasing the Configuration

To delete the startup-config file on a Cisco router, use the command `erase startup-config`, like this:

```
Router#erase startup-config
Erasing the nvram filesystem will remove all configuration files! Continue?
[confirm][enter]
[OK]
Erase of nvram: complete
*Mar  7 17:56:20.407: %SYS-7-NV_BLOCK_INIT: Initialized the geometry of nvram
Router#reload
System configuration has been modified. Save? [yes/no]:n
Proceed with reload? [confirm][enter]
 *Mar  7 17:56:31.059: %SYS-5-RELOAD: Reload requested by console. Reload
Reason: Reload Command.
```

This command deletes the contents of NVRAM on the router. By typing **reload** at privileged mode and typing **no** to saving the changes, the router will reload and come up into setup mode.

Using the Cisco IOS File System to Manage Your Router's Configuration (Cisco IFS)

Using the old, faithful `copy` command is still useful, and I recommend it. However, you still need to know about the Cisco IFS. I'll first show how to use the `show file` command to see the contents of NVRAM and RAM:

```
Router#show file information nvram:startup-config
nvram:startup-config:
  type is config
Router#cd nvram:
Router#pwd
nvram:/
Router#dir
Directory of nvram:/

  190  -rw-         830                    <no date>  startup-config
  191  ----           5                    <no date>  private-config
```

```
  192  -rw-         830                   <no date>  underlying-config
    1  -rw-           0                   <no date>  ifIndex-table
196600 bytes total (194689 bytes free)
Router#cd system:
Router#pwd
system:/
Router#dir ?
  /all              List all files
  /recursive        List files recursively
  all-filesystems   List files on all filesystems
  archive:          Directory or file name
  cns:              Directory or file name
  flash:            Directory or file name
  null:             Directory or file name
  nvram:            Directory or file name
  system:           Directory or file name
  xmodem:           Directory or file name
  ymodem:           Directory or file name
  <cr>
Router#dir
Directory of system:/

    3  dr-x           0                   <no date>  lib
   33  dr-x           0                   <no date>  memory
    1  -rw-         750                   <no date>  running-config
    2  dr-x           0                   <no date>  vfiles
Router#config net
Host or network configuration file [host]?[enter]
This command has been replaced by the command:
         'copy <url> system:/running-config'
Address or name of remote host [255.255.255.255]?
Router#copy tftp://1.1.1.2/todd-confg system://running-config
Destination filename [running-config]?[enter]
Accessing tftp://1.1.1.2/todd-confg...Loading todd-confg from 1.1.1.2 (via
FastEthernet0/0): !
[OK - 776 bytes]
[OK]
776 bytes copied in 13.816 secs (56 bytes/sec)
Router#
*Mar 10 22:12:59.819: %SYS-5-CONFIG_I: Configured from tftp://1.1.1.2/todd-
confg by console
```

Using Cisco Discovery Protocol (CDP)

Cisco Discovery Protocol (CDP) is a proprietary protocol designed by Cisco to help administrators collect information about both locally attached and remote devices. By using CDP, you can gather hardware and protocol information about neighbor devices, which is useful information for troubleshooting and documenting the network!

In the following sections, I'll discuss the CDP timer and CDP commands used to verify your network.

Getting CDP Timers and Holdtime Information

I'll start with the basic commands that describe how CDP works, and then I'll show how to use CDP to gather more advanced information. Table 2.10 shows a list of the CDP commands. You must know these!

TABLE 2.10 Cisco Discovery Protocol

Command	Meaning
`show CDP`	Displays CDP timer and holdtime values
`CDP holdtime`	Configures the CDP holdtimer
`CDP timer`	Configures the CDP timer
`CDP enable`	Globally enables CDP; to disable, use the `no` form of the command
`show CDP neighbor`	Displays information about directly connected neighbors
`show CDP neighbor detail`	Displays detailed information about neighbors including IOS and layer-3 information
`show CDP entry * protocol`	Displays just the layer-3 information, such as the IP address
`show CDP entry * version`	Displays the version information of directly connected neighbors
`show CDP traffic`	Displays interface CDP traffic statistics
`show CDP interface`	Displays interface status information

The cdp timer and holdtime is typically never changed, but you can and here is how you would do that:

- The *CDP timer* is how often CDP packets are transmitted to all active interfaces.
- The *CDP holdtime* is the amount of time that the device will hold packets received from neighbor devices.

```
Router#sh cdp
Global CDP information:
        Sending CDP packets every 60 seconds
        Sending a holdtime value of 180 seconds
        Sending CDPv2 advertisements is  enabled
Router(config)#cdp ?
  advertise-v2      CDP sends version-2 advertisements
  holdtime          Specify the holdtime (in sec) to be sent in packets
  log               Log messages generated by CDP
  run               Enable CDP
  source-interface  Insert the interface's IP in all CDP packets
  timer             Specify rate (in sec) at which CDP packets are sent  run
Router (config)#cdp holdtime ?
  <10-255>  Length  of time  (in sec) that receiver must keep this packet
Router (config)#cdp timer ?
  <5-254>  Rate at which CDP packets are sent (in  sec)
```

Gathering Neighbor Information

I can't stress to you enough how important CDP is. Let's go through the CDP commands and please study the output.

The following output shows the `show cdp neighbor` command used on my ISR router:

```
Router#sh cdp neighbors
Capability Codes: R - Router, T - Trans Bridge, B - Source Route Bridge
                  S - Switch, H - Host, I - IGMP, r - Repeater
Device ID    Local Intrfce   Holdtme    Capability  Platform  Port ID
ap          Fas 0/1           165         T I       AIR-AP124 Fas 0
R2          Ser 0/1/0         140        R S I      2801      Ser 0/2/0
R3          Ser 0/0/1         157        R S I      1841      Ser 0/0/1
R1          Ser 0/2/0         154        R S I      1841      Ser 0/0/1
R1          Ser 0/0/0         154        R S I      1841      Ser 0/0/0
Router#
```

Another command that will deliver the goods on neighbor information is the `show cdp neighbor detail` command (`show cdp nei de` for short). This command can be run on both routers and switches, and it displays detailed information about each device connected to the device on which you're running the command. Check out this router output for an example:

```
Router#sh cdp neighbors detail
-------------------------
Device ID: R2
Entry address(es):
  IP address: 10.4.4.2
Platform: Cisco 2801,  Capabilities: Router Switch IGMP
Interface: Serial0/1/0,  Port ID (outgoing port): Serial0/2/0
Holdtime : 135 sec

Version :
Cisco IOS Software, 2801 Software (C2801-ADVENTERPRISEK9-M), Experimental
Version 12.4(20050525:193634) [jezhao-ani 145]
Copyright (c) 1986-2005 by Cisco Systems, Inc.
Compiled Fri 27-May-05 23:53 by jezhao

advertisement version: 2
VTP Management Domain: ''

Corp#
Corp#show cdp entry * protocol
Protocol information for ap :
  IP address: 10.1.1.2
Protocol information for R2 :
  IP address: 10.4.4.2
Protocol information for R3 :
  IP address: 10.5.5.1
Protocol information for R1 :
  IP address: 10.3.3.2
Protocol information for R1 :
  IP address: 10.2.2.2
Corp#show cdp entry * version
Version information for ap :
  Cisco IOS Software, C1240 Software (C1240-K9W7-M), Version 12.3(8)JEA,
RELEASE SOFTWARE (fc2)
Technical Support: http://www.cisco.com/techsupport
Copyright (c) 1986-2006 by Cisco Systems, Inc.
Compiled Wed 23-Aug-06 16:45 by kellythw
```

```
Version information for R2 :
  Cisco IOS Software, 2801 Software (C2801-ADVENTERPRISEK9-M), Experimental
Version 12.4(20050525:193634) [jezhao-ani 145]
Copyright (c) 1986-2005 by Cisco Systems, Inc.
Compiled Fri 27-May-05 23:53 by jezhao

Version information for R3 :
  Cisco IOS Software, 1841 Software (C1841-IPBASE-M), Version 12.4(1c), RELEASE
SOFTWARE (fc1)
Technical Support: http://www.cisco.com/techsupport
Copyright (c) 1986-2005 by Cisco Systems, Inc.
Compiled Tue 25-Oct-05 17:10 by evmiller

 --More–
[output cut]
```

Gathering Interface Traffic Information

The `show cdp traffic` command displays information about interface traffic, including the number of CDP packets sent and received and the errors with CDP.

The following output shows the `show cdp traffic` command used on the Corp router:

```
Router#sh cdp traffic
CDP counters :
        Total packets output: 911, Input: 524
        Hdr syntax: 0, Chksum error: 0, Encaps failed: 2
        No memory: 0, Invalid packet: 0, Fragmented: 0
        CDP version 1 advertisements output: 0, Input: 0
        CDP version 2 advertisements output: 911, Input: 524
Router#
```

Gathering Port and Interface Information

The `show cdp interface` command gives you the CDP status on router interfaces or switch ports:

```
Router#sh cdp interface
FastEthernet0/0 is administratively down, line protocol is down
  Encapsulation ARPA
  Sending CDP packets every 60 seconds
  Holdtime is 180 seconds
```

```
FastEthernet0/1 is up, line protocol is up
  Encapsulation ARPA
  Sending CDP packets every 60 seconds
  Holdtime is 180 seconds
Serial0/0/0 is up, line protocol is up
  Encapsulation HDLC
  Sending CDP packets every 60 seconds
  Holdtime is 180 seconds
Serial0/0/1 is up, line protocol is up
  Encapsulation HDLC
  Sending CDP packets every 60 seconds
  Holdtime is 180 seconds
Serial0/1/0 is up, line protocol is up
  Encapsulation HDLC
  Sending CDP packets every 60 seconds
  Holdtime is 180 seconds
Serial0/2/0 is up, line protocol is up
  Encapsulation HDLC
  Sending CDP packets every 60 seconds
  Holdtime is 180 seconds
```

Using Telnet

Telnet, part of the TCP/IP protocol suite, is a powerful program that allows your computer to act like a dumb terminal and run programs on another computer. Table 2.11 shows the commands you need to know:

TABLE 2.11 Telnet Commands

Command	Meaning
`telnet`	Makes your terminal a dumb terminal. You can only run programs on another computer, not copy files.
`show sessions`	Shows the routers into which you are telnetted.
`show users`	Shows the routers that are telnetted into your router.

TABLE 2.11 Telnet Commands *(continued)*

Command	Meaning
`exit`	Closes a Telnet session.
`disconnect`	Closes a remote Telnet session.
`clear line line-number`	Clears a session connected to your router.

Telnet is a virtual terminal protocol that allows you to connect to remote devices, gather information, and run programs.

You can issue the `telnet` command from any router prompt, like this:

```
Router#telnet 10.2.2.2
Trying 10.2.2.2 ... Open

Password required, but none set

[Connection to 10.2.2.2 closed by foreign host]
Router#
```

As you can see, I didn't set my passwords—how embarrassing! Remember that the VTY ports on a router are configured as `login`, meaning you have to either set the VTY passwords or use the `no login` command.

On a Cisco router, you don't need to use the `telnet` command; you can just type in an IP address from a command prompt, and the router will assume you want to telnet to the device. Here's how that looks by using just the IP address:

```
Router#10.2.2.2
Trying 10.2.2.2 ... Open

Password required, but none set

[Connection to 10.2.2.2 closed by foreign host]
Router#
```

Telnetting into Multiple Devices Simultaneously

If you telnet to a router or switch, you can end the connection by using `exit` at any time. But what if you want to keep your connection to a remote device but still come back to your original router console? To do that, you can press the Ctrl+Shift+6 key combination, release it, and then press X.

Here's an example of connecting to multiple devices from my console:

```
Router#10.2.2.2
Trying 10.2.2.2 ... Open

User Access Verification

Password:
R1>
Router#
```

In this example, I telnetted to the R1 router and then typed the password to enter user mode. I next pressed Ctrl+Shift+6 and then X (but you can't see that because it doesn't show on the screen output). Notice that my command prompt is now back at the Router# prompt.

Checking Telnet Connections

To see the connections made from your router to a remote device, use the show sessions command, like so:

```
Corp#sh sessions
Conn Host                Address             Byte  Idle Conn Name
   1 10.2.2.2            10.2.2.2               0     0 10.2.2.2
*  2 10.1.1.2            10.1.1.2               0     0 10.1.1.2
Corp#
```

See that asterisk (*) next to connection 2? It means that session 2 was your last session. You can return to your last session by pressing Enter twice. You can also return to any session by typing the number of the connection and pressing Enter.

Checking Telnet Users

You can list all active consoles and VTY ports in use on your router with the show users command:

```
Corp#sh users
    Line       User       Host(s)              Idle       Location
*  0 con 0                10.1.1.2             00:00:01
     10.2.2.2             00:01:06
```

In the command's output, con represents the local console. In this example, the console is connected to two remote IP addresses or, in other words, two devices. In the next example, I typed **sh users** on the ap device that the Corp router had telnetted into and that is connected via line 1:

```
Corp#sh sessions
Conn Host                Address             Byte  Idle Conn Name
   1 10.1.1.2            10.1.1.2               0     0 10.1.1.2
*  2 10.2.2.2            10.2.2.2               0     0 10.2.2.2
Corp#1
[Resuming connection 1 to 10.1.1.2 ... ]
ap>sh users
    Line       User       Host(s)              Idle       Location
*  1 vty 0                idle                 00:00:00 10.1.1.1
ap>
```

This output shows that the console is active and that VTY port 1 is being used. The asterisk represents the current terminal session from which the `show user` command was entered.

Closing Telnet Sessions

You can end Telnet sessions a few different ways—using `exit` or `disconnect` is probably the easiest and quickest:

```
ap>exit

[Connection to 10.1.1.2 closed by foreign host]
Corp#
```

Since the ap device was my last session, I just pressed Enter twice to return to that session.

To end a session from a local device, use the `disconnect` command:

```
Corp#sh session
Conn Host                Address             Byte  Idle Conn Name
   2 10.2.2.2            10.2.2.2               0     0 10.2.2.2
Corp#disconnect ?
  <0-0>  The number of an active network connection
  qdm    Disconnect QDM web-based clients
  ssh    Disconnect an active SSH connection
Corp#disconnect 2
Closing connection to 10.2.2.2 [confirm][enter]
Corp#
```

If you want to end a session of a device attached to your local device through Telnet, you should first check to see whether any devices are telnetted into your router. To get that information, use the `show users` command like this:

```
R1#sh users
    Line       User       Host(s)              Idle       Location
*  0 con 0                idle                 00:00:00
  vty 194                 idle                 00:00:21 10.2.2.1
```

This output shows that VTY has IP address 10.2.2.1 connected. That's the Corp router. Also notice that the Corp router connected to line 194—remember, you cannot choose which line you connect to! This is why I set the same password on all lines.

To clear the connection, use the `clear line #` command:

```
R1#clear line 194
[confirm][enter]
 [OK]
R1#sh users
    Line       User       Host(s)              Idle        Location
*  0 con 0                idle                 00:00:00
```

This output confirms that the line has been cleared.

Resolving Hostnames

To use a hostname rather than an IP address to connect to a remote device, the device that you are using to make the connection must be able to translate the hostname to an IP address.

You can resolve hostnames to IP addresses in two ways: building a host table on each router or building a Domain Name System (DNS) server, which is similar to a dynamic host table. Table 2.12 is a list of important commands that can be used to help you resolve hostnames on a router:

TABLE 2.12 Hosts Table Commands

Command	Meaning
`ip host`	Creates a static host table on your router
`show hosts`	Displays the host table on your router
`ip domain-lookup`	Enables the DNS service

TABLE 2.12 Hosts Table Commands *(continued)*

Command	Meaning
`ip name-server`	Configures your device with the IP address of a DNS server
`ip domain-name`	Configures domain suffix for fully qualified domain name

Building a Host Table

A *host table* provides name resolution only on the router that it was built upon. The command to build a host table on a router is as follows:

```
ip host host_name tcp_port_number ip_address
```

The default is TCP port number 23, but you can create a session using Telnet with a different TCP port number if you want. You can also assign up to eight IP addresses to a hostname.

Here's an example of configuring a host table on the Corp router with two entries to resolve the names for the R1 router and the `ap` device:

```
Corp#config t
Enter configuration commands, one per line.  End with CNTL/Z.
Corp(config)#ip host R1 ?
  <0-65535>   Default telnet port number
  A.B.C.D     Host IP address
  additional  Append addresses
  mx          Configure a MX record
  ns          Configure an NS record
  srv         Configure a SRV record
Corp(config)#ip host R1 10.2.2.2 ?
  A.B.C.D  Host IP address
  <cr>
Corp(config)#ip host R1 10.2.2.2
Corp(config)#ip host ap 10.1.1.2
```

Notice in the previous router configuration that I can just keep adding IP addresses to reference a host, one after another, up to eight IP address. And to see the newly built host table, just use the `show hosts` command:

```
Corp(config)#do show hosts
Default domain is not set
Name/address lookup uses domain service
Name servers are 255.255.255.255
```

```
Codes: UN - unknown, EX - expired, OK - OK, ?? - revalidate
       temp - temporary, perm - permanent
       NA - Not Applicable None - Not defined
Host                      Port  Flags      Age Type   Address(es)
ap                        None  (perm, OK)  0   IP    10.1.1.2
R1                        None  (perm, OK)  0   IP    10.2.2.2
Corp(config)#^Z
Corp#
```

You can see the two hostnames plus their associated IP addresses in the preceding router output. The `perm` in the `Flags` column means the entry is manually configured. If it said `temp`, it would be an entry that was resolved by DNS. Here is an example of a router resolving a hostname and then telnetting to the resolved IP address:

```
Corp#r1
Trying R1 (10.2.2.2)... Open

User Access Verification

Password:
R1>Ctrl+Shift+6
Corp#ap
Trying ap (10.1.1.2)... Open

User Access Verification

Password:
ap>Ctrl+Shift+6
Corp#
Corp#sh sessions
Conn Host                Address             Byte  Idle Conn Name
   1 r1                  10.2.2.2               0     1 r1
*  2 ap                  10.1.1.2               0     0 ap
Corp#
```

If you want to remove a hostname from the table, just use the `no ip host` command, like this:

```
RouterA(config)#no ip host R1
```

The problem with the host table method is that you would need to create a host table on each router to be able to resolve names. And if you have a whole bunch of routers and want to resolve names, using DNS is a much better choice!

Using DNS to Resolve Names

If you have a lot of devices and don't want to create a host table in each device, you can use a DNS server to resolve hostnames.

Anytime a Cisco device receives a command it doesn't understand, it will try to resolve it through DNS by default. Watch what happens when I type the special command **todd** at a Cisco router prompt:

```
Corp#todd
Translating "todd"...domain server (255.255.255.255)
Translating "todd"...domain server (255.255.255.255)
Translating "todd"...domain server (255.255.255.255)
% Unknown command or computer name, or unable to find
  computer address
Corp#
```

You can get around this and prevent a time-consuming DNS lookup by using the `no ip domain-lookup` command on your router from global configuration mode.

If you have a DNS server on your network, you need to add a few commands to make DNS name resolution work:

```
Corp#config t
Corp(config)#ip domain-lookup
Corp(config)#ip name-server ?
  A.B.C.D  Domain server IP address (maximum of 6)
Corp(config)#ip name-server 192.168.0.70
Corp(config)#ip domain-name lammle.com
Corp(config)#^Z
Corp#
```

After the DNS configurations are set, you can test the DNS server by using a hostname to ping or telnet a device like this:

```
Corp#ping R1
Translating "R1"...domain server (192.168.0.70) [OK]
Type escape sequence to abort.
Sending 5, 100-byte ICMP Echos to 10.2.2.2, timeout is
  2 seconds:
!!!!!
Success rate is 100 percent (5/5), round-trip min/avg/max
  = 28/31/32 ms
```

Checking Network Connectivity and Troubleshooting

You can use the `ping` and `traceroute` commands to test connectivity to remote devices, and you can use both of them with many protocols, not just IP.

The `debug` command and the `show processes` command you need to troubleshoot a router are listed in Table 2.13:

TABLE 2.13 Troubleshooting Commands

Command	Meaning
`ping`	Tells you whether a host on an internetwork has an IP stack enabled
`traceroute`	Tells you the path a packet takes to find a remote host
`debug`	Enables packet-level debugging used for troubleshooting a router or network
`undebug`	The undebug command will disable debugging output on the router
`show processes`	Show the processes used on a router and CPU cycles

Using the *ping* Command

So far, you've seen many examples of pinging devices to test IP connectivity and name resolution using the DNS server. To see all the different protocols that you can use with the `ping` program, type **ping ?**, like so:

```
Corp#ping ?
  WORD  Ping destination address or hostname
  clns  CLNS echo
  ip    IP echo
  srb   srb echo
  tag   Tag encapsulated IP echo
  <cr>
```

The `ping` output displays the minimum, average, and maximum times it takes for a `ping` packet to find a specified system and return. Here's an example:

```
Corp#ping R1
Translating "R1"...domain server (192.168.0.70)[OK]
Type escape sequence to abort.
```

```
Sending 5, 100-byte ICMP Echos to 10.2.2.2, timeout
  is 2 seconds:
!!!!!
Success rate is 100 percent (5/5), round-trip min/avg/max
  = 1/2/4 ms
Corp#
```

Using the *traceroute* Command

The traceroute command (or trace for short) shows the path a packet takes to get to a remote device. It uses time to live (TTL) timeouts and ICMP error messages to outline the path a packet takes through an internetwork to arrive at a remote host. Let's take a look at the traceroute command being used on a router:

```
Corp#traceroute ?
  WORD        Trace route to destination address or hostname
  appletalk   AppleTalk Trace
  clns        ISO CLNS Trace
  ip          IP Trace
  ipv6        IPv6 Trace
  ipx         IPX Trace
  <cr>
```

The trace command shows the hops that a packet traverses on its way to a remote device. Here's an example:

```
Corp#traceroute r1

Type escape sequence to abort.
Tracing the route to R1 (10.2.2.2)

  1 R1 (10.2.2.2) 4 msec *  0 msec
Corp#
```

Debugging

The debug command is a troubleshooting command that's available from privileged exec mode (of Cisco IOS). It's used to display information about various router operations and the related traffic generated or received by the router, plus any error messages.

```
Corp>debug ?
% Unrecognized command
Corp>en
Corp#debug ?
```

```
  aaa                     AAA Authentication, Authorization and Accounting
  access-expression       Boolean access expression
  adjacency               adjacency
  all                     Enable all debugging
[output cut]
```

If you have the freedom to pretty much take out a router and you really want to have some fun with debugging, use the **debug all** command:

```
Corp#debug all

This may severely impact network performance. Continue? (yes/[no]):yes

All possible debugging has been turned on

2d20h: SNMP: HC Timer 824AE5CC fired
2d20h: SNMP: HC Timer 824AE5CC rearmed, delay = 20000
2d20h: Serial0/0: HDLC myseq 4, mineseen 0, yourseen 0, line down
2d20h:
2d20h: Rudpv1 Sent: Pkts 0,  Data Bytes 0,  Data Pkts 0
2d20h: Rudpv1 Rcvd: Pkts 0,  Data Bytes 0,  Data Pkts 0
2d20h: Rudpv1 Discarded: 0,  Retransmitted 0
2d20h:
2d20h: RIP-TIMER: periodic timer expired
2d20h: Serial0/0: HDLC myseq 5, mineseen 0, yourseen 0, line down
2d20h: Serial0/0: attempting to restart
2d20h: PowerQUICC(0/0): DCD is up.
2d20h: is_up: 0 state: 4 sub state: 1 line: 0
2d20h:
2d20h: Rudpv1 Sent: Pkts 0,  Data Bytes 0,  Data Pkts 0
2d20h: Rudpv1 Rcvd: Pkts 0,  Data Bytes 0,  Data Pkts 0
2d20h: Rudpv1 Discarded: 0,  Retransmitted 0
2d20h: un all
All possible debugging has been turned off
Corp#
```

To disable debugging on a router, just use the command **no** in front of the **debug** command:

```
Corp#no debug all
```

I typically just use the **undebug all** command since it is so easy when using the shortcut:

```
Corp#un all
```

Remember that instead of using the `debug all` command, it's almost always better to use specific commands—and only for short periods of time. Here's an example of deploying `debug ip rip` that will show you rip updates being sent and received on a router:

```
Corp#debug ip rip
RIP protocol debugging is on
Corp#
1w4d: RIP: sending v2 update to 224.0.0.9 via Serial0/0 (192.168.12.1)
1w4d: RIP: build update entries
1w4d:    10.10.10.0/24 via 0.0.0.0, metric 2, tag 0
1w4d:    171.16.125.0/24 via 0.0.0.0, metric 3, tag 0
1w4d:    172.16.12.0/24 via 0.0.0.0, metric 1, tag 0
1w4d:    172.16.125.0/24 via 0.0.0.0, metric 3, tag 0
1w4d: RIP: sending v2 update to 224.0.0.9 via Serial0/2 (172.16.12.1)
1w4d: RIP: build update entries
1w4d:    192.168.12.0/24 via 0.0.0.0, metric 1, tag 0
1w4d:    192.168.22.0/24 via 0.0.0.0, metric 2, tag 0
1w4d: RIP: received v2 update from 192.168.12.2 on Serial0/0
1w4d:     192.168.22.0/24 via 0.0.0.0 in 1 hops
Corp#un all
```

Using the *sh processes* Command

You really have to be careful when using the `debug` command on your devices. If your router's CPU utilization is consistently at 50 percent or more, it's probably not a good idea to type in the `debug all` command unless you want to see what a router looks like when it crashes!

```
Corp#sh processes
CPU utilization for five seconds: 2%/0%; one minute: 0%; five minutes: 0%
 PID QTy       PC Runtime (ms)    Invoked    uSecs     Stacks TTY Process
   1 Cwe 8034470C            0          1        0 5804/6000   0 Chunk Manager
   2 Csp 80369A88            4       1856        2 2616/3000   0 Load Meter
   3 M*         0          112         14   800010656/12000   0 Exec
   5 Lst 8034FD9C       268246      52101     5148 5768/6000   0 Check heaps
   6 Cwe 80355E5C           20          3     6666 5704/6000   0 Pool Manager
   7 Mst 802AC3C4            0          2        0 5580/6000   0 Timers
[output cut]
```

So basically, the output from the `show processes` command shows that the router is happily able to process debugging commands without being overloaded.

Chapter 3 IP Routing

In this chapter, I'll discuss the commands that configure the IP routing process. This is an important subject to understand since it pertains to all routers and configurations that use IP. *IP routing* is the process of moving packets from one network to another network using routers. And as before, by *routers* I mean Cisco routers, of course!

Once all routers know about all networks, a *routed protocol* can be used to send user data (packets) through the established enterprise. Routed protocols are assigned to an interface and determine the method of packet delivery. Examples of routed protocols are IP and IPv6.

For up-to-the minute updates for this chapter, please see `www.lammle.com` or `www.sybex.com/go/IOS`

Routing Basics

Once you create an internetwork by connecting your WANs and LANs to a router, you'll need to configure logical network addresses, such as IP addresses, to all hosts on the internetwork so that they can communicate across that internetwork.

If your network has no routers, then it should be apparent that you are not routing. Routers route traffic to all the networks in your internetwork. To be able to route packets, a router must know, at a minimum, the following:

- The destination address
- The neighbor routers from which it can learn about remote networks
- Possible routes to all remote networks
- The best route to each remote network
- How to maintain and verify routing information

The router learns about remote networks from neighbor routers or from an administrator. The router then builds a *routing table* (a map of the internetwork) that describes how to find the remote networks. If a network is directly connected, then the router already knows how to get to it.

If a network isn't directly connected to the router, the router must learn how to get to the remote network in one of two ways: by using *static routing*, meaning someone must type all network locations into the routing table, or by using something called *dynamic routing*.

Figure 3.1 shows a simple two-router network. Lab_A has one serial interface and three LAN interfaces.

FIGURE 3.1 A simple routing example

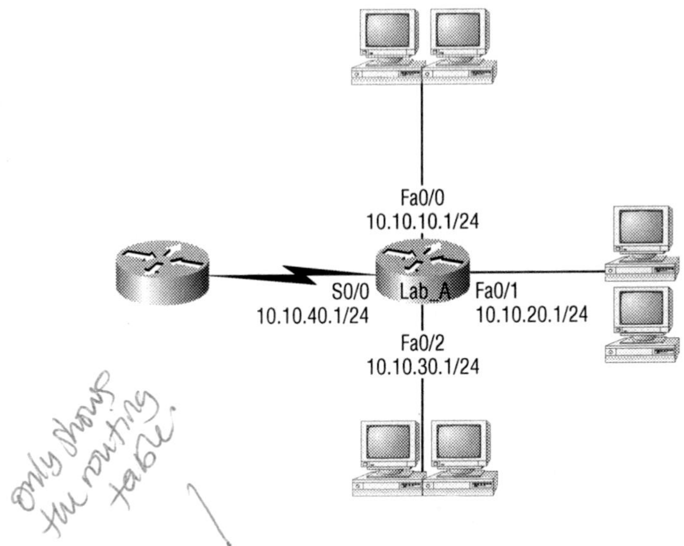

By using the command `show ip route` in Table 3.1, you can see the routing table (map of the internetwork) that Lab_A uses to make forwarding decisions:

TABLE 3.1 The show IP Route Command and Meaning

Command	Meaning
`show ip route`	Displays a routers table of known or learned destination networks.

And here is the output of the routing table:

```
Lab_A#sh ip route
[output cut]
Gateway of last resort is not set
C       10.10.10.0/24 is directly connected, FastEthernet0/0
C       10.10.20.0/24 is directly connected, FastEthernet0/1
C       10.10.30.0/24 is directly connected, FastEthernet0/2
C       10.10.40.0/24 is directly connected, Serial 0/0
```

Let's take a look at the information you get from the routing table. All the way to the left in each of the listings is a C. Now, if you look at a routing table on a real router, you will see a legend right above the table. The C tells you that each of these networks is directly connected to this router. I will be talking about many more of the codes in the legend as we go along. The next bit of information from the listings is the actual network that the router knows about. The table then tells you that each of the entries is directly connected and finally the interface you have to send packets out of to reach the given network.

For another example, look at the output of a corporate router's routing table, and it will say you have now turned on RIP:

```
Corp#sh ip route
[output cut]
R    192.168.215.0 [120/2] via 192.168.20.2, 00:00:23, Serial0/0
R    192.168.115.0 [120/1] via 192.168.20.2, 00:00:23, Serial0/0
R    192.168.30.0 [120/1] via 192.168.20.2, 00:00:23, Serial0/0
C    192.168.20.0 is directly connected, Serial0/0
C    192.168.214.0 is directly connected, FastEthernet0/0
```

You can now see there is a little bit more information the routing table is displaying to you. Again, from the far left there is an R. The R tells you that this entry or route was learned by the router through the RIP routing protocol. The entry displays the network for you again, but now you can see some new pieces. The two numbers in the brackets are important. The first number tells the administrative distance of the route. The second number gives you the metric of the route.

```
Corp#sh ip route
Codes: C - connected, S - static, R - RIP, M - mobile, B - BGP
       D - EIGRP, EX - EIGRP external, O - OSPF, IA - OSPF inter area
       N1 - OSPF NSSA external type 1, N2 - OSPF NSSA external type 2
       E1 - OSPF external type 1, E2 - OSPF external type 2
       i - IS-IS, su - IS-IS summary, L1 - IS-IS level-1, L2 - IS-IS level-2,
ia - IS-IS inter area, * - candidate default, U - per-user static route, o -
ODR, P - periodic downloaded static route

Gateway of last resort is not set

     10.0.0.0/24 is subnetted, 1 subnets
C       10.1.1.0 is directly connected, FastEthernet0/1
Corp#
```

Here is the output of the entire top portion of the routing table so you can see all the routing codes:

Static Routing

Now that you can get basic information from the router out of the routing table, you can start putting some information into the routing table. Static routing is a pretty simple way to put in information, and it is where we will start.

Static routing occurs when you manually add routes in each router's routing table. Static routing has pros and cons, but that's true for all routing processes.

Static routing has the following benefits:

- There is no overhead on the router CPU, which means you could buy a cheaper router than you would use if you were using dynamic routing.
- There is no bandwidth usage between routers, which means you could save money on WAN links.
- It adds security, because the administrator can choose to allow routing access to certain networks only.

Static routing has the following disadvantages:

- The administrator must really understand the internetwork and how each router is connected in order to configure routes correctly.
- If a network is added to the internetwork, the administrator has to add a route to it on all routers—by hand.
- It's not feasible in large networks because maintaining it would be a full-time job in itself.

That said, Table 3.2 lists the command syntax you use to add a static route to a routing table:

TABLE 3.2 The IP Route Command

Command	Meaning
`ip route`	Configures static route information for a router to possibly use in its routing table

Here are the options:

```
ip route [destination_network] [mask] [next-hop_address or
  exitinterface] [administrative_distance] [permanent]
```

Table 3.3 describes the command and each option in the string.

TABLE 3.3 Static Routing Commands and Options

Option	Meaning
destination_network	The network you're placing in the routing table.
mask	The subnet mask being used on the network.
next-hop_address	The address of the next-hop router that will receive the packet and forward it to the remote network. This is a router interface that's on a directly connected network.
exitinterface	Used in place of the next-hop address if you want and shows up as a directly connected route.
administrative_distance	By default, static routes have an administrative distance of 1 (or even 0 if you use an exit interface instead of a next-hop address).
permanent	If the interface is shut down or the router can't communicate to the next-hop router, the route will automatically be discarded from the routing table. Choosing the permanent option keeps the entry in the routing table no matter what happens.

Here is a sample static route, complete with the network to be added, its mask, and the next-hop address to which the data will be sent:

```
Router(config)#ip route 172.16.3.0 255.255.255.0 192.168.2.4
```

However, suppose the static route looked like this:

```
Router(config)#ip route 172.16.3.0 255.255.255.0 192.168.2.4 150
```

The 150, at the end of the command, changes the default administrative distance (AD) of 1 to 150. Remember that the AD is the trustworthiness of a route, where 0 is best and 255 is worst.

Here's one more example:

```
Router(config)#ip route 172.16.3.0 255.255.255.0 s0/0/0
```

Instead of using a next-hop address, you can use an exit interface that will make the route show up as a directly connected network. Functionally, the next-hop and exit interfaces work the same way.

Default Routing

You can use *default routing* to send packets with a remote destination network not in the routing table to the next-hop router. You should use default routing only on stub networks—those with only one exit path out of the network.

To configure a default route, you use wildcards in the network address and mask locations of a static route. In fact, you can just think of a default route as a static route that uses wildcards instead of network and mask information.

By using a default route, you can create just one static route entry instead. This sure is easier than typing in all those routes! Here is an example:

```
Router(config)#ip route 0.0.0.0 0.0.0.0 10.1.11.1
Router (config)#ip classless
Router (config)#do show ip route
  Gateway of last resort is 10.1.11.1 to network 0.0.0.0
 10.0.0.0/24 is subnetted, 2 subnets
C       10.1.11.0 is directly connected, Vlan1
C       10.1.12.0 is directly connected, Dot11Radio0
S*   0.0.0.0/0 [1/0] via 10.1.11.1
Router (config)#
```

If you look at the routing table, you'll see only the two directly connected networks plus an S*, which indicates this entry is a candidate for a default route. I could have completed the default `route` command another way:

```
Router (config)#ip route 0.0.0.0 0.0.0.0 Fa0/0
```

What this is telling you is that if you don't have an entry for a network in the routing table, just forward it out FastEthernet0/0. Table 3.4 defines the ip classless command:

TABLE 3.4 Default Routing

Command	Meaning
`ip classless`	Enables classless features, allowing different subnet sizes

All Cisco routers are classful routers, meaning they expect a default subnet mask on each interface of the router. When a router receives a packet for a destination subnet that's not in the routing table, it will drop the packet by default. If you're using default routing, you must use the `ip classless` command because it is possible that no remote subnets will be in the routing table. Here is example:

```
Router(config)#ip classless
```

Table 3.5 defines the ip default-network command used with RIP:

TABLE 3.5 Advanced Static Route Commands

Command	Meaning
`ip default-network`	Configures a gateway of last resort and allows it to be advertised

There's another command you can use to configure a gateway of last resort—the `ip default-network` command. Figure 3.2 shows a network that needs to have a gateway of last resort statement configured.

FIGURE 3.2 Configuring a gateway of last resort

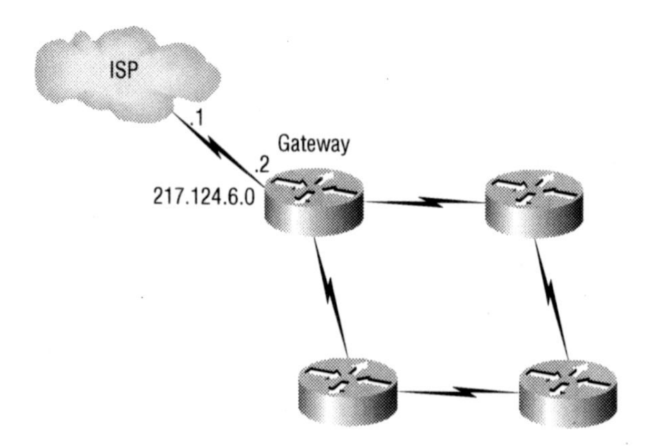

Here are three commands (all providing the same solution) for adding a gateway of last resort on the gateway router to the ISP:

```
Gateway(config)#ip route 0.0.0.0 0.0.0.0 217.124.6.1

Gateway(config)#ip route 0.0.0.0 0.0.0.0 s0/0

Gateway(config)#ip default-network 217.124.6.0
```

As I said before, all three of these commands would accomplish the goal of setting the gateway of last resort, but there are some small differences between them. First, the exit interface solution would be used over the other two solutions because it has an AD of 0. Also, the `ip default-network` command would advertise the default network when you configure an IGP (like RIP) on the router. This is so other routers in your internetwork will receive this route as a default route automatically.

I'll discuss one last topic before moving on to dynamic routing. If you have the routing table output as shown here, what happens if the router receives a packet from 10.1.6.100 destined for host 10.1.8.5?

```
Corp#sh ip route
[output cut]
Gateway of last resort is 10.1.5.5 to network 0.0.0.0

R     10.1.3.0 [120/1] via 101.2.2, 00:00:00, Serial 0/0
C     10.1.2.0  is directly connected, Serial0/0
C     10.1.5.0  is directly connected, Serial0/1
C     10.1.6.0  is directly connected, Fastethernet0/0
R*    0.0.0.0/0 [120/0] via 10.1.5.5, 00:00:00 Serial 0/1
```

This is a tad different from what I've shown you up until now because the default route is listed as R*, which means it's a RIP-injected route. This is because someone configured the `ip default-network` command on a remote router as well as configuring RIP, causing RIP to advertise this route through the internetwork as a default route. Since the destination address is 10.1.8.5 and there is no route to network 10.1.8.0, the router would use the default route and send the packet out serial 0/1.

Routing Protocol Basics

You should know some important facts about routing protocols before getting deeper into RIP. Specifically, you need to understand administrative distances, the three kinds of routing protocols, and routing loops. I'll cover each of these in more detail in the following sections.

Administrative Distances (ADs)

The *AD* is used to rate the trustworthiness of routing information received on a router from a neighbor router. An AD is an integer from 0 to 255, where 0 is the most trusted and 255 means no traffic will be passed via this route.

Table 3.6 shows the default administrative distances that a Cisco router uses to decide which route to take to a remote network.

TABLE 3.6 Default Administrative Distances

Route Source	Default AD
Connected interface	0
Static route	1

TABLE 3.6 Default Administrative Distances *(continued)*

Route Source	Default AD
EIGRP	90
IGRP	100
OSPF	110
RIP	120
External EIGRP	170
Unknown	255 (this route will never be used)

Table 3.7 defines the commands to change the AD of RIP on your router:

TABLE 3.7 Router Rip Commands

Command	Meaning
`router rip`	Enables RIP routing
`distance`	Changes the default administrative distance

Each routing protocol has a default AD; you can, however, change the AD for specific routes or for a routing protocol. Earlier when I added 150 to the end of the static route entry, I changed the AD for that specific route. If I want to change the AD for a routing protocol, I must use the `distance` command.

```
Router(config)#router rip
Router(config-router)#distance 150
```

Routing Information Protocol (RIP)

Routing Information Protocol (RIP) is a true distance-vector routing protocol. RIP sends the complete routing table to all active interfaces every 30 seconds. RIP uses the hop count only to determine the best way to a remote network, but it has a maximum allowable hop count of 15 by default, meaning that 16 is deemed unreachable. RIP works well in small networks, but it's inefficient on large networks with slow WAN links or on networks with a large number of routers installed.

RIP Timers

RIP uses four kinds of timers to regulate its performance; Table 3.8 describes them.

TABLE 3.8 RIP Timers

Timer	Meaning
`route update timer`	Sets the interval (typically 30 seconds) between periodic routing updates, in which the router sends a complete copy of its routing table to all neighbors.
`route invalid timer`	Determines the length of time that must elapse (180 seconds) before a router determines that a route has become invalid. It will come to this conclusion if it hasn't heard any updates about a particular route for that period. When that happens, the router will send out updates to all its neighbors letting them know that the route is invalid.
`holddown timer`	This sets the amount of time during which routing information is suppressed. Routes will enter into the holddown state when an update packet is received that indicates the route is unreachable. This continues either until an update packet is received with a better metric or until the holddown timer expires. The default is 180 seconds.
`route flush timer`	Sets the time between a route becoming invalid and its removal from the routing table (240 seconds). Before it's removed from the table, the router notifies its neighbors of that route's impending demise. The value of the route invalid timer must be less than that of the route flush timer. This gives the router enough time to tell its neighbors about the invalid route before the local routing table is updated.

Table 3.9 lists the commands to change the timers:

TABLE 3.9 RIP Timer Commands

Command	Meaning
`router rip`	Enables rip routing
`timers`	Changes the default RIP timers

The command to configure the RIP timers is `timers` under the RIP configuration mode. Here is an example of setting the timers to their defaults:

```
Router(config-router)#timers basic 30 180 180 240
```

Enabling RIP

To configure RIP routing, just turn on the protocol with the `router rip` command and tell the RIP routing protocol which networks to advertise. Table 3.10 shows the basic configuration of enabling RIP:

TABLE 3.10 RIP Commands

Command	Meaning
`router rip`	Starts and enable a RIP routing process
`network`	Configures a network to advertise and enable interfaces into the routing process

Here's an example:

```
Router#config t
Router(config)#router rip
Router(config-router)#network 10.0.0.0
```

That's it. Two or three commands, and you're done—that sure makes your job a lot easier than when using static routes, doesn't it? However, keep in mind the extra router CPU process and bandwidth you're consuming.

Notice I didn't type subnets, only the classful network address (all subnet bits and host bits off!). It is the job of the routing protocol to find the subnets and populate the routing tables. Since you have no router buddies running RIP, you won't see any RIP routes in the routing table yet.

Remember that RIP uses the classful address when configuring the network address. Because of this, all subnet masks must be the same on all devices in the network (this is called *classful routing*).

To clarify this, let's say you're using a Class B network address of 172.16.0.0/24 with subnets 172.16.10.0, 172.16.20.0, and 172.16.30.0. You would type only the classful network address of 172.16.0.0 and let RIP find the subnets and place them in the routing table.

Holding Down RIP Propagations

You probably don't want your RIP network advertised everywhere on your LAN and WAN. There's not a whole lot to be gained by advertising your RIP network to the Internet, now, is there?

To stop route updates from being sent out an interface, use the command in Table 3.11:

TABLE 3.11 Holding Down Rip Propagations

Command	Meaning
`passive-interface`	Prevents an interface from fully participating in a routing process

Here's an example of how to configure a passive interface on a router using the CLI:

```
Lab_A#config t
Lab_A(config)#router rip
Lab_A(config-router)#network 192.168.10.0
Lab_A(config-router)#passive-interface serial 0/0
```

This command will stop RIP updates from being propagated out serial interface 0/0, but serial interface 0/0 can still receive RIP updates.

RIP Version 2 (RIPv2)

I'll now spend a few paragraphs discussing RIPv2 before moving into the distance-vector, Cisco-proprietary routing protocol IGRP.

RIP version 2 (RIPv2) is mostly the same as RIP version 1 (RIPv1). Both RIPv1 and RIPv2 are *distance-vector protocols*, which means each router running RIP sends its complete routing tables out all active interfaces at periodic time intervals. Also, the timers and loop-avoidance schemes are the same in both RIP versions—that is, holddown timers and split horizon rule. Both RIPv1 and RIPv2 are configured as classful addressing (but RIPv2 is considered classless because subnet information is sent with each route update), and both have the same administrative distance (120). Table 3.12 describes the difference between the two protocols.

TABLE 3.12 RIPv1 vs. RIPv2

RIPv1	RIPv2
Distance vector	Distance vector
Maximum hop count of 15	Maximum hop count of 15

TABLE 3.12 RIPv1 vs. RIPv2 *(continued)*

RIPv1	RIPv2
Classful	Classless
Broadcast based	Uses Multicast 224.0.0.9
No support for VLSM	Supports VLSM networks
No authentication	Allows for MD5 authentication
No support for discontiguous networks	Supports discontiguous networks

Table 3.13 lists the commands for basic configuration of RIPv2 and for using authentication with RIPv2.

TABLE 3.13 RIPv2 Authentication Commands

Command	Meaning
`version`	Configures the version of RIP which is running
`key chain` *name*	This just creates a key chain name
`key` *key*	
`Key-string` *string*	This is the authentication string that is sent and received in the packets by the routing protocol being authenticated
`ip rip authentication key-chain` *chain_name*	Enables authentication on the interface and configures the key chain that will be used
`ip rip authentication mode md5`	Optional, but highly recommended. If you do not add the md5 authentication, then the key-chain is sent in clear text.

Configuring RIPv2 is pretty straightforward. Here's an example:

```
Lab_C(config)#router rip
Lab_C(config-router)#network 192.168.40.0
Lab_C(config-router)#network 192.168.50.0
Lab_C(config-router)#version 2
```

That's it–just add the command version 2 at the (config-router)# prompt, and you are now running RIPv2. Now, let's add authentication to the RIP route updates. Lab_C#**config t**

```
Lab_C(config)#key chain todd
Lab_C(config)#key 1
Lab_C(config)#key-string 12345
Lab_C(config)#interface serial 0/0
Lab_C(config-if)#ip rip authentication key-chain todd
Lab_C(config-if)#ip rip authentication mode md5
```

OK, let's verify RIP routing

Verifying RIP

The following commands in Table 3.14 are used for the verification of RIP routing.

TABLE 3.14 Verifying RIP

Command	Meaning
`show ip route`	Displays the routers routing table
`show ip protocols`	Displays the routing protocols and interfaces used with all routing protocols configured on your router
`debug ip rip`	Show rip updates being sent and received on your router

The *show ip protocols* Command

The `show ip protocols` command shows you the routing protocols that are configured on your router. Looking at the following output, you can see that RIP is running on the router and the timers that RIP uses:

```
R3#sh ip protocols
Routing Protocol is "rip"
  Outgoing update filter list for all interfaces is not set
  Incoming update filter list for all interfaces is not set
  Sending updates every 30 seconds, next due in 24 seconds
  Invalid after 180 seconds, hold down 180, flushed after 240
  Redistributing: rip
  Default version control: send version 1, receive version 1
```

```
    Interface             Send  Recv  Triggered RIP  Key-chain
    FastEthernet0/1       1     1
    Serial0/0/1           1     1
  Automatic network summarization is not in effect
  Maximum path: 4
  Routing for Networks:
    10.0.0.0
  Passive Interface(s):
    FastEthernet0/0
    Serial0/0/0
  Routing Information Sources:
    Gateway         Distance      Last Update
    10.1.11.2            120      00:00:10
    10.1.5.1             120      00:00:22
  Distance: (default is 120)
```

Let's discuss what the above output provides to us:

RIP is sending updates every 30 seconds, which is the default.

The timers used in distance vector are also shown.

Notice further down that RIP is routing for directly connected interfaces f0/1 and s0/0/0. To the right of the interfaces are the version listed—RIPv1.

F0/0 and s0/0/0 are listed as passive interfaces (they will not send RIP information out).

The neighbors it found are 10.1.11.2 and 10.1.5.1. The last entry is the default AD for RIP (120).

The *debug ip rip* Command

The `debug ip rip` command shows routing updates as they are sent and received on the router to the console session. If you are telnetted into the router, you'll need to use the `terminal monitor` command to be able to receive the output from the debug commands.

You can see in this output that RIP is both sending and receiving (the metric is the hop count):

```
R3#debug ip rip
RIP protocol debugging is on
R3#terminal monitor
*Mar 17 19:08:34.371: RIP: sending v1 update to 255.255.255.255 via Serial0/0/1
(10.1.5.2)
*Mar 17 19:08:34.371: RIP: build update entries
*Mar 17 19:08:34.371:    subnet 10.1.10.0 metric 1
*Mar 17 19:08:34.371:    subnet 10.1.11.0 metric 1
*Mar 17 19:08:34.371:    subnet 10.1.12.0 metric 2
```

```
*Mar 17 19:08:40.107: RIP: received v1 update from 10.1.5.1 on Serial0/0/1
*Mar 17 19:08:40.107:      10.1.1.0 in 1 hops
*Mar 17 19:08:40.107:      10.1.2.0 in 1 hops
*Mar 17 19:08:40.107:      10.1.3.0 in 1 hops
*Mar 17 19:08:40.107:      10.1.4.0 in 1 hops
*Mar 17 19:08:40.107:      10.1.6.0 in 2 hops
*Mar 17 19:08:40.107:      10.1.7.0 in 2 hops
*Mar 17 19:08:40.107:      10.1.8.0 in 2 hops
*Mar 17 19:08:40.107:      10.1.9.0 in 2 hops
*Mar 17 19:08:47.535: RIP: sending v1 update to 255.255.255.255 via
FastEthernet0/1 (10.1.11.1)
*Mar 17 19:08:47.535: RIP: build update entries
*Mar 17 19:08:47.535:   subnet 10.1.1.0 metric 2
*Mar 17 19:08:47.535:   subnet 10.1.2.0 metric 2
*Mar 17 19:08:47.535:   subnet 10.1.3.0 metric 2
*Mar 17 19:08:47.535:   subnet 10.1.4.0 metric 2
*Mar 17 19:08:47.535:   subnet 10.1.5.0 metric 1
*Mar 17 19:08:47.535:   subnet 10.1.6.0 metric 3
*Mar 17 19:08:47.535:   subnet 10.1.7.0 metric 3
*Mar 17 19:08:47.535:   subnet 10.1.8.0 metric 3
*Mar 17 19:08:47.535:   subnet 10.1.9.0 metric 3
*Mar 17 19:08:47.535:   subnet 10.1.10.0 metric 1
*Mar 17 19:08:49.331: RIP: received v1 update from 10.1.11.2 on FastEthernet0/1
*Mar 17 19:08:49.331:      10.1.12.0 in 1 hops
R3#undeug all
```

Let's talk about the parts I highlighted in bold. First, RIP is sending v1 packet to 255.255.255.255—an "all-hands" broadcast, out interface Serial0/0/1, via 10.1.5.2. This is where RIPv2 will come in handy. Why? Well, RIPv2 doesn't send broadcasts; it used the multicast 224.0.0.9. So even though the RIP packets could be transmitted onto a network with no routers, all hosts would just ignore them, making RIPv2 a bit of an improvement over RIPv1. On this R3, I'm using the passive interface so I'm not sending broadcasts out to a LAN with any routers connected. Continuing with the `debug ip rip` command, let's take a quick look at a route update when using RIPv2 with MD5 authentication.

```
R3#debug ip rip
 RIP protocol debugging is on
*May  3 20:48:37.046: RIP: received packet with MD5 authentication
*May  3 20:48:37.046: RIP: received v2 update from 192.168.10.1 on Serial0/0
*May  3 20:48:37.050:  10.0.0.0/8 via 0.0.0.0 in 1 hops
```

Chapter 4

Enhanced IGRP (EIGRP) and Open Shortest Path First (OSPF)

Enhanced Interior Gateway Routing Protocol (EIGRP) is a proprietary Cisco protocol that runs on Cisco routers. It is important for you to understand EIGRP because it is probably one of the two most popular routing protocols in use today. In this chapter, I'll show you the many features of EIGRP and describe how it works, with particular focus on the unique way it discovers, selects, and advertises routes.

I'll also introduce you to the Open Shortest Path First (OSPF) routing protocol, which is the other popular routing protocol in use today. I'll explain commands to use in order to implement single-area OSPF in specific networking environments and demonstrate how to verify that everything is running smoothly.

For up-to-the minute updates for this chapter, please see `www.lammle.com` or `www.sybex.com/go/IOS`

Understanding EIGRP Basics

A number of powerful features make EIGRP a real standout from IGRP and other protocols. The main ones are listed here:

- Support for IP and IPv6 (and some other useless routed protocols) via protocol-dependent modules
- Considered classless (same as RIPv2 and OSPF)
- Support for VLSM/CIDR
- Support for summaries and discontiguous networks
- Efficient neighbor discovery
- Communication via Reliable Transport Protocol (RTP)
- Best path selection via Diffusing Update Algorithm (DUAL)

Configuring EIGRP

Although EIGRP can be configured for IP, IPv6, IPX, and AppleTalk, as a future Cisco Certified Network Associate, you really need to focus only on configuring IP for now.

You can enter EIGRP commands from two modes: router configuration mode and interface configuration mode. *Router configuration mode* enables the protocol, determines which networks will run EIGRP, and sets global characteristics. *Interface configuration mode* allows the customization of summaries, metrics, timers, and bandwidth.

To start an EIGRP session on a router, use the `router eigrp` command followed by the autonomous system number of your network. You then enter the network numbers connected to the router using the `network` command followed by the network number. Table 4.1 defines the minimum commands to enable EIGRP on your router:

TABLE 4.1 Basic EIGRP Commands

Command	Meaning
`router eigrp`	Starts an EIGRP routing process for a given autonomous system
`network`	Configures a network to be advertised in the routing protocol and the interface to enable and include in the process

Here's an example of enabling EIGRP for autonomous system 20 on a router connected to two networks, with the network numbers being 10.3.1.0/24 and 172.16.10.0/24:

```
Router#config t
Router(config)#router eigrp 20
Router(config-router)#network 172.16.0.0
Router(config-router)#network 10.0.0.0
```

Remember—as with RIP, you use the classful network address, which means all host bits are turned off.

Holding Down EIGRP Propagations

Say you need to stop EIGRP from working on a specific interface, such as a BRI interface or a serial connection to the Internet. To do that, you would flag the interface as passive using the `passive-interface` *`interface`* command, as discussed in Chapter 3 with RIP. The following command (Table 4.2) shows you how to make interface serial 0/1 a passive interface: The passive-interface command is configured under the routing protocol, not the interface:

TABLE 4.2 Holding Down EIGRP Propagations

Command	Meaning
`passive-interface`	Configuring in EIGRP prevents the interface from participating in the routing process by preventing the sending and receiving of hello packets.

Here are the commands used in context:

```
Router(config)#router eigrp 20
Router(config-router)#passive-interface serial 0/1
```

Doing this will prohibit the interface from sending or receiving hello packets and, as a result, stop it from forming adjacencies. This means it won't send or receive route information on this interface.

Setting Maximum Paths and Hop Count

By default, EIGRP can provide equal-cost load balancing of up to four links (actually, all routing protocols do this). However, you can have EIGRP actually load balance across up to six links (equal or unequal) by using the following command: Typically you would not need to configure these commands, but here (Table 4.3) is how you see the maximum paths and hop count:

TABLE 4.3 Advanced EIGRP Commands

Command	Meaning
`maximum-paths`	Displays a routers table of known or learned destination networks
`metric maximum-hops`	Changes the hop count for EIGRP up to a maximum of 255

Here are the commands used in context:

```
Pod1R1(config)#router eigrp 10
Pod1R1(config-router)#maximum-paths ?
  <1-6>  Number of paths
```

In addition, EIGRP has a maximum hop count of 100 but can be set up to 255. Chances are you wouldn't want to ever change this, but if you did, here is how you would do it:

```
Pod1R1(config)#router eigrp 10
Pod1R1(config-router)#metric maximum-hops ?
  <1-255>  Hop count
```

As you can see from this router output, EIGRP can be set to a maximum of 255 hops, and even though it doesn't use hop count in the path metric calculation, it still uses the maximum hop count to limit the scope of the Autonomous System.

Using Redistribution Commands

From a router named R3, you just need to add the redistribution commands under EIGRP and RIP. Listed in Table 4.4 are the commands:

TABLE 4.4 Routing Protocol Redistribution Commands

Command	Meaning
`redistribution`	Displays a routers table of known or learned destination networks
`metric`	Sets the parameters for redistribution
`bandwidth`	Configures the bandwidth used for routing calculations
`delay`	Sets the delay of the link used for routing calculations
`reliability`	Not used by default with EIGRP, but sets the reliability of the link used with routing calculations if administratively set
`load`	Not used by default with EIGRP, but sets the load of the link used with routing calculations if administratively set
`MTU`	Not used by default with EIGRP, but sets the maximum transmission unit of the link used with routing calculations if administratively set

The commands seem a little convoluted, but once you work through them a few times, you'll start to feel more comfortable with redistribution. Take a look:

```
R3#config t
R3(config)#router eigrp 10
R3(config-router)#redistribute rip ?
```

```
  metric     Metric for redistributed routes
  route-map  Route map reference
  <cr>
R3(config-router)#redistribute rip metric ?
  <1-4294967295>  Bandwidth metric in Kbits per second
R3(config-router)#redistribute rip metric 10000000 ?
  <0-4294967295>  EIGRP delay metric, in 10 microsecond units
R3(config-router)#redistribute rip metric 10000000 20000 ?
  <0-255>  EIGRP reliability metric where 255 is 100% reliable
R3(config-router)#redistribute rip metric 10000000 20000 255 ?
  <1-255>  EIGRP Effective bandwidth metric (Loading) where 255 is 100% loaded
R3(config-router)#redistribute rip metric 10000000 20000 255 1 ?
  <1-65535>  EIGRP MTU of the path
R3(config-router)#redistribute rip metric 10000000 20000 255 1 1500
R3(config-router)#do show run | begin router eigrp 10
router eigrp 10
 redistribute rip metric 10000000 20000 255 1 1500
 passive-interface FastEthernet0/0
 passive-interface Serial0/0/0
 network 10.0.0.0
 no auto-summary
!
```

As you can see, I needed to change RIP's metric of hop count to match EIGRP's bandwidth metric, delay, reliability, load, and MTU. Even though EIGRP may use only bandwidth and delay of the line by default, when you configure redistribution, you have to configure all metric values.

The following output shows I'm redistributing EIGRP into RIP and changing the metric to hop count:

```
R3(config)#router rip
R3(config-router)#redistribute eigrp 10 ?
  metric     Metric for redistributed routes
  route-map  Route map reference
  <cr>
R3(config-router)#redistribute eigrp 10 metric ?
  <0-16>       Default metric
  transparent  Transparently redistribute metric

R3(config-router)#redistribute eigrp 10 metric 1
```

Configuring Discontiguous Networks

1. You need to be aware of one more configuration, as listed in Table 4.5, that has to do with autosummarization:

TABLE 4.5 Solving Discontiguous Networks

Command	Meaning
`no auto-summary`	Configures manual summarization and the propagation of all subnet entries in the routing table

Without the option of the no auto-summary command for both RIPv2 and EIGRP, discontiguous networks will never work.

```
Lab_A#config t
Lab_A(config)#router eigrp 100
Lab_A(config-router)#network 172.16.0.0
Lab_A(config-router)#network 10.0.0.0
Lab_A(config-router)#no auto-summary

Lab_B#config t
Lab_B(config)#router eigrp 100
Lab_B(config-router)#network 172.16.0.0
Lab_B(config-router)#network 10.0.0.0
Lab_B(config-router)#no auto-summary
```

By using the `no auto-summary` command, EIGRP will advertise all the subnets between the two routers. If the networks were larger, you could then provide manual summarization on these same boundaries.

Load Balancing with EIGRP

1. You might know that by default EIGRP can load balance up to four equal-cost links. But did you know that you can configure EIGRP to load balance across up to six equal/unequal-cost links to a remote network? Well, you can, so let's take a some EIGRP commands (Table 4.6) and do some load balancing as well:

TABLE 4.6 Load Balancing

Command	Meaning
`show ip route`	Displays the router's routing table

TABLE 4.6 Load Balancing *(continued)*

Command	Meaning
`show ip eigrp topology`	Shows the topology table used with EIGRP
`variance`	Sets a variance used for unequal-cost load balancing

Take a look at a routing table with EIGRP routing configured on the network:

```
R1#sh ip route
     10.0.0.0/24 is subnetted, 12 subnets
D       10.1.11.0 [90/2684416] via 10.1.3.1, 00:50:37, Serial0/0/1
                  [90/2684416] via 10.1.2.1, 00:50:37, Serial0/0/0
D       10.1.10.0 [90/2707456] via 10.1.3.1, 01:04:40, Serial0/0/1
                  [90/2707456] via 10.1.2.1, 01:04:40, Serial0/0/0
D       10.1.9.0 [90/2707456] via 10.1.3.1, 01:24:09, Serial0/0/1
                 [90/2707456] via 10.1.2.1, 01:24:09, Serial0/0/0
D       10.1.8.0 [90/2707456] via 10.1.3.1, 01:24:09, Serial0/0/1
                 [90/2707456] via 10.1.2.1, 01:24:09, Serial0/0/0
D       10.1.12.0 [90/2684416] via 10.1.3.1, 00:10:10, Serial0/0/1
                  [90/2684416] via 10.1.2.1, 00:10:10, Serial0/0/0
C       10.1.3.0 is directly connected, Serial0/0/1
C       10.1.2.0 is directly connected, Serial0/0/0
D       10.1.1.0 [90/2172416] via 10.1.3.1, 01:24:11, Serial0/0/1
                 [90/2172416] via 10.1.2.1, 01:24:11, Serial0/0/0
C       10.1.7.0 is directly connected, FastEthernet0/1
C       10.1.6.0 is directly connected, FastEthernet0/0
D       10.1.5.0 [90/2681856] via 10.1.3.1, 01:24:11, Serial0/0/1
                 [90/2681856] via 10.1.2.1, 01:24:11, Serial0/0/0
D       10.1.4.0 [90/2681856] via 10.1.3.1, 01:24:11, Serial0/0/1
                 [90/2681856] via 10.1.2.1, 01:24:11, Serial0/0/0
```

You can see that here you have two links to every route in the internetwork, and again, EIGRP will load balance across the s0/0/0 and s0/0/1 links by default because they're the same metric.

But how about bundling links? Well, EIGRP can allow you to do this too—with just a slightly different configuration! I'll show you how this works by configuring the links between the Corp and R1 router with the same subnet, meaning both links will have all interfaces within the same subnet. Check out my configuration:

```
Corp#config t
Corp(config)#int s0/0/1
Corp(config-if)#ip address 10.1.2.4 255.255.255.0

R1#config t
R1(config)#int s0/0/1
R1(config-if)#ip address 10.1.2.3 255.255.255.0
R1(config-if)#do show run | begin interface
interface Serial0/0/0
 description 1st Connection to Corp Router
 ip address 10.1.2.2 255.255.255.0
!
interface Serial0/0/1
 description 2nd connection to Corp Router
 ip address 10.1.2.3 255.255.255.0
```

Now both links have all four interfaces in the same subnet:

```
R1(config-if)#do show ip route
     10.0.0.0/24 is subnetted, 12 subnets
D       10.1.11.0 [90/2684416] via 10.1.2.4, 00:04:44, Serial0/0/1
                  [90/2684416] via 10.1.2.1, 00:04:44, Serial0/0/0
D       10.1.10.0 [90/2707456] via 10.1.2.4, 00:04:44, Serial0/0/1
                  [90/2707456] via 10.1.2.1, 00:04:44, Serial0/0/0
D       10.1.9.0 [90/2707456] via 10.1.2.4, 00:04:44, Serial0/0/1
                 [90/2707456] via 10.1.2.1, 00:04:44, Serial0/0/0
D       10.1.8.0 [90/2707456] via 10.1.2.4, 00:04:44, Serial0/0/1
                 [90/2707456] via 10.1.2.1, 00:04:44, Serial0/0/0
D       10.1.12.0 [90/2684416] via 10.1.2.4, 00:04:44, Serial0/0/1
                  [90/2684416] via 10.1.2.1, 00:04:44, Serial0/0/0
D       10.1.3.0 [90/3193856] via 10.1.2.4, 00:04:44, Serial0/0/1
                 [90/3193856] via 10.1.2.1, 00:04:44, Serial0/0/0
C       10.1.2.0 is directly connected, Serial0/0/0
                 is directly connected, Serial0/0/1
D       10.1.1.0 [90/2172416] via 10.1.2.4, 00:03:56, Serial0/0/1
                 [90/2172416] via 10.1.2.1, 00:03:56, Serial0/0/0
C       10.1.7.0 is directly connected, FastEthernet0/1
```

```
C        10.1.6.0 is directly connected, FastEthernet0/0
D        10.1.5.0 [90/2681856] via 10.1.2.4, 00:04:46, Serial0/0/1
                  [90/2681856] via 10.1.2.1, 00:04:46, Serial0/0/0
D        10.1.4.0 [90/2681856] via 10.1.2.4, 00:04:46, Serial0/0/1
                  [90/2681856] via 10.1.2.1, 00:04:46, Serial0/0/0
```

Now I'll show what's in the Corp topology table by using the `show ip eigrp topology` command. I'll cover this command more specifically in the "Verifying EIGRP" section.

```
Corp# sh ip eigrp topology
IP-EIGRP Topology Table for AS(10)/ID(10.1.5.1)
Codes: P - Passive, A - Active, U - Update, Q - Query, R - Reply,
       r - reply Status, s - sia Status
P 10.1.11.0/24, 1 successors, FD is 2172416
        via 10.1.5.2 (2172416/28160), Serial0/2/0
P 10.1.10.0/24, 1 successors, FD is 2172416
        via 10.1.5.2 (2195456/281600), Serial0/2/0
P 10.1.9.0/24, 1 successors, FD is 2195456
        via 10.1.4.2 (2195456/281600), Serial0/1/0
P 10.1.8.0/24, 1 successors, FD is 2195456
        via 10.1.4.2 (2195456/72960), Serial0/1/0
P 10.1.12.0/24, 1 successors, FD is 2172416
        via 10.1.5.2 (2172416/28160), Serial0/2/0
P 10.1.3.0/24, 1 successors, FD is 76839936
        via Connected, Serial0/0/1
        via 10.1.2.2 (9849856/7719936), Serial0/0/0, serno 89
P 10.1.2.0/24, 1 successors, FD is 2169856
        via Connected, Serial0/0/0
        via 10.1.2.2 (2681856/551936), Serial0/0/0
P 10.1.1.0/24, 1 successors, FD is 28160
        via Connected, FastEthernet0/1
P 10.1.7.0/24, 1 successors, FD is 793600
        via 10.1.2.2 (2195456/281600), Serial0/0/0
        via 10.1.3.2 (77081600/281600), Serial0/0/1
P 10.1.6.0/24, 1 successors, FD is 793600
        via 10.1.2.2 (2195456/281600), Serial0/0/0
        via 10.1.3.2 (77081600/281600), Serial0/0/1
P 10.1.5.0/24, 1 successors, FD is 2169856
        via Connected, Serial0/2/0
P 10.1.4.0/24, 1 successors, FD is 2169856
        via Connected, Serial0/1/0
```

Each entry also indicates the *feasible distance (FD)* to each remote network plus the next-hop neighbor through which packets will travel to their destinations. Plus, each entry also has two numbers in parentheses. The first indicates the feasible distance, and the second one indicates the advertised distance to a remote network.

Now here's where things get interesting—notice that under the 10.1.7.0 and 10.1.6.0 outputs there are two links to each network and the feasible distance and advertised distance are different. What this means is that you have one successor to the networks and one feasible successor—a backup route!

For the route to be a feasible successor, its advertised distance must be less than the feasible distance of the successor route. That's so very cool! You need to remember that even though both routes to network 10.1.6.0 and 10.1.7.0 are in the topology table, only the successor route (the one with the lowest metrics) will be copied and placed into the routing table.

EIGRP will load balance across both links automatically when they are of equal variance (equal cost), but EIGRP can also load balance across unequal cost links if you use the `variance` command. Changing a variance value enables EIGRP to install multiple, loop-free routes with unequal cost in a local routing table.

For example, if the variance is set to 2, an unequal cost path with a metric less than two times the successor metric will be installed in the local routing table. Remember, an unequal cost path will be used only if it is a feasible successor.

Using Route Authentication with EIGRP

To enable authentication of EIGRP packets, use the following commands in Table 4.7 beginning in interface configuration mode:

TABLE 4.7 EIGRP Route Authentication

Command	Meaning
interface *interface*	configure an interface type and enter interface configuration mode
ip authentication mode eigrp *AS* md5	enable MD5 authentication in EIGRP route update packets
ip authentication key-chain eigrp as *key-chain*	enable authentication of EIGRP packets
key chain *name*	identify the key chain

TABLE 4.7 EIGRP Route Authentication *(continued)*

Command	Meaning
key *number*	In key chain configuration mode, identify the key number
key-string *text*	In key chain key configure mode, identify the key string
accept-lifetime *start-time*	(optional) specify the time period during which the key can be received
send-lifetime *start-time*	(optional) specify the time period during which the key can be sent

Let's take a look at these commands as used on a Cisco router:

```
Corp#config t
Corp(config)#int s0/0/1
Corp(config-if)#ip authentication mode eigrp 10 md5
Corp(config-if)#ip authentication key-chain eigrp 10 todd
Corp(config-if)#exit
Corp(config)#key chain todd
Corp(config-keychain)#key 1
Corp(config-keychain-key)#key-string 1234567890
Corp(config-keychain-key)#accept-lifetime 04:00:00 Jan  14 2008 infinite
Corp(config)#send-lifetime 04:00:00 Jan 14 2008 04:50:00 Jan 14 2008
```

Now, let's verify EIGRP.

Verifying EIGRP

You can use several commands, as defined in Table 4.8, on a router to help you troubleshoot and verify the EIGRP configuration:

TABLE 4.8 Verifying EIGRP

Command	Meaning
show ip route eigrp	Shows only EIGRP entries in the routing table
show ip eigrp neighbors	Shows all EIGRP neighbors

TABLE 4.8 Verifying EIGRP *(continued)*

Command	Meaning
`show ip eigrp topology`	Shows entries in the EIGRP topology table
`debug eigrp packet`	Shows hello packets sent/received between adjacent routers
`debug ip eigrp notification`	Shows EIGRP changes and updates as they occur on your network

Now return to the Corp router and see what it shows in the neighbor table:

```
Corp#sh ip eigrp neighbors
IP-EIGRP neighbors for process 10
H   Address       Interface  Hold Uptime    SRTT  RTO Q   Seq
                              (sec)         (ms)      Cnt Num
1   10.1.3.2      Se0/0/1     14 00:35:10    1    200  0  81
3   10.1.5.2      Se0/2/0     10 02:51:22    1    200  0  31
2   10.1.4.2      Se0/1/0     13 03:17:20    1    200  0  20
0   10.1.2.2      Se0/0/0     10 03:19:37    1    200  0  80
```

You can read the information in this output like this:

- The H field indicates the order in which the neighbor was discovered.
- The hold time is how long this router will wait for a hello packet to arrive from a specific neighbor.
- The uptime indicates how long the "neighborship" has been established.
- The SRTT field is the smooth round-trip timer—an indication of the time it takes for a round-trip from this router to its neighbor and back. This value is used to determine how long to wait after a multicast for a reply from this neighbor. If a reply isn't received in time, the router will switch to using unicasts in an attempt to complete the communication. The time between multicast attempts is specified by the Retransmission Time Out (RTO) field, described next.
- RTO is the amount of time EIGRP waits before retransmitting a packet from the retransmission queue to a neighbor.
- The Q value indicates whether there are any outstanding messages in the queue—consistently large values would indicate a problem.
- The Seq field indicates the sequence number of the last update from that neighbor—something that's used to maintain synchronization and avoid duplicate or out-of-sequence processing of messages.

Now let's see what's in the Corp topology table by using the `show ip eigrp topology` command. This should be interesting!

```
Corp#sh ip eigrp topology
IP-EIGRP Topology Table for AS(10)/ID(10.1.5.1)
Codes: P - Passive, A - Active, U - Update, Q - Query, R - Reply,
       r - reply Status, s - sia Status
P 10.1.11.0/24, 1 successors, FD is 2172416
        via 10.1.5.2 (2172416/28160), Serial0/2/0
P 10.1.10.0/24, 1 successors, FD is 2172416
        via 10.1.5.2 (2195456/281600), Serial0/2/0
P 10.1.9.0/24, 1 successors, FD is 2195456
        via 10.1.4.2 (2195456/281600), Serial0/1/0
P 10.1.8.0/24, 1 successors, FD is 2195456
        via 10.1.4.2 (2195456/72960), Serial0/1/0
P 10.1.12.0/24, 1 successors, FD is 2172416
        via 10.1.5.2 (2172416/28160), Serial0/2/0
P 10.1.3.0/24, 1 successors, FD is 76839936
        via Connected, Serial0/0/1
        via 10.1.2.2 (9849856/7719936), Serial0/0/0, serno 89
P 10.1.2.0/24, 1 successors, FD is 2169856
        via Connected, Serial0/0/0
        via 10.1.2.2 (2681856/551936), Serial0/0/0
```

- Notice that every route is preceded by a P. This means the route is in the *passive state*, which is good because routes in the *active state (A)* indicate that the router has lost its path to this network and is searching for a replacement. Each entry also indicates the FD to each remote network plus the next-hop neighbor through which packets will travel to their destinations. In addition, each entry also has two numbers in parentheses. The first indicates the feasible distance, and the second indicates the advertised distance to a remote network.

```
Corp#debug eigrp packet
EIGRP Packets debugging is on
    (UPDATE, REQUEST, QUERY, REPLY, HELLO, IPXSAP, PROBE, ACK, STUB, SIAQUERY,
SIAREPLY)
Corp#
*Mar 21 23:17:35.050: EIGRP: Sending HELLO on FastEthernet0/1
*Mar 21 23:17:35.050:   AS 10, Flags 0x0, Seq 0/0 idbQ 0/0 iidbQ un/rely 0/0
*Mar 21 23:17:35.270: EIGRP: Received HELLO on Serial0/1/0 nbr 10.1.4.2
*Mar 21 23:17:35.270:   AS 10, Flags 0x0, Seq 0/0 idbQ 0/0 iidbQ un/rely 0/0
peerQ un/rely 0/0
*Mar 21 23:17:35.294: EIGRP: Received HELLO on Serial0/0/0 nbr 10.1.2.2
```

```
*Mar 21 23:17:35.294:   AS 10, Flags 0x0, Seq 0/0 idbQ 0/0 iidbQ un/rely 0/0
peerQ un/rely 0/0
 *Mar 21 23:17:38.014: EIGRP: Received HELLO on Serial0/2/0 nbr 10.1.5.2
*Mar 21 23:17:38.014:   AS 10, Flags 0x0, Seq 0/0 idbQ 0/0 iidbQ un/rely 0/0
peerQ un/rely 0/0
```

- Since my Corp router is connected to three EIGRP neighbors and because the 224.0.0.10 multicast is sent out every five seconds, I didn't have any problem seeing the updates. The hello packets are sent out every active interface, as well as all the interfaces to which I have neighbors connected. Did you notice the AS number is provided in the update? This is because if a neighbor doesn't have the same AS number, the hello update would just be discarded.

I'll now show you one more important debugging command—the `debug ip eigrp notification` command (called `debug ip eigrp events` on pre-12.4 routers), plus the resulting output. The only time you'll see output from this command is if there's a problem on your network or you you've added or deleted a network from a router in your internetwork.

```
Corp(config)#int f0/1
Corp(config-if)#shut
*Mar 21 23:25:43.506: IP-EIGRP(Default-IP-Routing-Table:10): Callback: route_
adjust FastEthernet0/1
*Mar 21 23:25:43.506: IP-EIGRP: Callback: ignored connected AS 0 10.1.1.0/24
*Mar 21 23:25:43.506:           into: eigrp AS 10
*Mar 21 23:25:43.506: IP-EIGRP(Default-IP-Routing-Table:10): Callback:
callbackup_routes 10.1.1.0/24
Corp(config-if)#n
*Mar 21 23:25:45.506: %LINK-5-CHANGED: Interface FastEthernet0/1, changed state
to administratively down
*Mar 21 23:25:46.506: %LINEPROTO-5-UPDOWN: Line protocol on Interface
FastEthernet0/1, changed state to down
Corp(config-if)#no shut
Corp(config-if)#^Z
*Mar 21 23:25:49.570: %LINK-3-UPDOWN: Interface FastEthernet0/1, changed state
to up
*Mar 21 23:25:49.570: IP-EIGRP(Default-IP-Routing-Table:10): Callback:
lostroute 10.1.1.0/24
*Mar 21 23:25:49.570: IP-EIGRP(Default-IP-Routing-Table:0): Callback: redist
connected (config change) FastEthernet0/1
*Mar 21 23:25:49.570: IP-EIGRP(Default-IP-Routing-Table:0): Callback: redist
connected (config change) Serial0/0/0
*Mar 21 23:25:49.570: IP-EIGRP(Default-IP-Routing-Table:0): Callback: redist
connected (config change) Serial0/0/1
*Mar 21 23:25:49.570: IP-EIGRP(Default-IP-Routing-Table:0): Callback: redist
connected (config change) Serial0/1/0
```

```
*Mar 21 23:25:49.570: IP-EIGRP(Default-IP-Routing-Table:0): Callback: redist
connected (config change) Serial0/2/0
*Mar 21 23:25:49.570: IP-EIGRP(Default-IP-Routing-Table:10): Callback: route_
adjust FastEthernet0/1
*Mar 21 23:25:50.570: %LINEPROTO-5-UPDOWN: Line protocol on Interface
FastEthernet0/1, changed state to up
```

Understanding Open Shortest Path First (OSPF) Basics

Open Shortest Path First (OSPF) is an open standards routing protocol that has been implemented by a wide variety of network vendors, including Cisco.

This works by using the Dijkstra algorithm. First a shortest path tree is constructed, and then the routing table is populated with the resulting best paths. OSPF converges quickly, although perhaps not as quickly as EIGRP, and it supports multiple, equal-cost routes to the same destination. Like EIGRP, it does support both IP and IPv6 routed protocols.

OSPF provides the following features:

- Consists of areas and autonomous systems
- Minimizes routing update traffic
- Allows scalability
- Supports VLSM/CIDR
- Has unlimited hop count
- Allows multivendor deployment (open standard)

Table 4.9 describes the characteristics of the RIP and OSPF protocols discussed thus far.

TABLE 4.9 Protocol Characteristics

Characteristic	OSPF	RIPv2	RIPv1
Type of protocol	Link-state	Distance Vector	Distance-vector
Classless support	Yes	Yes	No
VLSM support	Yes	Yes	No
Auto summarization	No	Yes	Yes
Manual summarization	Yes	No	No

TABLE 4.9 Protocol Characteristics

Characteristic	OSPF	RIPv2	RIPv1
Discontiguous support	Yes	Yes	No
Route propagation	Multicast on change	Periodic multicast	Periodic broadcast
Path metric	Bandwidth	Hops	Hops
Hop count limit	None	15	15
Convergence	Fast	Slow	Slow
Peer authentication	Yes	Yes	No
Hierarchical network	Yes (using areas)	No (flat only)	No (flat only)
Updates	Event triggered	Route table updates	Route table updates
Route computation	Dijkstra	Bellman-Ford	Bellman-Ford

OSPF is supposed to be designed in a hierarchical fashion, which basically means you can separate the larger internetwork into smaller internetworks called *areas*. This is the best design for OSPF.

The reasons for creating OSPF in a hierarchical design include the following:

- To decrease routing overhead
- To speed up convergence
- To confine network instability to single areas of the network

Configuring OSPF

Configuring basic OSPF isn't as simple as RIP, IGRP, and EIGRP, and it can get really complex once you factor in the many options that are allowed within OSPF.

These two elements are the basic elements of OSPF configuration:

- Enabling OSPF
- Configuring OSPF areas

Enabling OSPF

The easiest and also least scalable way to configure OSPF is to use just a single area. Doing this requires a minimum of two commands.

The command you use to activate the OSPF routing process is as follows:

```
Lab_A(config)#router ospf ?
<1-65535>
```

A value in the range 1–65,535 identifies the OSPF process ID. It's a unique number on this router that groups a series of OSPF configuration commands under a specific running process. Different OSPF routers don't have to use the same process ID in order to communicate. It's purely a local value that essentially has little meaning, but it cannot start at 0. It has to start at a minimum of 1.

Configuring OSPF Areas

After identifying the OSPF process, you need to identify the interfaces that you want to activate OSPF communications on, as well as the area in which each resides. This will also configure the networks you're going to advertise to others. OSPF uses wildcards in the configuration.

Here's an OSPF basic configuration example for you:

```
Lab_A#config t
Lab_A(config)#router ospf 1
Lab_A(config-router)#network 10.0.0.0 0.255.255.255
 area ?
  <0-4294967295>  OSPF area ID as a decimal value
  A.B.C.D         OSPF area ID in IP address format
Lab_A(config-router)#network 10.0.0.0 0.255.255.255
 area 0
```

Verifying OSPF Configuration

There are several ways to verify proper OSPF configuration and operation, and in the following sections I'll show you the OSPF show commands you need to know in order to do this. I'll start by showing the routing table of the Corp router. Here in Table 4.10 are the commands we'll use to verify OSPF:

TABLE 4.10 Verifying OSPF

Command	Meaning
`show ip route`	Displays the router's routing table
`show ip ospf`	Displays OSPF information for one or all OSPF processes running on the router
`show ip ospf database`	Shows the topological database used in OSPF
`show ip ospf interface`	Displays all interface-related OSPF information
`show ip ospf neighbor`	Summarizes the pertinent OSPF information regarding neighbors and the adjacency state
`show ip ospf protocols`	Shows routing protocol information

So, let's issue a `show ip route` command on the Corp router:

```
     10.0.0.0/24 is subnetted, 12 subnets
O       10.1.11.0 [110/65] via 10.1.5.2, 00:01:31, Serial0/2/0
O       10.1.10.0 [110/65] via 10.1.5.2, 00:01:31, Serial0/2/0
O       10.1.9.0 [110/74] via 10.1.4.2, 00:01:31, Serial0/1/0
O       10.1.8.0 [110/65] via 10.1.4.2, 00:01:31, Serial0/1/0
O       10.1.12.0 [110/66] via 10.1.5.2, 00:01:31, Serial0/2/0
C       10.1.3.0 is directly connected, Serial0/0/1
C       10.1.2.0 is directly connected, Serial0/0/0
C       10.1.1.0 is directly connected, FastEthernet0/1
O       10.1.7.0 [110/74] via 10.1.3.2, 00:01:32, Serial0/0/1
                 [110/74] via 10.1.2.2, 00:01:32, Serial0/0/0
O       10.1.6.0 [110/74] via 10.1.3.2, 00:01:32, Serial0/0/1
                 [110/74] via 10.1.2.2, 00:01:32, Serial0/0/0
C       10.1.5.0 is directly connected, Serial0/2/0
C       10.1.4.0 is directly connected, Serial0/1/0
```

The Corp router shows the found routes for all 12 networks, with the O representing OSPF internal routes (the Cs are obviously the directly connected networks). It also found the dual routes to networks 10.1.6.0 and 10.1.7.0. OSPF uses bandwidth only to determine the best path to a network.

Using the *show ip ospf* Command

You can use the `show ip ospf` command to display OSPF information for one or all OSPF processes running on the router. Information contained therein includes the router ID, area information, SPF statistics, and LSA timer information. Here's the output from the Corp router:

```
Corp#sh ip ospf
 Routing Process "ospf 132" with ID 10.1.5.1
 Start time: 04:32:04.116, Time elapsed: 01:27:10.156
 Supports only single TOS(TOS0) routes
 Supports opaque LSA
 Supports Link-local Signaling (LLS)
 Supports area transit capability
 Router is not originating router-LSAs with maximum metric
 Initial SPF schedule delay 5000 msecs
 Minimum hold time between two consecutive SPFs 10000 msecs
 Maximum wait time between two consecutive SPFs 10000 msecs
 Incremental-SPF disabled
 Minimum LSA interval 5 secs
 Minimum LSA arrival 1000 msecs
 LSA group pacing timer 240 secs
 Interface flood pacing timer 33 msecs
 Retransmission pacing timer 66 msecs
 Number of external LSA 0. Checksum Sum 0x000000
 Number of opaque AS LSA 0. Checksum Sum 0x000000
 Number of DCbitless external and opaque AS LSA 0
 Number of DoNotAge external and opaque AS LSA 0
 Number of areas in this router is 1. 1 normal 0 stub 0 nssa
 Number of areas transit capable is 0
 External flood list length 0
    Area BACKBONE(0)
        Number of interfaces in this area is 5
        Area has no authentication
        SPF algorithm last executed 00:14:52.220 ago
        SPF algorithm executed 14 times
        Area ranges are
        Number of LSA 6. Checksum Sum 0x03C06F
        Number of opaque link LSA 0. Checksum Sum 0x000000
        Number of DCbitless LSA 0
        Number of indication LSA 0
        Number of DoNotAge LSA 0
        Flood list length 0
```

Notice the router ID (RID) of 10.1.5.1, which is the highest IP address configured on the router.

Using the *show ip ospf database* Command

Using the `show ip ospf database` command will give you information about the number of routers in the internetwork (AS) plus the neighboring router's ID, and it is the topology database I mentioned earlier. Unlike the `show ip eigrp topogogy` command, this command shows the OSPF routers, not each and every link in the AS like EIGRP does.

The output is broken down by area. Here's some sample output, again from Corp:

```
Corp#sh ip ospf database

            OSPF Router with ID (10.1.5.1) (Process ID 132)

                Router Link States (Area 0)

Link ID         ADV Router      Age         Seq#       Checksum Link count
10.1.5.1        10.1.5.1        72          0x80000002 0x00F2CA 9
10.1.7.1        10.1.7.1        83          0x80000004 0x009197 6
10.1.9.1        10.1.9.1        73          0x80000001 0x00DA1C 4
10.1.11.1       10.1.11.1       67          0x80000005 0x00666A 4
10.1.12.1       10.1.12.1       67          0x80000004 0x007631 2

                Net Link States (Area 0)

Link ID         ADV Router      Age         Seq#       Checksum
10.1.11.2       10.1.12.1       68          0x80000001 0x00A337
```

You can see all five routers and the RID of each router (the highest IP address on each router). The router output shows the link ID—remember that an interface is also a link—and the RID of the router on that link under the ADV router (or *advertising* router).

Using the *show ip ospf interface* Command

The `show ip ospf interface` command displays all interface-related OSPF information. Data is displayed about OSPF information for all interfaces or for specified interfaces:

```
Corp#sh ip ospf interface f0/1
FastEthernet0/1 is up, line protocol is up
  Internet Address 10.1.1.1/24, Area 0
  Process ID 132, Router ID 10.1.5.1, Network Type BROADCAST, Cost: 1
  Transmit Delay is 1 sec, State DR, Priority 1
```

```
Designated Router (ID) 10.1.5.1, Interface address 10.1.1.1
No backup designated router on this network
Timer intervals configured, Hello 10, Dead 40, Wait 40, Retransmit 5
  oob-resync timeout 40
  Hello due in 00:00:01
Supports Link-local Signaling (LLS)
Index 1/1, flood queue length 0
Next 0x0(0)/0x0(0)
Last flood scan length is 0, maximum is 0
Last flood scan time is 0 msec, maximum is 0 msec
Neighbor Count is 0, Adjacent neighbor count is 0
Suppress hello for 0 neighbor(s)
```

The information displayed by this command includes the following:

- Interface IP address
- Area assignment
- Process ID
- Router ID
- Network type
- Cost
- Priority
- DR/BDR election information (if applicable)
- Hello and dead timer intervals
- Adjacent neighbor information

The reason I used the `show ip ospf interface f0/1` command is because I knew that there would be a designated router elected on the FastEthernet broadcast multiaccess network.

Using the *show ip ospf neighbor* Command

The `show ip ospf neighbor` command is really useful because it summarizes the pertinent OSPF information regarding neighbors and the adjacency state. If a DR or BDR exists, that information will also be displayed. Here's a sample:

```
Corp#sh ip ospf neighbor
Neighbor ID  Pri  State    Dead Time   Address     Interface
10.1.11.1      0  FULL/  - 00:00:37   10.1.5.2     Serial0/2/0
10.1.9.1       0  FULL/  - 00:00:34   10.1.4.2     Serial0/1/0
10.1.7.1       0  FULL/  - 00:00:38   10.1.3.2     Serial0/0/1
10.1.7.1       0  FULL/  - 00:00:34   10.1.2.2     Serial0/0/0
```

This is an important command to understand because it's extremely useful in production networks! Here are the R3 and 871W routers' outputs:

```
R3#sh ip ospf neighbor
Neighbor ID   Pri   State    Dead Time     Address        Interface
10.1.5.1        0   FULL/  -  00:00:39     10.1.5.1       Serial0/0/1
10.1.11.2       1   FULL/BDR  00:00:31     10.1.11.2      FastEthernet0/1
871W#sh ip ospf nei
Neighbor ID     Pri  State    Dead Time     Address        Interface
10.1.11.1       1   FULL/DR   00:00:30     10.1.11.1       Vlan1
```

Since there's an Ethernet link (broadcast multiaccess) on the Corp router, there's going to be an election to determine which router will be the designated router and which router will be the nondesignated router. You can see that the 871W became the designate router, and it won because it had the highest IP address on the network. You can change this, but that's the default.

The reason that the Corp connections to R1, R2, and R3 don't have a DR or BDR listed in the output is that by default elections don't happen on point-to-point links. But you can see that the Corp router is fully adjacent to all three routers (and on both connections to R1) from its output.

Using the *show ip protocols* Command

The `show ip protocols` command is also useful whether you're running OSPF, EIGRP, IGRP, RIP, BGP, IS-IS, or any other routing protocol that can be configured on your router. It provides an excellent overview of the actual operation of all currently running protocols.

Check out the output from the Corp router:

```
Corp#sh ip protocols
Routing Protocol is "ospf 132"
  Outgoing update filter list for all interfaces is not set
  Incoming update filter list for all interfaces is not set
  Router ID 10.1.5.1
  Number of areas in this router is 1. 1 normal 0 stub 0 nssa
  Maximum path: 4
  Routing for Networks:
    10.1.1.1 0.0.0.0 area 0
    10.1.2.1 0.0.0.0 area 0
    10.1.3.1 0.0.0.0 area 0
    10.1.4.1 0.0.0.0 area 0
    10.1.5.1 0.0.0.0 area 0
 Reference bandwidth unit is 100 mbps
```

```
Routing Information Sources:
  Gateway         Distance      Last Update
  10.1.11.1            110      00:28:53
  10.1.11.2            110      00:28:53
  10.1.9.1             110      00:28:53
  10.1.7.1             110      00:28:53
Distance: (default is 110)
```

Checking out this output, you can determine the OSPF process ID, OSPF router ID, type of OSPF area, networks and areas configured for OSPF, and the OSPF router IDs of neighbors—that's a lot. Read, that's efficient! And hold on a second. Did you notice the absence of timers like the ones you saw earlier in the RIP outputs from this command? That's because Link State routing protocols don't use timers to keep the network stable like Distance Vector routing algorithms do.

Debugging OSPF

Debugging is a great tool for any protocol, so let's take a look at Table 4.11 and a few debugging commands for troubleshooting OSPF:

TABLE 4.11 Debugging OSPF

Command	Meaning
`dubug ip ospf packet`	Shows hello packets being sent and received on your router.
`debug ip ospf hello`	Shows hello packets being sent and received on your router. Shows more detail than the `debug ip ospf packet` output.
`debug ip ospf adj`	Shows DR and DBR elections on a broadcast and nonbroadcast multiaccess network.

I'll start by showing you the output from the Corp router I got using the `debug ip ospf packet` command:

```
Corp#debug ip ospf packet
OSPF packet debugging is on
*Mar 23 01:20:42.199: OSPF: rcv. v:2 t:1 l:48 rid:172.16.10.3
      aid:0.0.0.0 chk:8075 aut:0 auk: from Serial0/1/0
Corp#
*Mar 23 01:20:45.507: OSPF: rcv. v:2 t:1 l:48 rid:172.16.10.2
      aid:0.0.0.0 chk:8076 aut:0 auk: from Serial0/0/0
```

```
*Mar 23 01:20:45.531: OSPF: rcv. v:2 t:1 l:48 rid:172.16.10.2
      aid:0.0.0.0 chk:8076 aut:0 auk: from Serial0/0/1
*Mar 23 01:20:45.531: OSPF: rcv. v:2 t:1 l:48 rid:172.16.10.4
      aid:0.0.0.0 chk:8074 aut:0 auk: from Serial0/2/0
*Mar 23 01:20:52.199: OSPF: rcv. v:2 t:1 l:48 rid:172.16.10.3
      aid:0.0.0.0 chk:8075 aut:0 auk: from Serial0/1/0
*Mar 23 01:20:55.507: OSPF: rcv. v:2 t:1 l:48 rid:172.16.10.2
      aid:0.0.0.0 chk:8076 aut:0 auk: from Serial0/0/0
*Mar 23 01:20:55.527: OSPF: rcv. v:2 t:1 l:48 rid:172.16.10.2
      aid:0.0.0.0 chk:8076 aut:0 auk: from Serial0/0/1
*Mar 23 01:20:55.531: OSPF: rcv. v:2 t:1 l:48 rid:172.16.10.4
      aid:0.0.0.0 chk:8074 aut:0 auk: from Serial0/2/0
```

In the previous output, you can see that the router is both sending and receiving hello packets every 10 seconds from neighbor (adjacent) routers. The next command will provide you with the same information but with more detail. For example, you can see the multicast address used (224.0.0.5) and the area:

```
Corp#debug ip ospf hello
*Mar 23 01:18:41.103: OSPF: Send hello to 224.0.0.5 area 0 on Serial0/1/0 from
10.1.4.1
*Mar 23 01:18:41.607: OSPF: Send hello to 224.0.0.5 area 0 on FastEthernet0/1
from 10.1.1.1
*Mar 23 01:18:41.607: OSPF: Send hello to 224.0.0.5 area 0 on Serial0/0/0 from
10.1.2.1
*Mar 23 01:18:41.611: OSPF: Send hello to 224.0.0.5 area 0 on Serial0/2/0 from
10.1.5.1
*Mar 23 01:18:41.611: OSPF: Send hello to 224.0.0.5 area 0 on Serial0/0/1 from
10.1.3.1
*Mar 23 01:18:42.199: OSPF: Rcv hello from 172.16.10.3 area 0 from Serial0/1/0
10.1.4.2
*Mar 23 01:18:42.199: OSPF: End of hello processing
*Mar 23 01:18:45.519: OSPF: Rcv hello from 172.16.10.2 area 0 from Serial0/0/0
10.1.2.2
*Mar 23 01:18:45.519: OSPF: End of hello processing
*Mar 23 01:18:45.543: OSPF: Rcv hello from 172.16.10.2 area 0 from Serial0/0/1
10.1.3.2
*Mar 23 01:18:45.543: OSPF: End of hello processing
*Mar 23 01:18:45.543: OSPF: Rcv hello from 172.16.10.4 area 0 from Serial0/2/0
10.1.5.2
*Mar 23 01:18:45.543: OSPF: End of hello processing
```

The last debug command I'll show you is the **debug ip ospf adj** command, which will show you elections as they occur on broadcast and nonbroadcast multiaccess networks:

```
Corp#debug ip ospf adj
OSPF adjacency events debugging is on
*Mar 23 01:24:34.823: OSPF: Interface FastEthernet0/1 going Down
*Mar 23 01:24:34.823: OSPF: 172.16.10.1 address 10.1.1.1 on FastEthernet0/1 is
dead, state DOWN
*Mar 23 01:24:34.823: OSPF: Neighbor change Event on interface FastEthernet0/1
*Mar 23 01:24:34.823: OSPF: DR/BDR election on FastEthernet0/1
*Mar 23 01:24:34.823: OSPF: Elect BDR 0.0.0.0
*Mar 23 01:24:34.823: OSPF: Elect DR 0.0.0.0
*Mar 23 01:24:34.823: OSPF: Elect BDR 0.0.0.0
*Mar 23 01:24:34.823: OSPF: Elect DR 0.0.0.0
*Mar 23 01:24:34.823:        DR: none    BDR: none
*Mar 23 01:24:34.823: OSPF: Flush network LSA immediately
*Mar 23 01:24:34.823: OSPF: Remember old DR 172.16.10.1 (id)
*Mar 23 01:24:35.323: OSPF: We are not DR to build Net Lsa for interface
FastEthernet0/1
*Mar 23 01:24:35.323: OSPF: Build router LSA for area 0, router ID 172.16.10.1,
seq 0x80000006
*Mar 23 01:24:35.347: OSPF: Rcv LS UPD from 172.16.10.2 on Serial0/0/1 length
148 LSA count 1
*Mar 23 01:24:40.703: OSPF: Interface FastEthernet0/1 going Up
*Mar 23 01:24:41.203: OSPF: Build router LSA for area 0, router ID 172.16.10.1,
seq 0x80000007
*Mar 23 01:24:41.231: OSPF: Rcv LS UPD from 172.16.10.2 on Serial0/0/1 length
160 LSA count 1
```

Chapter 5

Layer-2 Switching and Spanning-Tree Protocol (STP)

When Cisco discusses switching, it's talking about layer-2 switching unless otherwise mentioned. *Layer-2 switching* is the process of using the hardware address of devices on a LAN to segment a network. In this chapter I'll focus on the particulars of layer-2 switching so you can understand how it works.

OK, you know that switching breaks up large collision domains into smaller ones and that a collision domain is a network segment with two or more devices sharing the same bandwidth. A hub network is a typical example of this type of technology. But since each port on a switch is actually its own collision domain, you can make a much better Ethernet LAN network just by replacing your hubs with switches!

Routing protocols have processes for stopping network loops from occurring at the Network layer. However, if you have redundant physical links between your switches, routing protocols won't do a thing to stop loops from occurring at the Data Link layer. That's exactly the reason Spanning-Tree Protocol was developed—to put a stop to loops in a layer-2 switched network.

For up-to-the minute updates for this chapter, please see `www.lammle.com` or `www.sybex.com/go/IOS`

Switching Services

Unlike bridges, which use software to create and manage filter tables, switches use application-specific integrated circuits (ASICs) to build and maintain their filter tables. But it's still OK to think of a layer-2 switch as a multiport bridge because their basic purpose is the same: to break up collision domains.

Layer-2 switches and bridges are faster than routers because they don't take up time looking at the Network layer header information. Instead, they look at the frame's hardware addresses before deciding to either forward the frame or flood it.

Switches create private dedicated collision domains and provide independent bandwidth on each port, unlike hubs.

Layer 2 switching provides the following:

- Hardware-based bridging (ASIC)
- Wire speed
- Low latency
- Low cost

Three Switch Functions at Layer 2

Table 5.1 describes the three distinct functions of layer-2 switching (you need to remember these!).

TABLE 5.1 Functions of Layer-2 Switching

Function	Meaning
Address learning	Layer-2 switches and bridges remember the source hardware address of each frame received on an interface, and they enter this information into a MAC database called a *forward/filter table*.
Forward/filter decisions	When a frame is received on an interface, the switch looks at the destination hardware address and finds the exit interface in the MAC database. The frame is forwarded out the specified destination port only.
Loop avoidance	If multiple connections between switches are created for redundancy purposes, network loops can occur. Spanning-Tree Protocol is used to stop network loops while still permitting redundancy.

Now I'll show the output of a `show mac address-table` command. The MAC table, as it is often called, will display the hardware addresses that the switch has learned. From this table the forwarding decisions are also made.

The following command in Table 5.2 is used to display the forward/filter table on a switch:

TABLE 5.2 Command and Meaning

Command	Meaning
`show mac address-table`	Displays the cache table of learned hardware addresses

Here is the output for the sh mac address-table command:

```
Switch#sh mac address-table
Vlan    Mac Address       Type        Ports
----    -----------       --------    -----
   1    0005.dccb.d74b    DYNAMIC     Fa0/1
   1    000a.f467.9e80    DYNAMIC     Fa0/3
   1    000a.f467.9e8b    DYNAMIC     Fa0/4
   1    000a.f467.9e8c    DYNAMIC     Fa0/3
   1    0010.7b7f.c2b0    DYNAMIC     Fa0/3
   1    0030.80dc.460b    DYNAMIC     Fa0/3
   1    0030.9492.a5dd    DYNAMIC     Fa0/1
   1    00d0.58ad.05f4    DYNAMIC     Fa0/1
```

Basic Switch Configurations

Slightly different from configuring an interface on a router is configuring a switch to talk on the network. Remember, a switch operates at layer 2, and therefore its layer-2 ports do not get IP addresses. The only layer-3 function a switch has is a VLAN, so that is where you'll configure its IP address. For the switch to communicate with a device that is not on the same subnet, it will also have to know where to find a router. You configure the switch with a default gateway (much like a host) for this reason. Here in Table 5.3 are the commands you need:

TABLE 5.3 Command and Meaning

Command	Meaning
enable	Takes you to privileged mode
config t	Takes you to global configuration mode
interface vlan	Enter VLAN configuration mode to configure parameters such as the IP address and mask
ip default-gateway	Configures a default gateway on a switch

Remember, you do not need an IP address on a switch, but here is an example of setting an IP address, mask and default-gateway on a switch:

```
Core>enable
Core#config t
Core(config)#int vlan 1
Core(config-if)#ip address 192.168.10.19 255.255.255.240
Core(config-if)#no shut
```

```
Core#config t
Core(config)#ip default-gateway 192.168.10.30
Core(config)#exit
Core#
```

Switch Security

So, just how do you stop someone from simply plugging a host into one of your switch ports—or worse, adding a hub, switch, or access point into the Ethernet jack in their office? By default, MAC addresses will just dynamically appear in your MAC forward/filter database. You can stop them in their tracks by using port security by using the following command from Table 5.4:

TABLE 5.4 Command and Meaning

Command	Maning
`switchport port-security`	Configures access control of a switch port

To enable port security on a switch port, use the following:

```
Switch#config t
Switch(config)#int f0/1
Switch(config-if)#switchport port-security
```

Table 5.5 lists your options for the `switchport port-security` command.

TABLE 5.5 Options for *switchport port-security*

Options	Meaning
`aging`	Configures a timer for dynamically learned addresses to decay out of the cache.
`mac-address`	Configures a statically assigned secure hardware address for a given ports table.
`maximum`	Configures a max number of secure addresses for a given port.
`violation`	Configures an action should a violation on the port occur. There are three violation modes: protect, restrict, and shutdown.

Here is an example of setting port security on a switch port:

```
Switch#config t
Switch(config)#int f0/1
Switch(config-if)#switchport port-security ?
aging        Port-security aging commands
mac-address  Secure mac address
maximum      Max secure addresses
violation    Security violation mode
<cr>
```

If you want to set up a switch port to allow only one host per port and shut down the port if this rule is violated, use the following commands:

```
Switch#config t
Switch(config)#int f0/1
Switch(config-if)#switchport port-security maximum 1
Switch(config-if)#switchport port-security violation shutdown
```

These commands are probably the most popular because they prevent users from connecting to a switch or access point into their office. A `maximum` of 1 means only one MAC address can be used on that port, and if the user tries to add another host on that segment, the switch port will then shut down. If that happens, you'd have to manually go into the switch and enable the port with a `no shutdown` command.

Probably one of my favorite commands is the `sticky` command. Not only does it perform a cool function, but it has a cool name! You can find this command under the `mac-address` command:

```
Switch(config-if)#switchport port-security mac-address sticky
Switch(config-if)#switchport port-security maximum 2
Switch(config-if)#switchport port-security violation shutdown
```

Basically, this provides static MAC address security without having to type in everyone's MAC address on the network!

Assigning Static MAC Addresses

If you use static mac-address assignments on every switch port, I hope you like to type a lot. If you do, Table 5.6 shows you how to do it:

TABLE 5.6 Command and Meaning

Command	Meaning
`static`	Sets a static MAC address on a switch interface

You can set a static MAC address in the MAC address table, but like setting static MAC port security, it's a ton of work. But in case you want to do it, here's how it's done:

```
S1#config t
S1(config)#mac-address-table static aaaa.bbbb.cccc vlan 1 int fa0/5
S1(config)#do show mac address-table
          Mac Address Table
-------------------------------------------

Vlan    Mac Address       Type        Ports
----    -----------       --------    -----
 All    0100.0ccc.cccc    STATIC      CPU
[output cut]
   1    0002.1762.b235    DYNAMIC     Po1
   1    0009.b79f.c080    DYNAMIC     Po1
   1    000d.29bd.4b87    DYNAMIC     Po1
   1    000d.29bd.4b88    DYNAMIC     Po1
   1    0016.4662.52b4    DYNAMIC     Fa0/4
   1    0016.4677.5eab    DYNAMIC     Po1
   1    001a.2f52.49d8    DYNAMIC     Po1
   1    001a.2fe7.4170    DYNAMIC     Fa0/8
   1    001a.e2ce.ff40    DYNAMIC     Po1
   1    0050.0f02.642a    DYNAMIC     Fa0/3
   1    aaaa.bbbb.cccc    STATIC      Fa0/5
Total Mac Addresses for this criterion: 31
S1(config)#
```

Here you can see that a static MAC address is now assigned permanently to interface fa0/5 and that it's also assigned to VLAN 1 only.

Spanning-Tree Operations

Spanning-Tree Protocol (STP) allows a switch to perform its third function loop avoidance. Its job is to find all links in the network and shut down any redundant ones, thereby preventing network loops from occurring.

Let's look at changing the priority to force a switch to become the root of your STP network. Use the following command in Table 5.7 to change the bridge priority on a Catalyst switch:

TABLE 5.7 Command and Meaning

Command	Meaning
`spanning-tree`	Configures Spanning-Tree Protocol options

Table 5.8 shows the options for the `spanning-tree` command.

TABLE 5.8 Options for *spanning-tree*

Option	Meaning
`vlan 1 priority`	Configures a switch VLAN to have a specific STP priority
`show spanning-tree`	Shows the spanning-tree configuration for each VLAN

You need to set the priority per-vlan, as shown here:

```
Switch B(config)#spanning-tree vlan 1 priority ?
  <0-61440>  bridge priority in increments of 4096
Switch B(config)#spanning-tree vlan 1 priority 4096
```

You can set the priority to any value from 0 through 61440. Setting it to zero (0) means the switch will always be the root, and the highest setting means it never will. The bridge priority is set in increments of 4096. If you want to set a switch to be the root bridge for every VLAN in your network, then you have to change the priority for each VLAN.

Check out the following output—now that I've changed the priority of Switch B for VLAN 1 to the lowest possible priority, I've successfully forced this switch to become the root:

```
SwitchB#show spanning-tree
VLAN0001
  Spanning tree enabled protocol ieee
  Root ID    Priority    4097
             Address     0012.7f52.0280
             This bridge is the root
             Hello Time   2 sec  Max Age 20 sec  Forward Delay 15 sec

  Bridge ID  Priority    4097   (priority 4096 sys-id-ext 1)
             Address     0012.7f52.0280
             Hello Time   2 sec  Max Age 20 sec  Forward Delay 15 sec
             Aging Time 15
[output cut]
```

Optimizing Spanning-Tree Operations

There are a couple of enhancements that have been made to the original STP standard. A few of these started out as Cisco proprietary features and then later were changed and made into the new version of STP called *Rapid STP* (RSTP).

Table 5.9 lists the options, which are pretty simple.

TABLE 5.9 Options for RSTP

Option	Meaning
portfast	Configures a switch port to immediately transition to forwarding and not wait for the STP timer
interface range	Allows you to choose a range of interfaces to configure
bpdufilter	Filters BPDUs from entering a switch port
bpduguard	Shuts down a switch port if it receives a BPDU
uplinkfast	Configures spanning tree to find and maintain a secondary link to the root bridge
backbonefast	Configures spanning tree to maintain an alternate path to the root bridge in case there is a failure that is not directly connected to itself
mode	Configures the spanning tree mode to either MST, PVST, or Rapd-pvst it's ok

Spanning-Tree PortFast

If you have a server or other devices connected into your switch that you're totally sure won't create a switching loop if STP is disabled, you can use something called PortFast on these ports. Using it means the port won't spend the usual 50 seconds to come up into forwarding mode while STP is converging.

```
Switch(config-if)#spanning-tree portfast ?
  disable  Disable portfast for this interface
  trunk    Enable portfast on the interface even in trunk mode
  <cr>
```

Let's take a look at the message I get when I turn PortFast on an interface:

```
Switch(config-if)#spanning-tree portfast
%Warning: portfast should only be enabled on ports connected to a
   single host. Connecting hubs, concentrators, switches, bridges,
   etc... to this interface  when portfast is enabled, can cause
   temporary bridging loops.
 Use with CAUTION
```

```
%Portfast has been configured on FastEthernet0/1 but will only
 have effect when the interface is in a non-trunking mode.
Switch(config-if)#
```

Interface Range

A helpful interface command is the `range` command; you can use it on switches to help you configure multiple ports at the same time. Here's an example that allows you to configure 12 interfaces at one time!

```
Switch(config)#int range fastEthernet 0/1 - 12
Switch(config-if-range)#spanning-tree portfast
```

BPDUFilter

Another helpful command to use with PortFast is BPDUFilter. Since a switch port that has PortFast enabled will still receive BPDUs by default, you can use the BPDUFilter to stop BPDUs coming into that port completely. BPDU filtering not only blocks just the BPDUs, but it takes the port out of PortFast status and forces the port to be a part of the STP topology again.

```
S1(config-if-range)#spanning-tree bpdufilter ?
  disable  Disable BPDU filtering for this interface
  enable   Enable BPDU filtering for this interface
S1(config-if-range)#spanning-tree bpdufilter enable
```

BPDUGuard

I talked about this a bit earlier—if you turn on PortFast for a switch port, turning on BPDU-Guard is a really good idea. If a switch port that has PortFast enabled receives a BPDU on that port, it will shut that port down and put it into an error-disabled state.

```
S1(config-if-range)#spanning-tree bpduguard ?
  disable  Disable BPDU guard for this interface
  enable   Enable BPDU guard for this interface
S1(config-if-range)#spanning-tree bpduguard enable
```

UplinkFast

UplinkFast allows a switch to find alternate paths to the root bridge before the primary link fails. What this means is that if the primary link fails, the secondary link would come up more quickly—the port wouldn't wait for the normal STP convergence time of 50 seconds.

```
Switch(config)#spanning-tree uplinkfast ?
  max-update-rate  Rate at which station address updates are sent
  <cr>
UplinkFast is enabled

Station update rate set to 150 packets/sec.

UplinkFast statistics
-----------------------
Number of transitions via uplinkFast (all VLANs)            : 1
Number of proxy multicast addresses transmitted (all VLANs) : 8

Name                 Interface List
-------------------- ------------------------------------
VLAN0001             Fa0/1(fwd), Fa0/2
S1(config)#
```

The uplinkfast command is a global command, and it's enabled on every port.

BackboneFast

Unlike UplinkFast that's used to determine and quickly fix link failures on the local switch, another Cisco-propriety STP extension called BackboneFast is used for speeding up convergence when a link that's not directly connected to the switch fails. If a switch running BackboneFast receives an inferior BPDU from its designated bridge, it knows that a link on the path to the root has failed. Just to make sure you're clear on this: an inferior BPDU is one that lists the same switch for the root bridge and the designated bridge.

```
Switch(config)#spanning-tree backbonefast ?
  <cr>
BackboneFast is enabled

BackboneFast statistics
-----------------------
Number of transition via backboneFast (all VLANs)           : 0
Number of inferior BPDUs received (all VLANs)               : 2
Number of RLQ request PDUs received (all VLANs)             : 0
Number of RLQ response PDUs received (all VLANs)            : 1
Number of RLQ request PDUs sent (all VLANs)                 : 1
Number of RLQ response PDUs sent (all VLANs)                : 0
S2(config)#
```

RSTP (802.1w)

Configuring RSTP is as easy as it is for any of the other 802.1d extensions. Considering how much better it is than 802.1d, you'd think the configuration would be more complex, but you're in luck—it's not. So let's turn in on the Core switch now and see what happens:

```
Core#config t
Core(config)#spanning-tree mode ?
  mst         Multiple spanning tree mode
  pvst        Per-Vlan spanning tree mode
  rapid-pvst  Per-Vlan rapid spanning tree mode
Core(config)#spanning-tree mode rapid-pvst
Core(config)#
1d02h: %LINEPROTO-5-UPDOWN: Line protocol on Interface Vlan1, changed state to down
1d02h: %LINEPROTO-5-UPDOWN: Line protocol on Interface Vlan1, changed state to up
```

Sweet! The Core switch is now running the 802.1w STP. Let's verify that:

```
Core#show spanning-tree
VLAN0001
  Spanning tree enabled protocol rstp
  Root ID    Priority    32769
             Address     000d.29bd.4b80
             This bridge is the root
             Hello Time   2 sec  Max Age 20 sec  Forward Delay 15 sec

  Bridge ID  Priority    32769  (priority 32768 sys-id-ext 1)
             Address     000d.29bd.4b80
             Hello Time   2 sec  Max Age 20 sec  Forward Delay 15 sec
             Aging Time 300

Interface        Role Sts Cost      Prio.Nbr Type
---------------- ---- --- --------- -------- ------------
Fa0/5            Desg FWD 19        128.5    P2p Peer(STP)
Fa0/6            Desg FWD 19        128.6    P2p Peer(STP)
Fa0/7            Desg FWD 19        128.7    P2p Peer(STP)
Fa0/8            Desg FWD 19        128.8    P2p Peer(STP)
```

EtherChannel

I'll discuss the CLI because you need to know CLI commands too. Remember, there are two versions of EtherChannel, the Cisco version and the IEEE version. I'll show how to use the Cisco version in this section and bundle the links between the S1 switch and the Core.

I'll use the `interface port-channel` global command and the `channel-group` and `channel-protocol` interface commands on the S1 and Core switches. Here (in Table 5.10) are the commands we'll use for etherchannel:

TABLE 5.10 Command and Meaning

Command	Meaning
`interface port-channel`	Configures the virtual port or interface that will serve as the new single-bundled interface
`channel-group`	Configures the virtual link that binds the physical interfaces to the virtual interface bundle
`channel-protocol`	Configures the EtherChannel protocol to be used

Here's what that looks like:

```
S1#config t
S1(config)#int port-channel 1
S1(config-if)#int range f0/1-2
S1(config-if-range)#switchport mode trunk
1d03h: %SPANTREE_FAST-7-PORT_FWD_UPLINK: VLAN0001 FastEthernet0/2 moved to
Forwarding (UplinkFast).
S1(config-if-range)#switchport nonegotiate
S1(config-if-range)#channel-group 1 mode desirable
S1(config-if-range)#do sh int fa0/1 etherchannel
Port state     = Up Sngl-port-Bndl Mstr Not-in-Bndl
Channel group = 1             Mode = Desirable-Sl     Gcchange = 0
Port-channel  = null          GC   = 0x00010001       Pseudo port-channel = Po1
Port index    = 0             Load = 0x00             Protocol =    PAgP
[output cut]

Core#config t
Core(config)#int port-channel 1
Core(config-if)#int range f0/7-8
Core(config-if-range)#switchport trunk encap dot1q
Core(config-if-range)#switchport mode trunk
1d03h: %SPANTREE_FAST-7-PORT_FWD_UPLINK: VLAN0001 FastEthernet0/2 moved to
Forwarding (UplinkFast).
```

```
Core(config-if-range)#switchport nonegotiate
Core(config-if-range)#channel-group 1 mode desirable
1d04h: %SPANTREE_FAST-7-PORT_FWD_UPLINK: VLAN0001 FastEthernet0/2 moved to
Forwarding (UplinkFast).
1d04h: %SPANTREE_FAST-7-PORT_FWD_UPLINK: VLAN0001 FastEthernet0/2 moved to
Forwarding (UplinkFast).
1d04h: %LINK-3-UPDOWN: Interface Port-channel1, changed state to up
1d04h: %LINEPROTO-5-UPDOWN: Line protocol on Interface Port-channel1, changed
state to up
Core(config-if-range)#do show int port-channel 1
Port-channel1 is up, line protocol is up (connected)
  Hardware is EtherChannel, address is 001b.2b55.7501 (bia 001b.2b55.7501)
  MTU 1500 bytes, BW 200000 Kbit, DLY 100 usec,
     reliability 255/255, txload 1/255, rxload 1/255
  Encapsulation ARPA, loopback not set
  Full-duplex, 100Mb/s, link type is auto, media type is unknown
[output cut]
```

I added the `switchport nonegotiate` interface command to stop the switches from trying to autodetect the link types and to automatically set up trunking. Instead, I statically configured my trunk links. The two links between the S1 and the Core are now bundled using the Cisco EtherChannel version of Port Aggregation Protocol (PAgP).

Verifying Cisco Catalyst Switches

Table 5.11 lists the most important basic commands you can use on a switch for verification purposes:

TABLE 5.11 Command and Meaning

Command	Meaning
`show interface`	Displays statistics for a given interface
`show mac address-table`	Displays the cache table of learned hardware addresses
`show spanning-tree`	Displays the spanning tree statistics, including information about the root bridge and port status

show interface

To verify the IP address set on a switch, you can use the `show interface` command. Here is the output:

```
S1#sh int vlan 1
Vlan1 is up, line protocol is up
  Hardware is EtherSVI, address is 001b.2b55.7540 (bia 001b.2b55.7540)
  Internet address is 192.168.10.17/28
  MTU 1500 bytes, BW 1000000 Kbit, DLY 10 usec,
     reliability 255/255, txload 1/255, rxload 1/255
  Encapsulation ARPA, loopback not set, reliability 255/255, txload 1/255,
rxload 1/255
  [output cut]
```

show mac address-table

I'm sure you remember being shown the `show mac address-table` command earlier in the chapter. Using it displays the forward filter table also called a *content addressable memory* (CAM) table. Here's the output from the S1 switch:

```
S1#sh mac address-table
          Mac Address Table
-------------------------------------------
Vlan    Mac Address       Type        Ports
----    -----------       --------    -----
 All    0100.0ccc.cccc    STATIC      CPU
 All    ffff.ffff.ffff    STATIC      CPU
[output cut]
   1    0002.1762.b235    DYNAMIC     Po1
   1    0009.b79f.c080    DYNAMIC     Po1
   1    000d.29bd.4b87    DYNAMIC     Po1
   1    000d.29bd.4b88    DYNAMIC     Po1
   1    0016.4662.52b4    DYNAMIC     Fa0/4
   1    0016.4677.5eab    DYNAMIC     Po1
   1    001a.2f52.49d8    DYNAMIC     Po1
   1    001a.2fe7.4170    DYNAMIC     Fa0/8
   1    001a.e2ce.ff40    DYNAMIC     Po1
   1    0050.0f02.642a    DYNAMIC     Fa0/3
Total Mac Addresses for this criterion: 31
S1#
```

The switches use what are called *base MAC addresses* that are assigned to the CPU, and the 2960s use 20. From the previous output, you can see that I have five MAC addresses dynamically assigned to EtherChannel port 1. Ports Fa0/3, Port8, and Fa0/4 have only one MAC address assigned, and all ports are assigned to VLAN 1. This code has been described many times in this chapter.

```
S2#sh mac address-table
          Mac Address Table
-------------------------------------------

Vlan    Mac Address       Type        Ports
----    -----------       --------    -----
 All    0008.205a.85c0    STATIC      CPU
 All    0100.0ccc.cccc    STATIC      CPU
 All    0100.0ccc.cccd    STATIC      CPU
 All    0100.0cdd.dddd    STATIC      CPU
[output cut]
   1    0002.1762.b235    DYNAMIC     Fa0/3
   1    000d.29bd.4b80    DYNAMIC     Fa0/1
   1    000d.29bd.4b85    DYNAMIC     Fa0/1
   1    0016.4662.52b4    DYNAMIC     Fa0/1
   1    0016.4677.5eab    DYNAMIC     Fa0/4
   1    001b.2b55.7540    DYNAMIC     Fa0/1
Total Mac Addresses for this criterion: 26
S2#
```

You can see in the previous output that I have four MAC addresses assigned to Fa0/1. And of course, you can also see that you have one connection for each host on ports 3 and 4. But where's port 2? Since port 2 is a redundant link, STP placed fa0/2 into blocking mode.

show spanning-tree

By this time you know that the `show spanning-tree` command is important. With it, you can see who the root bridge is and what the priorities are set to for each VLAN.

Understand that Cisco switches run what is called *Per-VLAN Spanning-Tree* (PVST), which basically means that each VLAN runs its own instance of STP. If you typed **show spanning-tree**, you'd receive information for each VLAN, starting with VLAN 1. So, say you have multiple VLANs and you want to see what's up with VLAN 2—you'd type the command **show spanning-tree vlan 2**.

Here is an output from the `show spanning-tree` command from switch S1. Since I'm using only VLAN 1, I don't need to add the VLAN number to the command:

```
S1#sh spanning-tree
VLAN0001
  Spanning tree enabled protocol ieee
```

```
  Root ID    Priority    32769
             Address     000d.29bd.4b80
             Cost        3012
             Port        56 (Port-channel1)
             Hello Time   2 sec  Max Age 20 sec  Forward Delay 15 sec

  Bridge ID  Priority    49153  (priority 49152 sys-id-ext 1)
             Address     001b.2b55.7500
             Hello Time   2 sec  Max Age 20 sec  Forward Delay 15 sec
             Aging Time 15
  Uplinkfast enabled

Interface        Role Sts Cost      Prio.Nbr Type
---------------- ---- --- --------- -------- ----------
Fa0/3            Desg FWD 3100      128.3    Edge Shr
Fa0/4            Desg FWD 3019      128.4    Edge P2p
Fa0/8            Desg FWD 3019      128.8    P2p
Po1              Root FWD 3012      128.56   P2p
```

Since I have only VLAN 1 configured, there's no more output for this command, but if I had more, I would get another page for each VLAN configured on the switch. The default priority is 32768, but there's something called the *system ID extension* (`sys-id-ext`), which is the VLAN identifier. The bridge ID priority is incremented by the number of that VLAN. And since I have only VLAN 1, I increment by 1 to 32769. Understand, by default, BackboneFast raises the default priority to 49152 to prevent the bridge from becoming the root.

The top of the output shows you who the root bridge is:

```
VLAN0001
    Root ID  Priority    32769
             Address     000d.29bd.4b80
             Cost        3012
             Port        56 (Port-channel1)
             Hello Time   2 sec  Max Age 20 sec  Forward Delay 15 sec
```

EtherChannel Port 1 is the root port, which means that it's the chosen path to the root bridge, and it has an identifier of 000d.29bd.4b80. That can be either the Core switch or S2 only, and you'll find out which one it is in a minute.

The last output from the command displays the ports that are running STP and have a connection to another device. Because I'm running EtherChannel, I have no blocked ports. One way to determine whether your bridge is the root is to look to see whether there are any Altn BLK ports (meaning a blocked port that is an alternate). A root bridge would never have a blocked port on any interface, but all the ports on S1 show Forwarding (FWD) because of the EtherChannel configuration.

Determining the Root Bridge

TABLE 5.12 Command and Meaning

Command	Meaning
`spanning-tree vlan` *`vlan`* `priority` *`priority`*	Changes the STP priority of the PVST
`spanning-tree vlan` *`vlan`* `root primary`	Sets the switch to be the primary root bridge of the PVST
`spanning-tree vlan` *`vlan`* `root secondary`	Sets the switch to be the secondary root of the PVST

Look at Table 5.12. To determine your root bridge, you would obviously use the `show spanning-tree` command. Let's take a look at the other two switches and see which switch is the default root bridge. Make a mental note of the bridge ID MAC address as well as the priority of the S1 switch. Here's the S2 output:

```
S2#sh spanning-tree

VLAN0001
  Spanning tree enabled protocol ieee
  Root ID    Priority    32769
             Address     000d.29bd.4b80
             Cost        3019
             Port        2 (FastEthernet0/1)
             Hello Time   2 sec  Max Age 20 sec  Forward Delay 15 sec

  Bridge ID  Priority    49153  (priority 49152 sys-id-ext 1)
             Address     001a.e2ce.ff00
             Hello Time   2 sec  Max Age 20 sec  Forward Delay 15 sec
             Aging Time 300
  Uplinkfast enabled

Interface        Role Sts Cost      Prio.Nbr Type
---------------- ---- --- --------- -------- ------------
Fa0/1            Root FWD 3019      128.2    P2p
Fa0/2            Altn BLK 3019      128.3    P2p
Fa0/3            Desg FWD 3100      128.4    Edge Shr
Fa0/4            Desg FWD 3019      128.5    Edge P2p
S2#
```

You can see that port Fa0/2 is blocked, so this cannot be your root bridge! A root bridge cannot have blocked ports. Again, pay special attention to the bridge ID MAC address and the priority. Here's the output from the Core switch:

```
Core#sh spanning-tree
VLAN0001
  Spanning tree enabled protocol rstp
  Root ID     Priority     32769
              Address      000d.29bd.4b80
              This bridge is the root
              Hello Time    2 sec   Max Age 20 sec   Forward Delay 15 sec

  Bridge ID   Priority     32769  (priority 32768 sys-id-ext 1)
              Address      000d.29bd.4b80
              Hello Time    2 sec   Max Age 20 sec   Forward Delay 15 sec
              Aging Time 300

Interface        Role Sts Cost      Prio.Nbr Type
---------------- ---- --- --------- -------- --------------
Fa0/5            Desg FWD 19        128.5    P2p Peer(STP)
Fa0/6            Desg FWD 19        128.6    P2p Peer(STP)
Po1              Desg FWD 12        128.66   P2p Peer(STP)
```

Well there you have it. "This bridge is the root."

But think about this—why does the Core switch have just the default of 32768 and not 49152 like the other switches? Well, it's running the 802.1w version of STP and BackboneFast is disabled by default.

Let's take a look at the bridge MAC address of each switch:

- *S1 address:* 001b.2b55.7500
- *S2 address:* 001a.e2ce.ff00
- *Core address:* 000d.29bd.4b80

If all switches are set to the default priority, which switch do you think will be the root switch? Start reading the MAC addresses from the left, moving toward the right. Core is obviously the lowest MAC address, and by looking at the output of the `show spanning-tree` command, you can see that it is, indeed, the root bridge (even if all switches had the same priority). It's just good practice to figure out the root bridge by comparing the MAC addresses of the switches once in awhile.

Setting the Root Bridge

It's kind of convenient that the Core switch is the root bridge by default because that's right where I'd typically choose to set the root. But just for fun, let's change it. Here's how you can do that:

```
S1#config t
S1(config)#spanning-tree vlan 1 priority ?
  <0-61440>  bridge priority in increments of 4096
S1(config)#spanning-tree vlan 1 priority 16384
S1(config)#do show spanning-tree
VLAN0001
Spanning tree enabled protocol ieee
  Root ID    Priority    16385
             Address     001b.2b55.7500
             This bridge is the root
             Hello Time   2 sec  Max Age 20 sec  Forward Delay 15 sec

  Bridge ID  Priority    16385  (priority 16384 sys-id-ext 1)
             Address     001b.2b55.7500
             Hello Time   2 sec  Max Age 20 sec  Forward Delay 15 sec
             Aging Time 300

Interface          Role Sts Cost      Prio.Nbr Type
---------------- ---- --- --------- -------- -----------
Fa0/3              Desg FWD 100       128.3    Edge Shr
Fa0/4              Desg FWD 19        128.4    Edge P2p
Fa0/8              Desg FWD 19        128.8    P2p
Po1                Desg FWD 12        128.56   P2p
```

By lowering the S1 priority to 16384, the S1 switch immediately became the root bridge. You can set your priorities all the way from 0 to 61440. Zero (0) means that the switch will always be the root bridge, and 61440 means the switch will never be a root.

There's one last command I want to tell you about; if you want to skip all this verification and configuration of the root bridge stuff—and no, you don't get to skip all that if you want to pass the Cisco exams—here's a simple command you can run on a switch to set it as a root bridge:

```
S1(config)#spanning-tree vlan 1 root ?
  primary    Configure this switch as primary root for this spanning tree
  secondary  Configure switch as secondary root
S1(config)#spanning-tree vlan 1 root primary
```

Understand that this does not override a low-priority switch; this command would work for you only if all your switches had the same priority, or higher, set.

Chapter 6

Virtual LANs (VLANs)

In this chapter, you'll learn the commands on how to create VLANs, put ports into VLANs, configure trunks and trunking protocols, configure VTP and all its options, configure inter-VLAN routing, and look at VLAN verification information.

For up-to-the minute updates for this chapter, please see `www.lammle.com` or `www.sybex.com/go/IOS`

Understanding VLAN Basics

Here's a short list of ways that configuring VLANs can help simplify network management:

- Network adds, moves, and changes are achieved with ease by just configuring a port into the appropriate VLAN.
- A group of users that needs an unusually high level of security can be put into their own VLAN so that users outside the VLAN can't communicate with them.
- As a logical grouping of users by function, VLANs can be considered independent from their physical or geographic locations.
- VLANs greatly enhance network security.
- VLANs increase the number of broadcast domains while decreasing their size.

Configuring VLANs

It may come as a surprise to you, but configuring VLANs is actually pretty easy. Figuring out which users you want in each VLAN is not. It's time-consuming, but once you've decided on the number of VLANs you want to create and established which users you want to belong to each one, it's time to bring your first VLAN into the world!

To configure VLANs on a Cisco Catalyst switch, use the global configuration `vlan` command. In the following example, I'll demonstrate how to configure VLANs on the S1 switch by creating three VLANs for three different departments—again, remember that VLAN 1 is the native and administrative VLAN by default.

Creating VLANs is very simple. Here in Table 6.1 is the command:

TABLE 6.1 Creating A VLAN

Command	Meaning
vlan	Creates or allows the modification of a VLAN in the VLAN database
name	Configures a name for a given VLAN from the VLAN configuration mode

Here is how you simply create VLANs on a switch:

```
S1#config t
S1(config)#vlan ?
  WORD      ISL VLAN IDs 1-4094
  internal  internal VLAN
S1(config)#vlan 2
S1(config-vlan)#name Sales
S1(config-vlan)#vlan 3
S1(config-vlan)#name Marketing
S1(config-vlan)#vlan 4
S1(config-vlan)#name Accounting
S1(config-vlan)#^Z
S1#
```

From the previous output, you can see that you can create VLANs from 2-4094. This is only mostly true. Like I said, VLANs can really be created only up to 1005, and you can't use, change, rename, or delete VLANs 1 and 1002 through 1005 because they're reserved. The previous VLAN numbers are called *extended* VLANs and won't be saved in the database unless your switch is set to VTP Transparent mode. You won't see these VLAN numbers used too often in production. Here's an example of setting my S1 switch to VLAN 4000 when my switch is set to VTP Server mode (the default VTP mode):

```
S1#config t
S1(config)#vlan 4000
S1(config-vlan)#^Z
% Failed to create VLANs 4000
Extended VLAN(s) not allowed in current VTP mode.
%Failed to commit extended VLAN(s) changes.
```

Verifying VLAN Creation

Once the VLANs are created, verify your configuration with the `show vlan` command in Table 6.2 (`sh vlan` for short):

TABLE 6.2 Verifying a VLAN

Command	Meaning
`show vlan`	Displays the contents or list of VLANs stored in the VLAN database file. (The VLAN database file is called `vlan.dat` and can be seen with the `show flash` command.)

Here is the output:

```
S1#sh vlan

VLAN Name                    Status    Ports
---- ----------------------------------------------------------
1    default                  active    Fa0/3, Fa0/4, Fa0/5, Fa0/6
                                        Fa0/7, Fa0/8, Gi0/1
2    Sales                    active
3    Marketing                active
4    Accounting               active
 [output cut]
```

Assigning Switch Ports to VLANs

You configure a port to belong to a VLAN by assigning a membership mode that specifies the kind of traffic the port carries, plus the number of VLANs to which it can belong. You can configure each port on a switch to be in a specific VLAN (access port) by using the interface `switchport` command. You can also configure multiple ports at the same time with the `interface range` command.

Here in Table 6.3 are the basic switch VLAN commands used on a switch port:

TABLE 6.3 Assigning Switch Port Memberships

Command	Meaning
`interface`	Enters the interface configuration mode and allows the configuration of a specific interface.

TABLE 6.3 Assigning Switch Port Memberships *(continued)*

Command	Meaning
`interface range`	Allows the selection of multiple ports for the purpose of configuring the same functions on all of those ports.
`switchport mode`	The `switchport` command is used to modify most layer-2 properties of a switch port. The mode option allows the modification of how a switch port will handle traffic for a specific VLAN or set of VLANs.
`switchport access`	Configures the port into a specific VLAN for the purpose of allowing only traffic from that VLAN to pass to and from that port.

Here's an example of setting a switch port assignment to VLAN 3

```
S1#config t
S1(config)#int fa0/3
S1(config-if)#switchport ?
  access        Set access mode characteristics of the interface
  backup        Set backup for the interface
  block         Disable forwarding of unknown uni/multi cast addresses
  host          Set port host
  mode          Set trunking mode of the interface
44  nonegotiate   Device will not engage in negotiation protocol on this
                interface
  port-security Security related command
  priority      Set appliance 802.1p priority
  protected     Configure an interface to be a protected port
  trunk         Set trunking characteristics of the interface
  voice         Voice appliance attributes
S1(config-if)#switchport mode ?
  access   Set trunking mode to ACCESS unconditionally
  dynamic  Set trunking mode to dynamically negotiate access or
trunk mode
  trunk    Set trunking mode to TRUNK unconditionally

S1(config-if)#switchport mode access
S1(config-if)#switchport access vlan 3
```

Configuring Trunk Ports

The 2960 switch runs the IEEE 802.1q encapsulation method only. To configure trunking on a Fast Ethernet port, use the interface command `trunk [parameter]`. It's a tad different on the 3560 switch, and I'll show you that in the next section.

The following switch output shows the trunk configuration on interface fa0/8 as set to trunk on:

```
S1#config t
S1(config)#int fa0/8
S1(config-if)#switchport mode trunk
```

Table 6.4 lists the trunk commands you can use:

TABLE 6.4 Configuring Trunk Ports

Mode	Meaning
`access`	This places a port into permanent nontrunking mode.
`dynamic auto`	This port state is able to convert to a trunk link if the neighbor interface is set to become a trunk and can negotiate with DTP.
`dynamic desirable`	Through the use of dynamic trunking protocol (DTP) this port mode attempts to convert the link into a trunk.
`trunk`	This sets the port state to permanent trunking mode and negotiates to make the neighbor interface a trunk port as well.
`nonegotiate`	This command can be used with access and trunk modes. It disables the sending of DTP packets out the interface, thereby disabling the ability to negotiate the trunk status.

Here is a list of the various trunk modes on a switch port:

switchport mode access This puts the interface (access port) into permanent nontrunking mode and negotiates to convert the link into a nontrunk link. The interface becomes a nontrunk interface regardless of whether the neighboring interface is a trunk interface. This port would be a dedicated layer-2 port.

switchport mode dynamic auto This mode makes the interface able to convert the link to a trunk link. The interface becomes a trunk interface if the neighboring interface is set to trunk or desirable mode. This is now the default switchport mode for all Ethernet interfaces on all new Cisco switches.

switchport mode dynamic desirable This one makes the interface actively attempt to convert the link to a trunk link. The interface becomes a trunk interface if the neighboring interface is set to trunk, desirable, or auto mode. I used to see this mode as the default on some older switches, but not any longer. The default is `dynamic auto` now.

switchport mode trunk This puts the interface into permanent trunking mode and negotiates to convert the neighboring link into a trunk link. The interface becomes a trunk interface even if the neighboring interface isn't a trunk interface.

switchport nonegotiate This prevents the interface from generating DTP frames. You can use this command only when the interface switchport mode is `access` or `trunk`. You must manually configure the neighboring interface as a trunk interface to establish a trunk link.

Trunking with the Cisco Catalyst 3560 Switch

In this section, you'll look at one more switch—the Cisco Catalyst 3560. The configuration is pretty much the same as it is for a 2960 with the exception being that the 3560 can provide layer-3 services and the 2960 can't. Plus, the 3560 can run both the ISL and the IEEE 802.1Q trunking encapsulation methods—the 2960 can run 802.1Q only. With all this in mind, let's just take a quick look at the VLAN encapsulation difference regarding the 3560 switch.

With a higher end switch, you have the option to set the encapsulation method, as highlighted in Table 6.5:

TABLE 6.5 Configuring Trunk Encapsulations

Command	Meaning
`switchport trunk encapsulation`	Allows the configuration of an encapsulation type. The type of encapsulation used can vary depending on the device or the type used on the other end of the trunk link.

For the 3560, you have the `encapsulation` command that the 2960 switch doesn't:

```
Core(config-if)#switchport trunk encapsulation ?
  dot1q      Interface uses only 802.1q trunking encapsulation
 when trunking
  isl        Interface uses only ISL trunking encapsulation
 when trunking
  negotiate  Device will negotiate trunking encapsulation with peer on
             interface
Core(config-if)#switchport trunk encapsulation dot1q
Core(config-if)#switchport mode trunk
```

Here in Table 6.6 are the two options:

TABLE 6.6 Encapsulation options

Command	Meaning
dot1q	Specifies the IEEE specification 802.1q encapsulation. This type of encapsulation is an open standard and is supported by almost all switches.
ISL	Specifies the ISL standard of encapsulation that is a Cisco proprietary standard of encapsulation. This encapsulation type is being phased out of use. Cisco doesn't even support it on their lower-level switches any more.

As you can see, we have the option to add either the IEEE 802.1Q (dot1q) encapsulation or the ISL encapsulation to the 3560 switch. After you set the encapsulation, you still have to set the interface mode to trunk.

Defining the Allowed VLANs on a Trunk

As I've mentioned, trunk ports send and receive information from all VLANs by default, and if a frame is untagged, it's sent to the management VLAN. This applies to the extended range VLANs as well.

But you can remove VLANs from the allowed list to prevent traffic from certain VLANs from traversing a trunked link. Table 6.7 lists the command for how you'd do that:

TABLE 6.7 Removing VLANs from Traversing a Trunk

Command	Meaning
switchport trunk allowed	Allows the configuration of a specific list of VLANs to be carried over a trunk link

Here is an example of using the command:

```
S1#config t
S1(config)#int f0/1
S1(config-if)#switchport trunk allowed vlan ?
  WORD     VLAN IDs of the allowed VLANs when this port is in
trunking mode
  add      add VLANs to the current list
  all      all VLANs
```

```
  except  all VLANs except the following
  none    no VLANs
  remove  remove VLANs from the current list
S1(config-if)#switchport trunk allowed vlan remove ?
  WORD  VLAN IDs of disallowed VLANS when this port is in trunking mode
S1(config-if)#switchport trunk allowed vlan remove 4
```

The previous command stopped the trunk link configured on S1 port f0/1, causing it to drop all traffic sent and received for VLAN 4.

Changing or Modifying the Trunk Native VLAN

Cisco doesn't recommend that you change the trunk port native VLAN from VLAN 1, but you can, and some people do it for security reasons. To change the native VLAN, use the command in Table 6.8:

TABLE 6.8 Changing the native VLAN

Command	Meaning
`switchport trunk native`	Allows the configuration of the native VLAN on a trunk link. The native VLAN is important for the proper operation of 802.1q encapsulation because it specifies what VLAN will carry any traffic that is not tagged.

Because nontagged traffic is considered a security threat, the recommended configuration for the native VLAN is a parked VLAN. A parked VLAN is a real VLAN that exists in the VLAN database but is not used to carry any enterprise data. This means you create the VLAN and assign no ports or data to it. This way, if there is any untagged data, it will be placed in this parked VLAN and go nowhere, causing no harm.

```
S1#config t
S1(config)#int f0/1
S1(config-if)#switchport trunk ?
  allowed  Set allowed VLAN characteristics when interface is
in trunking mode
  native   Set trunking native characteristics when interface
is in trunking mode
  pruning  Set pruning VLAN characteristics when interface is
in trunking mode
S1(config-if)#switchport trunk native ?
  vlan  Set native VLAN when interface is in trunking mode
```

```
S1(config-if)#switchport trunk native vlan ?
  <1-4094>  VLAN ID of the native VLAN when this port is in
 trunking mode
S1(config-if)#switchport trunk native vlan 40
S1(config-if)#^Z
```

Configuring Inter-VLAN Routing

By default, only hosts that are members of the same VLAN can communicate. To change this and allow inter-VLAN communication to be possible, you need a router or a layer-3 switch.

To support ISL or 802.1Q routing on a Fast Ethernet interface, the router's interface is divided into logical interfaces—one for each VLAN. These are called *subinterfaces*. Anyway, from a Fast Ethernet or Gigabit interface, you can set the interface to trunk with the `encapsulation` command:

The configuration of the switch would look something like this:

```
2960#config t
2960(config)#int f0/1
2960(config-if)#switchport mode trunk
2960(config-if)#int f0/2
2960(config-if)#switchport access vlan 1
2960(config-if)#int f0/3
2960(config-if)#switchport access vlan 1
2960(config-if)#int f0/4
2960(config-if)#switchport access vlan 3
2960(config-if)#int f0/5
2960(config-if)#switchport access vlan 3
2960(config-if)#int f0/6
2960(config-if)#switchport access vlan 2
```

Before you configure the router, you need to design your logical network:

VLAN 1: 192.168.10.16/28

VLAN 2: 192.168.10.32/28

VLAN 3: 192.168.10.48/28

The configuration of the router would then look like this:

```
ISR#config t
ISR(config)#int f0/0
ISR(config-if)#no ip address
```

```
ISR(config-if)#no shutdown
ISR(config-if)#int f0/0.1
ISR(config-subif)#encapsulation dotlq 1
ISR(config-subif)#ip address 192.168.10.17 255.255.255.240
ISR(config-subif)#int f0/0.2
ISR(config-subif)#encapsulation dotlq 2
ISR(config-subif)#ip address 192.168.10.33 255.255.255.240
ISR(config-subif)#int f0/0.3
ISR(config-subif)#encapsulation dotlq 3
ISR(config-subif)#ip address 192.168.10.49 255.255.255.240
```

The hosts in each VLAN would be assigned an address from their subnet range, and the default gateway would be the IP address assigned to the router's subinterface in that VLAN.

Configuring VTP

All Cisco switches are configured to be VTP servers by default. To configure VTP, first you have to configure the domain name you want to use. And of course, once you configure the VTP information on a switch, you need to verify it.

When you create the VTP domain, you have a bunch of options, including setting the domain name, password, operating mode, and pruning capabilities of the switch. Use the `vtp` global configuration mode command to set all this information. In the following example, I'll set the S1 switch to a `vtp server`, the VTP domain to `Lammle`, and the VTP password to `todd`:

Here in Table 6.9 are the commands you need:

TABLE 6.9 VTP Commands

Command	Meaning
`vtp mode server`	Configures a switch to be a VTP server. In Server mode, the VLAN database is allowed to be modified. VLANs can be added, deleted, modified or changed. Server is the default vtp mode for a Cisco switch. Changing the `server` option to `client` or `transparent` would configure the switch to that mode.
`vtp domain`	Configures the VTP domain name for a group of switches in the layer-2 switch fabric.

TABLE 6.9 VTP Commands *(continued)*

Command	Meaning
`vtp password`	Configures a password to be used by the switches in a VTP domain. The password serves two purposes. It allows updates to be authenticated, ensuring the update came from the correct server. With that authentication, it then adds a step in preventing an incorrect server from joining the domain and wiping out the VLAN database.
`show vtp status`	Displays all the configured options for VTP on the current switch. This is one of the most useful commands when troubleshooting VTP, because it allows the domain name, revision number, and other settings to easily be verified.

Let's take a look at an example on how to use these commands:

```
S1#config t
S1#(config)#vtp mode server
Device mode already VTP SERVER.
S1(config)#vtp domain Lammle
Changing VTP domain name from null to Lammle
S1(config)#vtp password todd
Setting device VLAN database password to todd
S1(config)#do show vtp password
VTP Password: todd
S1(config)#do show vtp status
VTP Version                     : 2
Configuration Revision          : 0
Maximum VLANs supported locally : 255
Number of existing VLANs        : 8
VTP Operating Mode              : Server
VTP Domain Name                 : Lammle
VTP Pruning Mode                : Disabled
VTP V2 Mode                     : Disabled
VTP Traps Generation            : Disabled
MD5 digest                      : 0x15 0x54 0x88 0xF2 0x50 0xD9 0x03 0x07
Configuration last modified by 192.168.24.6 at 3-14-93 15:47:32
Local updater ID is 192.168.24.6 on interface Vl1 (lowest numbered VLAN
interface found)
```

Let's go to the Core and S2 switches and set them into the Lammle VTP domain. It is important to remember that the VTP domain name is case sensitive! VTP is not forgiving—one teeny small mistake, and it just won't work!

```
Core#config t
Core(config)#vtp mode client
Setting device to VTP CLIENT mode.
Core(config)#vtp domain Lammle
Changing VTP domain name from null to Lammle
Core(config)#vtp password todd
Setting device VLAN database password to todd
Core(config)#do show vtp status
VTP Version                     : 2
Configuration Revision          : 0
Maximum VLANs supported locally : 1005
Number of existing VLANs        : 5
VTP Operating Mode              : Server
VTP Domain Name                 : Lammle
VTP Pruning Mode                : Disabled
VTP V2 Mode                     : Disabled
VTP Traps Generation            : Disabled
MD5 digest                      : 0x2A 0x6B 0x22 0x17 0x04 0x4F 0xB8 0xC2
Configuration last modified by 192.168.10.19 at 3-1-93 03:13:16
Local updater ID is 192.168.24.7 on interface Vl1 (first interface found)
```

Here's how to use the `show vlan brief` command on the Core and S2 switch:

```
Core#sh vlan brief
VLAN Name                 Status    Ports
---- ------------------ --------- ---------------------
1    default              active    Fa0/1,Fa0/2,Fa0/3,Fa0/4
                                    Fa0/9,Fa0/10,Fa0/11,Fa0/12
Fa0/13,Fa0/14,Fa0/15,         Fa0/16,Fa0/17, Fa0/18, Fa0/19, Fa0/20,Fa0/21, Fa0/
22, Fa0/23, Fa0/24, Gi0/1, Gi0/2
2    Sales                 active
3    Marketing             active
4    Accounting            active
[output cut]
```

Telephony: Configuring Voice VLANs

The voice VLAN feature enables access ports to carry IP voice traffic from an IP phone. When a switch is connected to a Cisco IP Phone, the phone sends voice traffic with layer-3 IP precedence and layer-2 class of service (CoS) values, which are both set to 5 for voice traffic; all other traffic defaults to 0. Because the sound quality of an IP phone call can deteriorate if the data is unevenly sent, the switch supports quality of service (QoS) based on IEEE 802.1p CoS (802.1p provides a mechanism for implementing QoS at the MAC level). The 802.1p field is carried in the 802.1q trunk header. If you look at the fields in an 802.1q tag, you will see a field called the *priority field*, which is where the 802.1p information goes. QoS uses classification and scheduling to send network traffic from the switch in an organized, predictable manner.

The Cisco IP Phone is a configurable device, and you can configure it to forward traffic with an IEEE 802.1p priority. You can also configure the switch to either trust or override the traffic priority assigned by a Cisco IP Phone—which is exactly what I'll show how to do here. The Cisco phone basically has a three-port switch: one to connect to the Cisco switch, one to a PC device, and one to the actual phone, which is internal.

You can also configure an access port with an attached Cisco IP Phone to use one VLAN for voice traffic and another VLAN for data traffic from a device attached to the phone—like a PC. You can configure access ports on the switch to send Cisco Discovery Protocol (CDP) packets that instruct an attached Cisco IP Phone to send voice traffic to the switch in any of these ways:

- In the voice VLAN, tagged with a layer-2 CoS priority value
- In the access VLAN, tagged with a layer-2 CoS priority value
- In the access VLAN, untagged (no layer-2 CoS priority value)

The switch can also process tagged data traffic (traffic in IEEE 802.1Q or IEEE 802.1p frame types) from the device attached to the access port on the Cisco IP Phone. You can configure layer-2 access ports on the switch to send CDP packets that instruct the attached Cisco IP Phone to configure the phone access port in one of these modes:

- In trusted mode, all traffic received through the access port on the Cisco IP Phone passes through the phone unchanged.
- In untrusted mode, all traffic in IEEE 802.1Q or IEEE 802.1p frames received through the access port on the Cisco IP Phone receive a configured layer-2 CoS value. The default layer-2 CoS value is 0. Untrusted mode is the default.

Configuring the Voice VLAN

By default, the voice VLAN feature is disabled, and you enable it by using the interface command `switchport voice vlan`. When the voice VLAN feature is enabled, all untagged traffic is sent according to the default CoS priority of the port. The CoS value is not trusted for IEEE 802.1p or IEEE 802.1Q tagged traffic.

These are the voice VLAN configuration guidelines:

- You should configure voice VLAN on switch access ports; voice VLAN isn't supported on trunk ports, even though you can actually configure it!
- The voice VLAN should be present and active on the switch for the Cisco IP Phone to correctly communicate on it. Use the `show vlan` privileged exec command to see whether the VLAN is present—if it is, it'll be listed in the display.
- Before you enable the voice VLAN, it's recommend you enable QoS on the switch by entering the `mls qos` global configuration command and set the port trust state to trust by entering the `mls qos trust cos` interface configuration command.
- You must make sure that CDP is enabled on the switch port connected to the Cisco IP Phone to send the configuration. This is on by default, so unless you disabled it, you shouldn't have a problem.
- The PortFast feature is automatically enabled when the voice VLAN is configured, but when you disable the voice VLAN, the PortFast feature isn't automatically disabled.
- To return the port to its default setting, use the `no switchport voice vlan` interface configuration command.

Here in Table 6.10 are the commands you need:

TABLE 6.10 Configuring Voice Switch Ports

Command	Meaning
`mls qos`	Configured from global configuration mode, this command enables globally on the switch the feature set to run QOS.
`switchport voice vlan`	This configures a switch port association into a voice VLAN. The voice VLAN used to be called an *auxiliary VLAN* and allows an access port to be associated to a data and voice VLAN simultaneously.
`mls qos trust cos`	This configures a switch port to trust the frame's COS priority tag. If a frame is untagged, then the port's default COS value will be used.
`switchport priority extend cos`	Configures the switchport to override or rewrite the 802.1p (COS) value that is in an incoming frame's header. This is establishing your QOS policy at the edge or your network. With regard to QOS, the edge of the network is also called the *trust boundary.*
`switchport priority extend trust`	This configures the switchport to trust or leave the 802.1p (COS) value that is in an incoming frame's header. This is establishing your QOS policy at the edge or your network. With regard to QOS, the edge of the network is also called the *trust boundary.*

TABLE 6.10 Configuring Voice Switch Ports *(continued)*

Command	Meaning
`mls qos trust device cisco-phone`	This configures the switchport to trust the priority marking coming from the Cisco phone. This configuration will work only with a Cisco phone because the switch and the phone communicate using CDP.

OK, here goes, this is the hardest part of the book, but take a look at how I did it and try it for yourself if possible:

```
Switch#configure t
Switch(config)#mls qos
Switch(config)#interface f0/1
Switch(config-if)#switchport priority extend ?
  cos    Override 802.1p priority of devices on appliance
  trust  Trust 802.1p priorities of devices on appliance
Switch(config-if)#switchport priority extend trust
Switch(config-if)#mls qos trust cos
Switch(config-if)#switchport voice vlan dot1p
Switch(config-if)#switchport mode access
Switch(config-if)#switchport access vlan 3
Switch(config-if)#switchport voice vlan 10
```

The command `mls qos trust cos` will configure the interface to classify incoming traffic packets by using the packet CoS value. For untagged packets, the port's default CoS value will be used. But before configuring the port trust state, you must first globally enable QoS by using the `mls qos` global configuration command.

Chapter 7 Security

In this chapter, you'll learn a lot about deterring the most commonly attempted threats to your network's security with Cisco routers and IOS firewalls that together offer quite a powerful, integrated detection package against many types of invasion. I'll cover how Cisco IOS Firewall puts actual security and policy enforcement for your internal and external networking needs. I'll also show you how to create secure connections to any remote locations you may have living on the fringes, too!

Access lists are an integral part of Cisco's security solution, and I'll show you the keys of both simple and advanced access lists that will equip you with the ability to ensure internetwork security as well as mitigate most security-oriented network threats.

For up-to-the minute updates for this chapter, please see `www.lammle.com` or `www.sybex.com/go/IOS`

Perimeter Routers, Firewalls, and Internal Routers

Typically, medium to large enterprise networks base their various strategies for security on some recipe of internal and perimeter routers plus firewall devices. Internal routers provide additional security to the network by screening traffic to various parts of the protected corporate network, and they do this using access lists. Figure 7.1 shows where you can find each of these types of devices.

I'll first discuss the security threats a typical secured internetwork faces, and then I'll provide some ways of protecting the internetwork using the Cisco IOS Firewall feature set and access lists.

FIGURE 7.1 A typical secured network

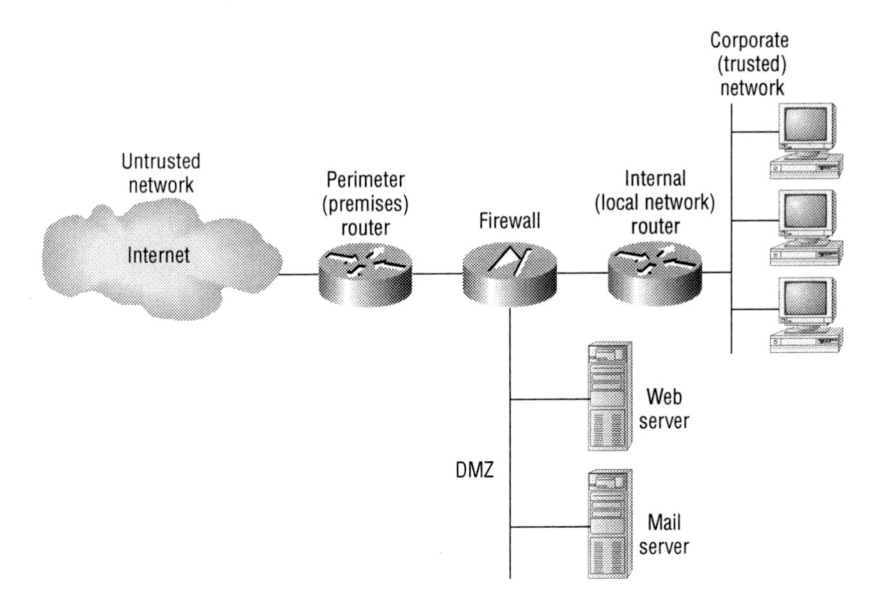

Recognizing Security Threats

You see, it all comes down to planning—or, rather, a lack thereof. Basically, the vital tool that the Internet has become to us today was absolutely unforeseen by those who brought it into being. This is a big reason why security is now such an issue—most IP implementations are innately insecure. No worries, though. Cisco can help us with this. But first, let's examine some common attack profiles:

- Application-layer attacks
- Autorooters
- Backdoors
- Denial of Service (DoS) and Distributed Denial of Service (DDoS) attacks
  - TCP SYN flood
  - "Ping of Death" attacks
  - Tribe Flood Network (TFN) and Tribe Flood Network 2000 (TFN2K)
  - Stacheldraht

- IP spoofing
- Man-in-the-middle attacks
- Network reconnaissance
- Packet sniffers
- Password attacks
- Brute-force attack
- Port redirection attacks
- Trojan horse attacks and viruses
- Trust exploitation attacks

Using Cisco IOS Firewall

Here's where you'll find out how to mitigate some of the more common security threats on the list in the previous section using the following Cisco IOS Firewall features:

Stateful IOS firewall inspection engine This is your perimeter protection feature, because it gives your internal users secure access control on a per-application basis. People often call it *context-based access control* (CBAC).

Intrusion detection This is a deep packet inspection tool that lets you monitor, intercept, and respond to abuse in real-time by referencing 102 of the most common attack and intrusion detection signatures.

Firewall voice traversal This is an application-level feature based on the protocol's understanding of call flow, as well as the relevant open channels. It supports both the H.323v2 and Session Initiation Protocol (SIP) voice protocols.

ICMP inspection Basically, this permits responses to ICMP packets such as `ping` and `traceroute` that come from inside your firewall while denying other ICMP traffic.

Authentication proxy This is a feature that makes users authenticate any time they want to access the network's resources through HTTP, HTTPS, FTP, and Telnet. It keeps personal network access profiles for users, and it automatically gets them for you from a RADIUS or TACACS+ server and applies them as well.

Destination URL policy management This is a buffet of features that's commonly referred to as *URL filtering*.

Per-user firewalls These are basically personalized, user-specific, downloadable firewalls obtained through service providers. You can also get personalized ACLs and other settings via AAA server profile storage.

Cisco IOS router and firewall provisioning This allows for no-touch router provisioning, version updates, and security policies.

DoS detection and prevention This is a feature that checks packet headers and drops any packets it finds suspicious.

Dynamic port mapping This is a sort of adapter that permits applications supported by firewalls on nonstandard ports.

Java applet blocking This protects you from any strange, unrecognized Java applets.

You can use standard, extended, and even dynamic ACLs such as lock-and-key traffic filtering with Cisco IOS Firewall. And you get to apply access controls to any network segment you want. Plus, you can specify the exact kind of traffic you want to allow to pass through any segment.

Policy-based, multi-interface support This allows you to control user access by IP address and interface depending on your security policy.

Network Address Translation (NAT) This conceals the internal network from the outside, which increases security.

Time-based access lists This determines security policies based upon the exact time of day and the particular day of week.

Peer router authentication This guarantees that routers are getting dependable routing information from actual, trusted sources. (For this to work, you need a routing protocol that supports authentication such as RIPv2, EIGRP, or OSPF.)

Introduction to Access Lists

Creating access lists is really a lot like programming a series of `if-then` statements—if a given condition is met, then a given action is taken. If the specific condition isn't met, nothing happens, and the next statement is evaluated. Access-list statements are basically packet filters that packets are compared against, categorized by, and acted upon accordingly. Once the lists are built, they can be applied to either inbound or outbound traffic on any interface. Applying an access list causes the router to analyze every packet crossing that interface in the specified direction and take the appropriate action.

A packet follows a few important rules when it's being compared to an access list:

- It's always compared to each line of the access list in sequential order; in other words, it'll always start with the first line of the access list, then go to line 2, then line 3, and so on.
- It's compared to lines of the access list only until a match is made. Once the packet matches the condition on a line of the access list, the packet is acted upon, and no further comparisons take place.
- There is an implicit "deny" at the end of each access list; this means that if a packet doesn't match the condition on any of the lines in the access list, the packet will be discarded.

There are two main types of access lists:

Standard access lists These use only the source IP address in an IP packet as the condition test. All decisions are made based on the source IP address. This means standard access lists basically permit or deny an entire suite of protocols. They don't distinguish between any of the many types of IP traffic such as WWW, Telnet, UDP, and so on.

Extended access lists Extended access lists can evaluate many of the other fields in the layer-3 and layer-4 headers of an IP packet. They can evaluate source and destination IP addresses, the protocol field in the Network layer header, and the port number at the Transport layer header. This gives extended access lists the ability to make much more granular decisions when controlling traffic.

Named access lists Hey, wait a minute—I said two types of access lists but listed three! Well, technically there really are only two since *named access lists* are either standard or extended and not actually a new type. I'm just distinguishing them because they're created and referred to differently than standard and extended access lists. But they're functionally the same.

Here's a list of the many security threats you can mitigate with ACLs:

- IP address spoofing—inbound
- IP address spoofing—outbound
- DoS TCP SYN attacks—blocking external attacks
- DoS TCP SYN attacks—using TCP intercept
- DoS smurf attacks
- Filtering ICMP messages—inbound
- Filtering ICMP messages—outbound
- Filtering `traceroute`

It's generally wise not to allow any IP packets coming into a private network that contain the source address of any internal hosts or networks—just don't do it!

Here's a list of rules to live by when configuring ACLs from the Internet to your production network to mitigate security problems:

- Deny any addresses from your internal networks.
- Deny any local host addresses (127.0.0.0/8).
- Deny any reserved private addresses.
- Deny any addresses in the IP multicast address range (224.0.0.0/4).

Standard Access Lists

Standard IP access lists filter network traffic by examining the source IP address in a packet. You create a *standard IP access list* by using the access-list numbers 1–99 or 1300–1999 (expanded range). Access-list types are generally differentiated using a number. Based on the number used when the access list is created, the router knows which type of syntax to expect as the list is entered. By using numbers 1–99 or 1300–1999, you're telling the router you want to create a standard IP access list, so the router will expect syntax specifying only the source IP address in the test lines.

Here in Table 7.1 are the basic access-list commands that will get your configuration started:

TABLE 7.1 Creating an Access-list and Applying it to an Interface

Command	Meaning
access-list	Configures a single access-list statement into a router's memory for use in a complete access list that will be applied to an interface
ip access-group	Places an access list on a device's physical interface

Table 7.2 lists the options for these commands:

TABLE 7.2 Access-list Command Options

Option	Meaning
<ID number>	Identifies an access list by number as a standard or extended list. Also allows the creation and separation of multiple access lists.
permit or deny	Specifies the effect of the access-list statement as allowing or blocking the traffic specified.
hostname or IP address	Specifies the hostname or device's IP address that will be acted upon in the access-list statement.
host	Specifies a single specific host for the statement.
any	Specifies that regardless of the host or device IP, it will match the statement.

The following is an example of the many access-list number ranges that you can use to filter traffic on your network (the protocols for which you can specify access lists depend on your IOS version):

```
Corp(config)#access-list ?
  <1-99>            IP standard access list
  <100-199>         IP extended access list
  <1100-1199>       Extended 48-bit MAC address access list
  <1300-1999>       IP standard access list (expanded range)
  <200-299>         Protocol type-code access list
  <2000-2699>       IP extended access list (expanded range)
  <700-799>         48-bit MAC address access list
  compiled          Enable IP access-list compilation
  dynamic-extended  Extend the dynamic ACL absolute timer
  rate-limit        Simple rate-limit specific access list
```

Let's take a look at the syntax used when creating a standard access list:

```
Corp(config)#access-list 10 ?
  deny    Specify packets to reject
  permit  Specify packets to forward
  remark  Access list entry comment
```

As I said, by using the access-list numbers between 1–99 or 1300–1999, you're telling the router that you want to create a standard IP access list.

After you choose the access-list number, you need to decide whether you're creating a permit or deny statement. For this example, you will create a deny statement:

```
Corp(config)#access-list 10 deny ?
  Hostname or A.B.C.D  Address to match
  any                  Any source host
  host                 A single host address
```

The next step requires a more detailed explanation. Three options are available. You can use the any parameter to permit or deny any host or network, you can use an IP address to specify either a single host or a range of them, or you can use the host command to specify a specific host only. The any command is pretty obvious—any source address matches the statement, so every packet compared against this line will match. The host command is relatively simple. Here's an example of how to use it:

```
Corp(config)#access-list 10 deny host ?
  Hostname or A.B.C.D  Host address
Corp(config)#access-list 10 deny host 172.16.30.2
```

This tells the list to deny any packets from host 172.16.30.2. The default parameter is host. In other words, if you type **access-list 10 deny 172.16.30.2**, the router assumes you mean host 172.16.30.2.

Wildcard Masking

Wildcards are used with access lists to specify an individual host, a network, or a certain range of a network or networks. To understand a *wildcard*, you need to understand what a *block size* is; it's used to specify a range of addresses. Some of the different block sizes available are 64, 32, 16, 8, and 4.

The following example tells the router to match the first three octets exactly but that the fourth octet can be anything:

```
Corp(config)#access-list 10 deny 172.16.10.0 0.0.0.255
```

The next example tells the router to match the first two octets and that the last two octets can be any value:

```
Corp(config)#access-list 10 deny 172.16.0.0
  0.0.255.255
```

Try to figure out this next line:

```
Corp(config)#access-list 10 deny 172.16.16.0 0.0.3.255
```

The previous configuration tells the router to start at network 172.16.16.0 and use a block size of 4. The range would then be 172.16.16.0 through 172.16.19.0.

Controlling VTY (Telnet) Access

You'll probably have a difficult time trying to stop users from telnetting to a large router because any active interface on a router is fair game for VTY access. You could try to create an extended IP access list that limits Telnet access to every IP address on the router. But if you did that, you'd have to apply it inbound on every interface, and that really wouldn't scale well to a large router with dozens, even hundreds, of interfaces, would it? Here's a much better solution: use a standard IP access list to control access to the VTY lines themselves.

Why does this work? Well, when you apply an access list to the VTY lines, you don't need to specify the Telnet protocol, since access to the VTY implies terminal access. You also don't need to specify a destination address, since it really doesn't matter which interface address the user used as a target for the Telnet session. You really need only to control where the user is coming from—their source IP address.

To perform this function, follow these steps:

1. Create a standard IP access list that permits only the host or hosts you want to be able to telnet into the routers.

2. Apply the access list to the VTY line with the `access-class` command. Here in Table 7.3 is the command you can configure on the VTY lines:

TABLE 7.3 Assigning and Access List to a VTY Line

Command	Meaning
access-class	Places an access list on the VTY lines of a device

Here is an example of allowing only host 172.16.10.3 to telnet into a router:

```
Lab_A(config)#access-list 50 permit 172.16.10.3
Lab_A(config)#line vty 0 4
Lab_A(config-line)#access-class 50 in
```

Because of the implied `deny any` at the end of the list, the access list stops any host from telnetting into the router except the host 172.16.10.3, regardless of which individual IP address on the router is used as a target.

Extended Access Lists

In the standard IP access list example shown previously, notice how you had to block all access from the sales LAN to the finance department. What if you needed sales to gain access to a certain server on the finance LAN but not to other network services for security reasons? With a standard IP access list, you can't allow users to get to one network service and not another. Said another way, when you need to make decisions based on both source and destination addresses, a standard access list won't allow you to do that since it makes decisions based on source address only.

But an *extended access list* will hook you up. That's because extended access lists allow you to specify source and destination addresses as well as the protocol and port number that identify the upper-layer protocol or application. By using extended access lists, you can effectively allow users access to a physical LAN and stop them from accessing specific hosts—or even specific services on those hosts.

Table 7.4 lists your basic access-list commands:

TABLE 7.4 Creating an Access List and Applying it to an Interface

Command	Meaning
access-list	Configures a single access-list statement into a router's memory for use in a complete access list that will be applied to an interface

TABLE 7.4 Creating an Access List and Applying it to an Interface *(continued)*

Command	Meaning
`ip access-group`	Places an access list on a device's physical interface

Choose a number to identify the list as standard or extended, then add your options (see Table 7.5):

TABLE 7.5 Extended Access List Options

Option	Meaning
`<ID number>`	Identifies an access list by number as a standard or extended list. Also allows the creation and separation of multiple access lists.
`permit` or `deny`	Specifies the effect of the access-list statement as allowing or blocking the traffic specified.
`protocol`	Specifies the protocol to be filtered in the access-list statement.
`hostname` or `IP address`	Specifies the hostname or device's IP address that will be acted upon in the access-list statement. In an extended access list, this field will be entered for both the source and destination host or device.
`host`	Specifies a single specific host for the statement.
`any`	Specifies that regardless of the host or device IP, it will match the statement.
`eq`	Means equal to, and specifies the application protocol to be filtered by the statement.
`<port # or ID>`	Lists the actual port number or protocol for filtering.

Here's an example of an extended IP access list:

```
Corp(config)#access-list ?
  <1-99>            IP standard access list
  <100-199>         IP extended access list
  <1100-1199>       Extended 48-bit MAC address access list
  <1300-1999>       IP standard access list (expanded range)
```

```
  <200-299>          Protocol type-code access list
  <2000-2699>        IP extended access list (expanded range)
  <700-799>          48-bit MAC address access list
  compiled           Enable IP access-list compilation
  dynamic-extended   Extend the dynamic ACL absolute timer
  rate-limit         Simple rate-limit specific access list
```

The first command shows the access-list numbers available. You'll use the extended access-list range from 100 to 199. Be sure to notice that the range 2000–2699 is also available for extended IP access lists.

At this point, you need to decide what type of list entry you are making. For this example, you'll choose a **deny** list entry:

```
Corp(config)#access-list 110 ?
  deny     Specify packets to reject
  dynamic  Specify a DYNAMIC list of PERMITs or DENYs
  permit   Specify packets to forward
  remark   Access list entry comment
```

Once you choose the access-list type, you then need to select a protocol field entry:

```
Corp(config)#access-list 110 deny ?
  <0-255>  An IP protocol number
  ahp      Authentication Header Protocol
  eigrp    Cisco's EIGRP routing protocol
  esp      Encapsulation Security Payload
  gre      Cisco's GRE tunneling
  icmp     Internet Control Message Protocol
  igmp     Internet Gateway Message Protocol
  ip       Any Internet Protocol
  ipinip   IP in IP tunneling
  nos      KA9Q NOS compatible IP over IP tunneling
  ospf     OSPF routing protocol
  pcp      Payload Compression Protocol
  pim      Protocol Independent Multicast
  tcp      Transmission Control Protocol
  udp      User Datagram Protocol
```

Here, you'll choose to filter an Application-layer protocol that uses TCP by selecting TCP as the protocol. You'll specify the specific TCP port later. Next, you will be prompted for the source IP address of the host or network (you can choose the **any** command to allow any source address):

```
Corp(config)#access-list 110 deny tcp ?
  A.B.C.D  Source address
```

```
  any       Any source host
  host      A single source host
```

After the source address is selected, the destination address is chosen:

```
Corp(config)#access-list 110 deny tcp any ?
  A.B.C.D   Destination address
  any       Any destination host
  eq        Match only packets on a given port number
  gt        Match only packets with a greater port number
  host      A single destination host
  lt        Match only packets with a lower port number
  neq       Match only packets not on a given port number
  range     Match only packets in the range of port numbers
```

In the following example, any source IP address that has a destination IP address of 172.16.30.2 has been denied:

```
Corp(config)#access-list 110 deny tcp any host 172.16.30.2 ?
  ack           Match on the ACK bit
  dscp          Match packets with given dscp value
  eq            Match only packets on a given port number
  established   Match established connections
  fin           Match on the FIN bit
  fragments     Check non-initial fragments
  gt            Match only packets with a greater port number
  log           Log matches against this entry
  log-input     Log matches against this entry, including input interface
  lt            Match only packets with a lower port number
  neq           Match only packets not on a given port number
  precedence    Match packets with given precedence value
  psh           Match on the PSH bit
  range         Match only packets in the range of port numbers
  rst           Match on the RST bit
  syn           Match on the SYN bit
  time-range    Specify a time-range
  tos           Match packets with given TOS value
  urg           Match on the URG bit
  <cr>
```

You can press Enter here and leave the access list as is. But if you do that, all TCP traffic to host 172.16.30.2 will be denied, regardless of the destination port. You can be even more specific: once you have the host addresses in place, just specify the type of service you are denying.

The following help output shows you the available options. You can choose a port number or use the application or protocol name:

```
Corp(config)#access-list 110 deny tcp any host 172.16.30.2 eq ?
  <0-65535>    Port number
  bgp          Border Gateway Protocol (179)
  chargen      Character generator (19)
  cmd          Remote commands (rcmd, 514)
  daytime      Daytime (13)
  discard      Discard (9)
  domain       Domain Name Service (53)
  drip         Dynamic Routing Information Protocol (3949)
  echo         Echo (7)
  exec         Exec (rsh, 512)
  finger       Finger (79)
  ftp          File Transfer Protocol (21)
  ftp-data     FTP data connections (20)
  gopher       Gopher (70)
  hostname     NIC hostname server (101)
  ident        Ident Protocol (113)
  irc          Internet Relay Chat (194)
  klogin       Kerberos login (543)
  kshell       Kerberos shell (544)
  login        Login (rlogin, 513)
  lpd          Printer service (515)
  nntp         Network News Transport Protocol (119)
  pim-auto-rp  PIM Auto-RP (496)
  pop2         Post Office Protocol v2 (109)
  pop3         Post Office Protocol v3 (110)
  smtp         Simple Mail Transport Protocol (25)
  sunrpc       Sun Remote Procedure Call (111)
  syslog       Syslog (514)
  tacacs       TAC Access Control System (49)
  talk         Talk (517)
  telnet       Telnet (23)
  time         Time (37)
  uucp         Unix-to-Unix Copy Program (540)
  whois        Nicname (43)
  www          World Wide Web (HTTP, 80)
```

At this point, let's block Telnet (port 23) to host 172.16.30.2 only. If the users want to FTP, fine—that's allowed. The `log` command is used to log messages every time the access list is hit. This can be an extremely cool way to monitor inappropriate access attempts. Here is how to do this:

```
Corp(config)#access-list 110 deny tcp any host 172.16.30.2 eq 23 log
```

You need to keep in mind that the next line is an implicit `deny any` by default. If you apply this access list to an interface, you might as well just shut the interface down, since by default there is an implicit `deny all` at the end of every access list. You have to follow up the access list with the following command:

```
Corp(config)#access-list 110 permit ip any any
```

Remember, `0.0.0.0 255.255.255.255` is the same command as `any`, so the command could look like this:

```
Corp(config)#access-list 110 permit ip 0.0.0.0 255.255.255.255 0.0.0.0
255.255.255.255
```

Once the access list is created, you need to apply it to an interface (it's the same command as the IP standard list), like so:

```
Corp(config-if)#ip access-group 110 in
```

or like so:

```
Corp(config-if)#ip access-group 110 out
```

Named Access Lists

Named access lists allow you to use names to both create and apply either standard or extended access lists. There is nothing new or different about these access lists aside from being able to refer to them in a way that makes sense to humans. But the syntax has some subtle changes so let's take a look at the commands in Table 7.6:

TABLE 7.6 Named Access List Commands

Command	Meaning
`ip access-list`	Configures a named access list
`ip access-group`	Places an access list on a device's physical interface

Here in Table 7.7 are the options you can use:

TABLE 7.7 Named Access List Options

Option	Meaning
standard or extended	In a named access list, the type must be specified because there is no number used for identification.
permit or deny	Specifies the effect of the access-list statement as allowing or blocking the traffic specified.
hostname or IP address	Specifies the hostname or device's IP address that will be acted upon in the access list statement.
host	Specifies a single specific host for the statement.
any	Specifies that regardless of the host or device IP, it will match the statement.

Let's take a look at an example using all the commands and options:

```
Lab_A#config t
Enter configuration commands, one per line.  End with CNTL/Z.
Lab_A(config)#ip access-list ?
  extended  Extended Acc
  logging   Control access list logging
  standard  Standard Access List
```

Notice that I started by typing **ip access-list**, not **access-list**. This allows me to enter a named access list. Next, I'll need to specify that it's to be a standard access list:

```
Lab_A(config)#ip access-list standard ?
  <1-99>  Standard IP access-list number
  WORD    Access-list name

Lab_A(config)#ip access-list standard BlockSales
Lab_A(config-std-nacl)#
```

I specified a standard access list and then added a name: BlockSales. Notice that I could have used a number for a standard access list, but instead, I chose to use a descriptive name. Also, notice that after entering the name, I hit Enter, and the router prompt changed. I'm now in named access list configuration mode and am entering the named access list:

```
Lab_A(config-std-nacl)#?
Standard Access List configuration commands:
  default  Set a command to its defaults
  deny     Specify packets to reject
  exit     Exit from access-list configuration mode
  no       Negate a command or set its defaults
  permit   Specify packets to forward

Lab_A(config-std-nacl)#deny 172.16.40.0 0.0.0.255
Lab_A(config-std-nacl)#permit any
Lab_A(config-std-nacl)#exit
Lab_A(config)#^Z
Lab_A#
```

I enter the access list and then exit out of configuration mode. Next, I'll take a look at the running configuration to verify that the access list is indeed in the router:

```
Lab_A#show running-config

!
ip access-list standard BlockSales
 deny   172.16.40.0 0.0.0.255
 permit any
!
```

The BlockSales access list has truly been created and is in the running-config file of the router. Next, I'll need to apply the access list to an interface:

```
Lab_A#config t
Enter configuration commands, one per line.  End with CNTL/Z.
Lab_A(config)#int e1
Lab_A(config-if)#ip access-group BlockSales out
Lab_A(config-if)#^Z
Lab_A#
```

Switch Port ACLs

You can apply port ACLs to only layer-2 interfaces on your switches. Why? They're supported only on physical interfaces, that's why. Another good thing to keep in mind is that you can apply them only as inbound lists on your interfaces as well.

Port ACLs control IP traffic via IP access lists. Any non-IP traffic is filtered through the use of MAC addresses. And even though you can apply both types of filter to a single interface, you get to apply only one of each. If you try a put an additional ACL of either type on an interface that already has them in place, the new one will override the one you had there before. So, it's a good idea to be careful here—look before you leap.

Let's check out the access list in Table 7.8 that we can use on a switch port:

TABLE 7.8 Switch Access List Commands

Command	Meaning
`mac access-list`	Configures a MAC access-list statement
`mac access-group`	Places a MAC access list on a device's physical interface

Table 7.9 lists the options:

TABLE 7.9 Switch Access List Options

Option	Meaning
`<word> name`	Identifies an access list by name. Also allows the creation and separation of multiple access lists.
`permit or deny`	Specifies the effect of the access-list statement as allowing or blocking the traffic specified.
`h.h.h mac address`	Specifies the device by MAC address that will be acted upon in the access-list statement.
`Host`	Specifies a single specific host for the statement
`Any`	Specifies that regardless of the host or device IP, it will match the statement.

Here's an example of this command:

```
S1#config t
S1(config)#mac access-list ?
  extended  Extended Access List
S1(config)#mac access-list extended ?
  WORD  access-list name
S1(config)#mac access-list extended Todd_MAC_List
S1(config-ext-macl)#deny ?
```

```
  H.H.H  48-bit source MAC address
  any    any source MAC address
  host   A single source host
S1(config-ext-macl)#deny any ?
  H.H.H  48-bit destination MAC address
  any    any destination MAC address
  host   A single destination host
S1(config-ext-macl)#deny any host ?
  H.H.H  48-bit destination MAC address
S1(config-ext-macl)#deny any host 000d.29bd.4b85
S1(config-ext-macl)#permit ?
  H.H.H  48-bit source MAC address
  any    any source MAC address
  host   A single source host
S1(config-ext-macl)#permit any any
S1(config-ext-macl)#do show access-list
Extended MAC access list Todd_MAC_List
    deny   any host 000d.29bd.4b85
    permit any any
S1(config-ext-macl)#
```

You can see that you can create only an extended named access list. You have no other options. And don't forget to add the `permit any any` at the end!

Here is how you would apply the list to a switch port:

```
S1(config-ext-macl)#int f0/6
S1(config-if)#mac access-group Todd_MAC_List in
```

This is pretty much the same as it is with an IP list, except you start with the command `mac`.

Although it's true there are special circumstances where you would deny based on MAC address, there is another option, and I think it's usually the better one: just deny access based on the `ether-type` field in the Ethernet frame header instead. Take a look:

```
S1(config-ext-macl)#deny any any ?
  <0-65535>      An arbitrary EtherType in decimal, hex, or octal
  aarp           EtherType: AppleTalk ARP
  amber          EtherType: DEC-Amber
  appletalk      EtherType: AppleTalk/EtherTalk
  cos            CoS value
  dec-spanning   EtherType: DEC-Spanning-Tree
  decnet-iv      EtherType: DECnet Phase IV
  diagnostic     EtherType: DEC-Diagnostic
  dsm            EtherType: DEC-DSM
```

```
etype-6000    EtherType: 0x6000
etype-8042    EtherType: 0x8042
lat           EtherType: DEC-LAT
lavc-sca      EtherType: DEC-LAVC-SCA
lsap          LSAP value
mop-console   EtherType: DEC-MOP Remote Console
mop-dump      EtherType: DEC-MOP Dump
msdos         EtherType: DEC-MSDOS
mumps         EtherType: DEC-MUMPS
netbios       EtherType: DEC-NETBIOS
vines-echo    EtherType: VINES Echo
vines-ip      EtherType: VINES IP
xns-idp       EtherType: XNS IDP
<cr>
```

Time-Based ACLs

Time-based ACLs work a lot like extended ACLs do, but their type of access control is totally time-oriented. Basically, you specify a certain time of day and week and then identify that particular period by giving it a name referenced by a task. So, by necessity, the reference function will fall under whatever time constraints you've dictated. The time period is based upon the router's clock, but I highly recommend using it in conjunction with Network Time Protocol (NTP) synchronization.

Here's an example of the command in Table 7.10:

TABLE 7.10 Timed Access List Commands

Command	Meaning
`time-range`	Configures a time range value to be added to an access list as an option to control traffic and access by time

and the options (see Table 7.11):

TABLE 7.11 Timed Access List Options

Option	Meaning
`<ID name>`	Identifies the time range by name for use in an access-list statement

TABLE 7.11 Timed Access List Options

Option	Meaning
`Periodic`	Specifies how the time range will act or be created, allowing specific time values to be set
`hh:mm`	Specifies time values for when the range will start and stop on specific days

Here is an example of the time-based ACL's:

```
Corp#config t
Corp(config)#time-range no-http
Corp(config-time-range)#periodic we?
Wednesday  weekdays  weekend
Corp(config-time-range)#periodic weekend ?
  hh:mm  Starting time
Corp(config-time-range)#periodic weekend 06:00 to 12:00
Corp(config-time-range)#exit
Corp(config)#time-range tcp-yes
Corp(config-time-range)#periodic weekend 06:00 to 12:00
Corp(config-time-range)#exit
Corp(config)#ip access-list extended Time
Corp(config-ext-nacl)#deny tcp any any eq www time-range no-http
Corp(config-ext-nacl)#permit tcp any any time-range tcp-yes
Corp(config-ext-nacl)#interface f0/0
Corp(config-if)#ip access-group Time in
Corp(config-if)#do show time-range
time-range entry: no-http (inactive)
   periodic weekdays 8:00 to 15:00
   used in: IP ACL entry
time-range entry: tcp-yes (inactive)
   periodic weekend 8:00 to 13:00
   used in: IP ACL entry
Corp(config-if)#
```

The `time-range` command is pretty flexible and will drive users crazy if you deny them access to basic network access or the Internet during off-hours. Be careful with the previous commands; make sure you test your list on a nonproduction network before you implement the lists on your production network.

Monitoring Access Lists

Again, it's always good to be able to verify a router's configuration. Table 7.12 lists the commands you can use:

TABLE 7.12 Access List Verification Commands

Command	Meaning
`show access-list`	Displays all access lists and their parameters configured on the router. This command does not show you which interface the list is set on.
`show access-list 110`	Shows only the parameters for the access list 110. This command does not show you the interface the list is set on.
`show ip access-list`	Shows only the IP access lists configured on the router.
`show ip interface`	Shows which interfaces have access lists set.
`show running-config`	Shows the access lists and which interfaces have access lists set.
`show mac access-group`	Displays MAC access lists applied to all layer-2 interfaces or the specified layer-2 interface (used on layer-2 switches only).

You've already seen how to use the `show running-config` command to verify that a named access list was in the router as well as a MAC access list on a layer-2 switch. So now I'll show the output from some of the other commands.

The `show access-list` command will list all access lists on the router, whether they're applied to an interface:

```
Lab_A#show access-list
Standard IP access list 10
    deny   172.16.40.0, wildcard bits 0.0.0.255
    permit any
Standard IP access list BlockSales
    deny   172.16.40.0, wildcard bits 0.0.0.255
    permit any
Extended IP access list 110
    deny tcp any host 172.16.30.5 eq ftp
    deny tcp any host 172.16.30.5 eq telnet
    permit ip any any
Lab_A#
```

First, notice that both access list 10 and the named access list appear on this list. Second, notice that even though I entered actual numbers for TCP ports in access list 110, the `show` command gives you the protocol names rather than TCP ports for readability (hey, not everyone has them all memorized!).

Here's the output of the `show ip interface` command:

```
Lab_A#show ip interface e1
Ethernet1 is up, line protocol is up
  Internet address is 172.16.30.1/24
  Broadcast address is 255.255.255.255
  Address determined by non-volatile memory
  MTU is 1500 bytes
  Helper address is not set
  Directed broadcast forwarding is disabled
  Outgoing access list is BlockSales
  Inbound  access list is not set
  Proxy ARP is enabled
  Security level is default
  Split horizon is enabled
  ICMP redirects are always sent
  ICMP unreachables are always sent
  ICMP mask replies are never sent
  IP fast switching is disabled
  IP fast switching on the same interface is disabled
  IP Null turbo vector
  IP multicast fast switching is disabled
  IP multicast distributed fast switching is disabled
  Router Discovery is disabled
  IP output packet accounting is disabled
  IP access violation accounting is disabled
  TCP/IP header compression is disabled
  RTP/IP header compression is disabled
  Probe proxy name replies are disabled
  Policy routing is disabled
  Network address translation is disabled
  Web Cache Redirect is disabled
  BGP Policy Mapping is disabled
Lab_A#
```

Be sure to notice the bold line indicating that the outgoing list on this interface is BlockSales, but the inbound access list isn't set.

As I've already mentioned, you can use the `show running-config` command to see all access lists. However, on a layer-2 switch, you can verify your interface configurations with the `show mac access-group` command:

```
S1#sh mac access-group
Interface FastEthernet0/1:
   Inbound access-list is not set
   Outbound access-list is not set
Interface FastEthernet0/2:
   Inbound access-list is not set
   Outbound access-list is not set
S1#
```

Depending on how many interfaces you set your MAC access lists on, you can use the interface command to view individual interfaces:

```
S1#sh mac access-group interface f0/6
Interface FastEthernet0/6:
   Inbound access-list is Todd_MAC_List
   Outbound access-list is not set
```

Chapter 8

Network Address Translation (NAT)

In this chapter, I'll give you the skinny on Network Address Translation (NAT); Dynamic NAT; and Port Address Translation (PAT), which is also known as NAT Overload. Of course, I'll demonstrate NAT, and then I'll finish this chapter by using SDM so you can see how you can configure NAT the easy way.

It will be helpful for you to read Chapter 7 before reading this chapter since you need to use access lists in your NAT configurations.

For up-to-the minute updates for this chapter, please see `www.lammle.com` or `www.sybex.com/go/IOS`

When Do We Use NAT?

Similar to Classless Inter-Domain Routing (CIDR), the original intention for NAT was to slow the depletion of available IP address space by allowing many private IP addresses to be represented by some smaller number of public IP addresses.

Since then, it has been discovered that NAT is also a useful tool for network migrations and mergers, server load sharing, and virtual server creation. So in this chapter, I'll describe the basics of NAT functionality and the terminology common to NAT.

At times, NAT really decreases the overwhelming amount of public IP addresses required in your networking environment. And NAT really comes in handy when two companies that have duplicate internal addressing schemes merge. NAT is also great to have around when an organization changes its Internet service provider (ISP) and the networking manager doesn't want the hassle of changing the internal address scheme.

Here are some situations when it's best to have NAT on your side:

- You need to connect to the Internet, and your hosts don't have globally unique IP addresses.
- You change to a new ISP that requires you to renumber your network.
- You need to merge two intranets with duplicate addresses.

You typically use NAT on a border router. For an illustration of this, see Figure 8.1.

FIGURE 8.1 Where to configure NAT

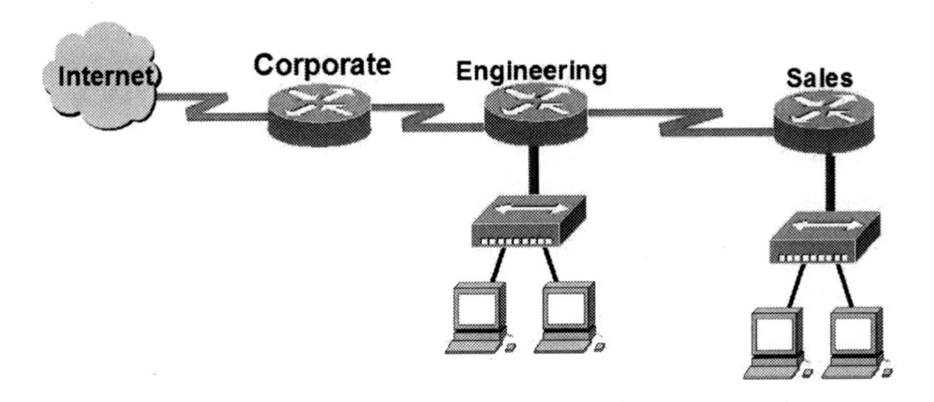

Now you may be thinking, "NAT's totally cool. It's the grooviest, greatest network gadget, and I just gotta have it." Well, hang on a minute. There are truly some serious snags related to NAT use. Oh, don't get me wrong—it really can save you sometimes, but it has a dark side you need to know about, too. For some of the pros and cons linked to using NAT, check out Table 8.1.

TABLE 8.1 Advantages and Disadvantages of Implementing NAT

Advantages	Disadvantages
Conserves legally registered addresses.	Translation introduces switching path delays.
Reduces address overlap occurrence.	Loss of end-to-end IP traceability.
Increases flexibility when connecting to Internet.	Certain applications will not function with NAT enabled.
Eliminates address renumbering as network changes.	

Types of Network Address Translation

In this section, I'll go over the three types of NAT with you:

Static NAT This type of NAT is designed to allow one-to-one mapping between local and global addresses. Keep in mind that the static version requires you to have one real Internet IP address for every host on your network.

Dynamic NAT This version gives you the ability to map an unregistered IP address to a registered IP address from out of a pool of registered IP addresses. You don't have to statically configure your router to map an inside to an outside address as you would using static NAT, but you do need to have enough real, bona fide IP addresses for everyone who is going to be sending packets to and receiving them from the Internet.

Overloading This is the most popular type of NAT configuration. Understand that overloading really is a form of dynamic NAT that maps multiple unregistered IP addresses to a single registered IP address—many-to-one—by using different ports. Now, why is this so special? Well, it's also known as Port Address Translation (PAT). And by using PAT (NAT Overload), you get to have thousands of users connect to the Internet using only one real global IP address—pretty slick, yeah? Seriously, NAT Overload is the real reason we haven't run out of valid IP address on the Internet. Really, I'm not joking.

NAT Names

The names we use to describe the addresses used with NAT are pretty simple. Addresses used after NAT translations are called *global* addresses. These are usually the public addresses used on the Internet, but remember, you don't need public addresses if you aren't going on the Internet.

Local addresses are the ones we use before NAT translation. So, the inside local address is actually the private address of the sending host that's trying to get to the Internet, while the outside local address is the address of the destination host. The latter is usually a public address (web address, mail server, and so on) and is how the packet begins its journey.

After translation, the inside local address is then called the *inside global address*, and the outside global address becomes the name of the destination host. Check out Table 8.2, which lists all this terminology, for a clear picture of the various names used with NAT.

TABLE 8.2 NAT Terms

Names	Meaning
Inside local	Name of inside source address before translation
Outside local	Name of destination host before translation
Inside global	Name of inside host after translation
Outside global	Name of outside destination host after translation

Static NAT Configuration

OK, let's start looking at some actual commands (see Table 8.3) used with NAT:

TABLE 8.3 Basic NAT Commands

Command	Meaning
`ip nat inside source static` *`inside_local inside_global`*	Statically maps a host with a private IP address to a global Internet address
`ip nat inside`	Sets the interface as an inside interface
`ip nat outside`	Sets the interface as an outside interface

Let's take a look at a simple basic static NAT configuration:

```
ip nat inside source static 10.1.1.1 170.46.2.2
!
interface Ethernet0
 ip address 10.1.1.10 255.255.255.0
 ip nat inside
!
interface Serial0
 ip address 170.46.2.1 255.255.255.0
 ip nat outside
!
```

In the preceding router output, the `ip nat inside source` command identifies which IP addresses will be translated. In this configuration example, the ip nat inside source command configures a static translation between the inside local IP address 10.1.1.1 to the outside global IP address 170.46.2.2.

If you look further down in the configuration, you can see an `ip nat` command under each interface. The `ip nat inside` command identifies that interface as the inside interface. The `ip nat outside` command identifies that interface as the outside interface. When you look back at the ip nat inside source command, you see that the command is referencing the inside interface as the source or starting point of the translation. The command could also be used like this—ip nat outside source—which is referencing the interface you designated as the outside interface to be the source or starting point for the translation.

Dynamic NAT Configuration

Table 8.4 lists the commands you'll need to create dynamic NAT:

TABLE 8.4 Dynamic NAT Commands

Command	Meaning
`ip nat pool` *pool_name starting_ address ending_address mask*	Creates a pool of inside global addresses for the inside local hosts to use
`ip nat inside source list` *list_number* `pool` *pool_name*	Sets the inside local hosts that match the access-list number to use the pool of addresses configured by the `ip nat pool` command
`ip nat inside`	Sets the inside local interface
`ip nat ouside`	Sets the inside global interface
`access-list` *list_number* `permit` *network inverse_mask*	Creates an access list that permits the inside local hosts to use the global pool of addresses

Dynamic NAT means we have a pool of addresses that we will use to provide real IP addresses to a group of users on the inside. We do not use port numbers, so we need to have real IP addresses for every user trying to get outside the local network.

Here is a sample output of a dynamic NAT configuration:

```
ip nat pool todd 170.168.2.2 170.168.2.254
    netmask 255.255.255.0
ip nat inside source list 1 pool todd
!
interface Ethernet0
 ip address 10.1.1.10 255.255.255.0
 ip nat inside
!
interface Serial0
 ip address 170.168.2.1 255.255.255.0
 ip nat outside
!
access-list 1 permit 10.1.1.0 0.0.0.255
!
```

The `ip nat inside source list 1 pool todd` command tells the router to translate IP addresses that match `access-list 1` to an address found in the IP NAT pool named `todd`. The access list in this case is not being used to permit or deny traffic as we would use it for security reasons to filter traffic. It is being used in this case to select or designate what we often call "interesting" traffic. When interesting traffic has been matched with the access list, it is pulled into the NAT process to be translated. This is a common use for access lists; they don't always have the dull job of just blocking traffic at an interface.

The `ip nat pool todd 170.168.2.2 192.168.2.254` command creates a pool of addresses that will be distributed to those hosts that require NAT.

PAT (Overloading) Configuration

As you'll see in Table 8.5, the commands used for PAT are similar to what we used for dynamic NAT:

TABLE 8.5 PAT Commands

Command	Meaning
`ip nat pool` *`pool_name starting_ address ending_address`* `mask`	Creates a pool of inside global addresses for the inside local hosts to use
`ip nat inside source list` *`list_number`* `pool` *`pool_name`* `overload`	Sets the inside local hosts that match the access-list number to use the pool of addresses configured by the `ip nat pool` command. The Overload command configures PAT.
`ip nat inside`	Sets the inside local interface
`ip nat ouside`	Sets the inside global interface
`access-list` *`list_number`* `permit network` *`inverse_mask`*	Creates an access list that permits the inside local hosts to use the global pool of addresses

This example shows how to configure inside global address overloading. This is the typical NAT you would use today. It is rare you would use static or dynamic NAT unless you were statically mapping an internal server, for example.

Here is a sample output of a PAT configuration:

```
ip nat pool globalnet 170.168.2.1 170.168.2.1
   netmask 255.255.255.0
```

```
ip nat inside source list 1 pool globalnet overload
!
interface Ethernet0/0
 ip address 10.1.1.10 255.255.255.0
 ip nat inside
!
interface Serial0/0
 ip address 170.168.2.1 255.255.255.0
 ip nat outside
!
access-list 1 permit 10.1.1.0 0.0.0.255
```

The nice feature of PAT is that the only differences between this configuration and the previous dynamic NAT configuration is that the pool of addresses has shrunk to only one IP address and at the end of the `ip nat inside source` command I included the `overload` command.

Notice in the example that the one IP address that is in the pool for you to use is the IP address of the outside interface. This is perfect if you are configuring NAT Overload for yourself at home or for a small office that has only one IP from your ISP. You could, however, use an additional address such as 170.168.2.2 if you had the address available to you. This could be helpful in a large implementation where you may have so many internal users that you need more than one overloaded IP address on the outside.

Simple Verification of NAT

Table 8.6 is a list of commands you can use to verify NAT on your router:

TABLE 8.6 NAT Verification Commands

Command	Meaning
`show ip nat translation`	Shows the basic translation table. This is probably one of the most important NAT command for verification.
`debug ip nat`	Shows the sending address, the translation, and the destination address on each debug line.
`show ip nat statistics`	Shows a summary of your configuration, your active translations, and the inside and outside interfaces that are being used.

Once you have configured the type of NAT you are going to use, typically Overload (PAT), you need to be able to verify the configuration.

To see basic IP address translation information, use the following command:

```
Router#show ip nat translation
```

When looking at the IP NAT translations, you may see many translations from the same host to the same host at the destination. This is typical of many connections to the Web. Here is an example:

```
Router#sh ip nat trans
Pro Inside global        Inside local         Outside local        Outside global
icmp 64.1.1.5:271        10.1.9.2:271         64.1.1.10:271        64.1.1.10:271
tcp 64.1.1.5:11000       10.1.9.2:11000       64.1.1.10:23         64.1.1.10:23
Corp#
```

In addition, you can verify your NAT configuration with the **debug ip nat** command. This output will show the sending address, the translation, and the destination address on each debug line:

```
Router#debug ip nat
*May  9 22:57:47.679: NAT*: TCP s=11000->1024, d=23
*May  9 22:57:47.679: NAT*: s=10.1.6.2->64.1.1.5, d=64.1.1.10 [0]
*May  9 22:57:47.683: NAT*: TCP s=23, d=1024->11000
*May  9 22:57:47.683: NAT*: s=64.1.1.10, d=64.1.1.5->10.1.6.2 [0]
*May  9 22:57:47.699: NAT*: TCP s=11000->1024, d=23
*May  9 22:57:47.699: NAT*: s=10.1.6.2->64.1.1.5, d=64.1.1.10 [1]
*May  9 22:57:47.703: NAT*: TCP s=23, d=1024->11000
*May  9 22:57:47.703: NAT*: s=64.1.1.10, d=64.1.1.5->10.1.6.2 [1]
*May  9 22:57:47.707: NAT*: TCP s=11000->1024, d=23
*May  9 22:57:47.707: NAT*: s=10.1.6.2->64.1.1.5, d=64.1.1.10 [2]
*May  9 22:57:47.711: NAT*: TCP s=11000->1024, d=23
*May  9 22:57:47.711: NAT*: s=10.1.6.2->64.1.1.5, d=64.1.1.10 [3]
*May  9 22:57:47.719: NAT*: TCP s=23, d=1024->11000
*May  9 22:57:47.719: NAT*: s=64.1.1.10, d=64.1.1.5->10.1.6.2 [2]
*May  9 22:57:47.723: NAT*: TCP s=23, d=1024->11000
*May  9 22:57:47.723: NAT*: s=64.1.1.10, d=64.1.1.5->10.1.6.2 [3]
*May  9 22:57:47.723: NAT*: TCP s=11000->1024, d=23
*May  9 22:57:47.723: NAT*: s=10.1.6.2->64.1.1.5, d=64.1.1.10 [4]
*May  9 22:57:47.731: NAT*: TCP s=11000->1024, d=23
*May  9 22:57:47.731: NAT*: s=10.1.6.2->64.1.1.5, d=64.1.1.10 [5]
*May  9 22:57:47.735: NAT*: TCP s=23, d=1024->11000
*May  9 22:57:47.735: NAT*: s=64.1.1.10, d=64.1.1.5->10.1.6.2 [4]
*May  9 22:57:47.735: NAT*: TCP s=11000->1024, d=23
*May  9 22:57:47.735: NAT*: s=10.1.6.2->64.1.1.5, d=64.1.1.10 [6]
*May  9 22:57:47.747: NAT*: TCP s=11000->1024, d=23
*May  9 22:57:47.747: NAT*: s=10.1.6.2->64.1.1.5, d=64.1.1.10 [7]
*May  9 22:57:47.951: NAT*: TCP s=11000->1024, d=23
*May  9 22:57:47.951: NAT*: s=10.1.6.2->64.1.1.5, d=64.1.1.10 [8]
*May  9 22:57:48.103: NAT*: TCP s=23, d=1024->11000
```

```
*May  9 22:57:48.103: NAT*: s=64.1.1.10, d=64.1.1.5->10.1.6.2 [5]
Corp#
```

Now, let's use the command `show ip nat statistics` on the router:

```
Corp#sh ip nat stat
Total active translations: 2 (0 static, 2 dynamic; 2 extended)
Outside interfaces:
  Serial0/2/0
Inside interfaces:
  FastEthernet0/1, Serial0/0/0, Serial0/0/1, Serial0/1/0
Hits: 269  Misses: 13
CEF Translated packets: 227, CEF Punted packets: 0
Expired translations: 27
Dynamic mappings:
-- Inside Source
[Id: 1] access-list 1 pool Todd refcount 2
 pool Todd: netmask 255.255.255.252
        start 64.1.1.5 end 64.1.1.5
        type generic, total addresses 1, allocated 1 (100%), misses 0
Queued Packets: 0
Corp#
```

What you can see here is a summary of the configuration, the two active translations, and the inside and outside interfaces that are being used. The pool is listed right there toward the bottom of the output. And it all looks good, so it's time to move on to configuring NAT using SDM.

Configuring NAT Using SDM

Configuring NAT using the SDM is really much easier than anyone would think—let's take a look a the simple wizards Cisco created within the SDM:

If you have not been introduced to SDM, please jump ahead to Chapter 12, and then head back here to read this section.

Basic NAT Wizard Use this wizard if you have some basic PCs/hosts on your trusted network that need access to the Internet. This wizard will guide you through the process of creating a basic NAT configuration.

Advanced NAT Wizard If you have a DMZ, or servers on your inside network that users from the outside need to access, you definitely want to opt for the advanced NAT configuration.

The first screen is the Create NAT Configuration screen.

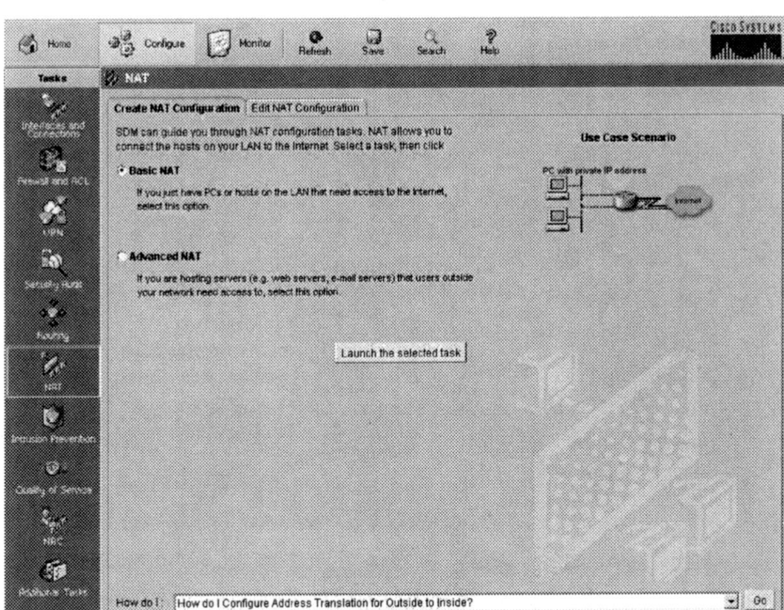

From here, I'll simply connect and create a basic NAT. After that, I click Launch the Selected Task and go to the next screen, which tells me what the Basic NAT Wizard is going to do.

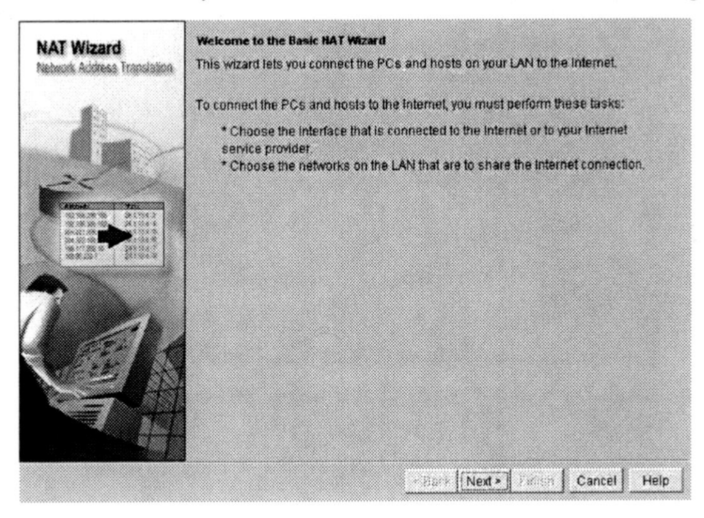

As you might guess, it rocks—all I have to do is to click Next to get to a screen from which I'm able to select all my inside and outside addresses.

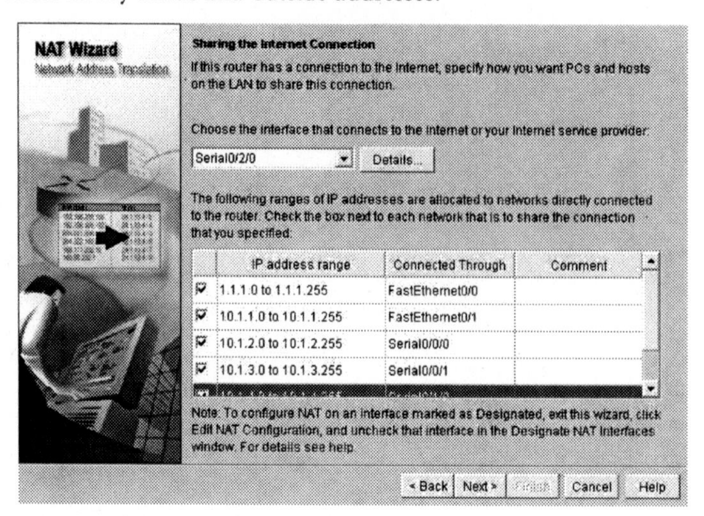

After choosing my inside and outside interfaces, I click Next. A NAT pool is created, and all my interfaces are assigned inside or outside configurations, just like that!

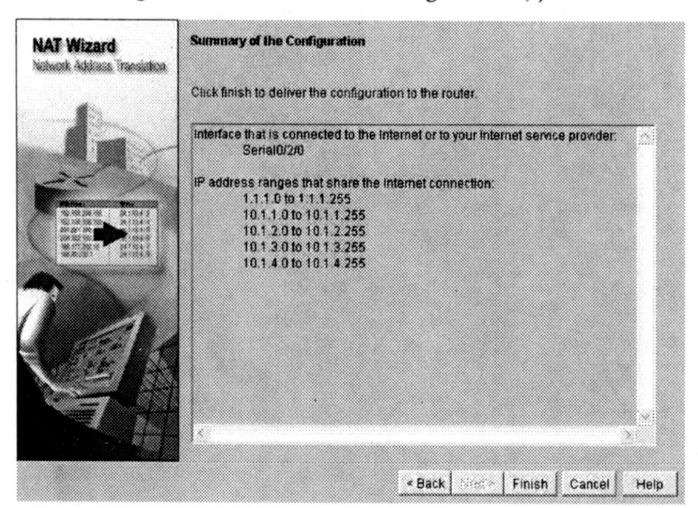

Finally, I click Finish. Let's see what doing that did to my router. Here are the interfaces it configured:

```
!
interface FastEthernet0/0
 ip address 1.1.1.1 255.255.255.0
 ip nat inside
```

```
 ip virtual-reassembly
 duplex auto
 speed auto
!
interface FastEthernet0/1
 description Connection to 1242 AP
 ip address 10.1.1.1 255.255.255.0
 ip nat inside
 ip virtual-reassembly
 duplex auto
 speed auto
!
[output cut]
!
interface Serial0/2/0
 description Connection to R3$FW_OUTSIDE$
 ip address 64.1.1.5 255.255.255.252
 ip access-group 103 in
 ip verify unicast reverse-path
 ip nat outside
 ip inspect SDM_LOW out
 ip virtual-reassembly
 clock rate 2000000
!
[output cut]
```

Here is the `ip nat inside source list` it created:

```
ip nat inside source list 2 interface Serial0/2/0 overload
!
[output cut]
```

And last, here is the access list created for each interface I chose as in inside network:

```
access-list 2 remark SDM_ACL Category=2
access-list 2 permit 1.1.1.0 0.0.0.255
access-list 2 permit 10.1.4.0 0.0.0.255
access-list 2 permit 10.1.1.0 0.0.0.255
access-list 2 permit 10.1.2.0 0.0.0.255
access-list 2 permit 10.1.3.0 0.0.0.255
```

I know I've said this over and over in the book, but SDM really is an incredibly useful tool for creating advanced configurations such as ACLs, VPNs, and NAT. This is one thing I think I've nailed down for you, and the last two chapters have really proven that!

Chapter 9

Cisco's Wireless Technologies

If you want to understand the basic wireless LANs (WLANs) that are most commonly used today, just think 10BaseT Ethernet with hubs. What this means is that WLANs typically run half-duplex communication—everyone is sharing the same bandwidth, and only one user is communicating at a time. This isn't necessarily bad; it's just not good enough. Because most people rely upon wireless networks today, it's critical that they evolve faster than greased lightening to keep up with our rapidly escalating needs. The good news is that this is actually happening—Cisco has reacted by coming up with an answer called the *Cisco Unified Wireless Solution* that works with all types of wireless connections. And it works securely too!

In this chapter, I will cover basic wireless LAN technologies and committees, as well as wireless security. For the current CCNA objectives, there are very few commands you must remember, so I'll actually cover more technology—wireless technology you must know—than I will commands in this chapter.

For up-to-the-minute updates on the topics covered in this chapter, please see `www.lammle.com` or `www.sybex.com/go/IOS`

Introducing Wireless Technology

Transmitting a signal using the typical 802.11 specifications works a lot like it does with a basic Ethernet hub: they're both two-way forms of communication, and they both use the same frequency to both transmit and receive, often referred to as *half-duplex* (mentioned earlier). WLANs use radio frequencies (RFs) that are radiated into the air from an antenna that creates radio waves. These waves can be absorbed, refracted, or reflected by walls, water, and metal surfaces, resulting in low signal strength. Because of this innate vulnerability to surrounding environmental factors, it's pretty apparent that wireless will never offer us the same robustness as wired networks can, but that still doesn't mean we're not going to run wireless. Believe me, we definitely will!

We can increase the transmitting power and gain a greater transmitting distance, but doing so can create some nasty distortion, so it has to be done carefully. By using higher frequencies, we can attain higher data rates, but this is, unfortunately, at the cost of decreased transmitting distances. And if we use lower frequencies, we get to transmit greater distances but at lower data rates. This should make it pretty clear to you that understanding all the various types of WLANs you can implement is imperative to creating the LAN solution that best meets the specific requirements of your unique situation.

Also important to note is that the 802.11 specifications were developed so that there would be no licensing required in most countries—to give the user the freedom to install and operate without any licensing or operating fees. This means any manufacturer can create products and sell them at a local computer store or wherever. It also means that all our computers should be able to communicate wirelessly without configuring much, if anything at all.

Various agencies have been around for a long time to help govern the use of wireless devices, frequencies, standards, and how the frequency spectrums are used. Table 9.1 shows the current agencies that help create, maintain, and even enforce wireless standards worldwide.

TABLE 9.1 Wireless Agencies and Standards

Agency	Purpose	Website
Institute of Electrical and Electronics Engineers (IEEE)	Creates and maintains operational standards	`www.ieee.org`
Federal Communications Commission (FCC)	Regulates the use of wireless devices in the United States	`www.fcc.gov`
European Telecommunications Standards Institute (ETSI)	Produces common standards in Europe	`www.etsi.org`
Wi-Fi Alliance	Promotes and tests for WLAN interoperability	`www.wi-fi.com`
WLAN Association (WLANA)	Educates and raises consumer awareness regarding WLANs	`www.wlana.org`

Because WLANs transmit over radio frequencies, they're regulated by the same types of laws used to govern devices such as AM/FM radios. The Federal Communications Commission (FCC) regulates the use of wireless LAN devices, and the Institute of Electrical and Electronics Engineers (IEEE) takes it from there and creates standards based on what frequencies the FCC releases for public use.

The FCC has released three unlicensed bands for public use: 900MHz, 2.4GHz, and 5.7GHz. The 900MHz and 2.4GHz bands are referred to as the *Industrial, Scientific, and Medical* (ISM) bands, and the 5GHz band is known as the *Unlicensed National Information Infrastructure* (UNII) band. Figure 9.1 shows where the unlicensed bands sit within the RF spectrum.

So it follows that if you opt to deploy wireless in a range outside of the three public bands shown in Figure 9.1, you need to get a specific license from the FCC to do so. Once the FCC opened the three frequency ranges for public use, many manufacturers were able to start offering myriad products that flooded the market, with 802.11b/g being the most widely used wireless network today.

The Wi-Fi Alliance grants certification for interoperability among 802.11 products offered by various vendors. This certification provides a sort of comfort zone for users purchasing many types of products, but in my experience, it's just a whole lot easier if you buy all your access points from the same manufacturer!

FIGURE 9.1 Unlicensed frequencies

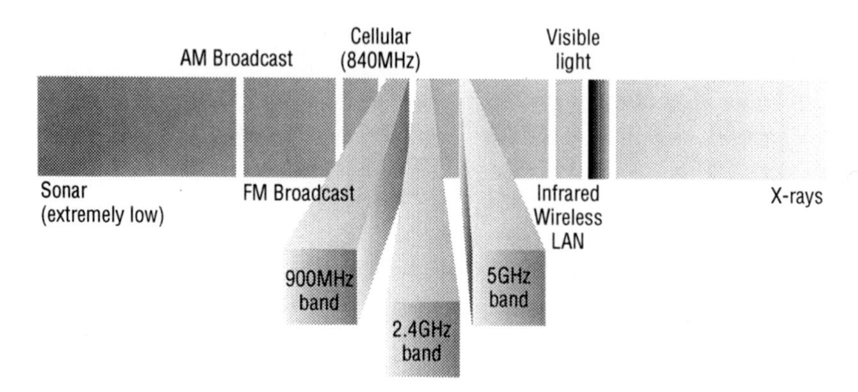

In the current U.S. wireless LAN market, there are several accepted operational standards and drafts created and maintained by the IEEE. I'll cover these standards next and then talk about how the most commonly used standards work.

The 802.11 Standards

Wireless networking has its own 802 standards group—remember, Ethernet's committee is 802.3. Wireless starts with 802.11, and there are various other up-and-coming standards groups as well, such as for 802.16 and 802.20. And there's no doubt that cellular networks will become huge players in our wireless future. But for now, I'll concentrate on the 802.11 standards committee and subcommittees.

IEEE 802.11 was the first, original standardized WLAN at 1Mbps and 2Mbps. It runs in the 2.4GHz radio frequency and was ratified in 1997 even though we didn't see many products pop up until around 1999 when 802.11b was introduced. All the committees listed in Table 9.2 are amendments to the original 802.11 standard except for 802.11F and 802.11T, which are both stand-alone documents.

TABLE 9.2 802.11 Committees and Subcommittees

Committee	Purpose
IEEE 802.11a	54Mbps, 5GHz standard
IEEE 802.11b	Enhancements to 802.11 to support 5.5Mbps and 11Mbps
IEEE 802.11c	Bridge operation procedures; included in the IEEE 802.1D standard
IEEE 802.11d	International roaming extensions
IEEE 802.11e	Quality of service

TABLE 9.2 802.11 Committees and Subcommittees *(continued)*

Committee	Purpose
IEEE 802.11F	Inter-Access Point Protocol
IEEE 802.11g	54Mbps, 2.4GHz standard (backward compatible with 802.11b)
IEEE 802.11h	Dynamic Frequency Selection (DFS) and Transmit Power Control (TPC) at 5GHz
IEEE 802.11i	Enhanced security
IEEE 802.11j	Extensions for Japan and U.S. public safety
IEEE 802.11k	Radio resource measurement enhancements
IEEE 802.11m	Maintenance of the standard; odds and ends
IEEE 802.11n	Higher throughput improvements using multiple input, multiple output (MIMO) antennas
IEEE 802.11p	Wireless Access for the Vehicular Environment (WAVE)
IEEE 802.11r	Fast roaming
IEEE 802.11s	Extended service set mesh networking
IEEE 802.11T	Wireless Performance Prediction (WPP)
IEEE 802.11u	Internetworking with non-802 networks (cellular, for example)
IEEE 802.11v	Wireless network management
IEEE 802.11w	Protected management frames
IEEE 802.11y	3650–3700 operation in the United States

I'll now discuss some of the most widely used unlicensed wireless networks in use today.

2.4GHz (802.11b)

The 802.11b standard was at one time the most widely deployed wireless standard, and it operates in the 2.4GHz unlicensed radio band that delivers a maximum data rate of 11Mbps. The 802.11b standard has been widely adopted by both vendors and customers who found that its 11Mbps data rate worked pretty well for most applications. But now that 802.11b has a big brother (802.11g), no one goes out and buys an 802.11b card or access point anymore, because why would you buy a 10Mbps Ethernet card when you can score a 10/100 Ethernet card for the same price?

An interesting feature of all Cisco 802.11 WLAN products is that they have the ability to data-rate shift while moving. This allows the person operating at 11Mbps to shift to 5.5Mbps and to 2Mbps and finally still communicate farthest from the access point at 1Mbps. And furthermore, this rate shifting happens without losing connection and with no interaction from the user. Rate shifting also occurs on a transmission-by-transmission basis. This is important because it means the access point can support multiple clients at varying speeds depending upon the location of each client.

The problem with 802.11b lies in how the Data Link layer is dealt with. To solve problems in the RF spectrum, a type of Ethernet collision detection was created called *Carrier Sense Multiple Access with Collision Avoidance* (CSMA/CA), as shown in Figure 9.2.

FIGURE 9.2 802.11b CSMA/CA

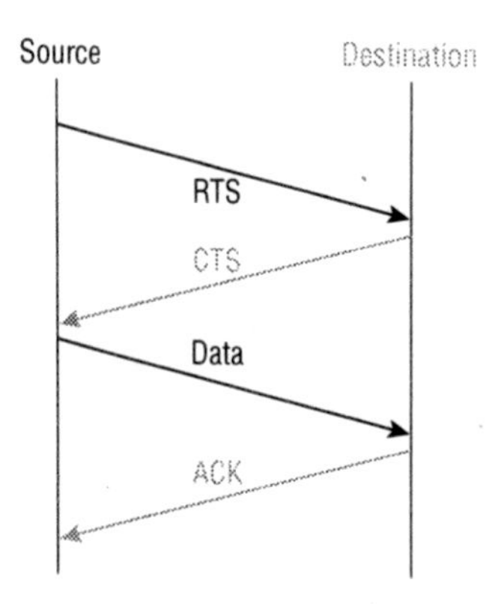

CSMA/CA is also called a Request to Send, Clear to Send (RTS/CTS) because of the way that hosts must communicate to the access point (AP). For every packet sent, an RTS/CTS and acknowledgment must be received, and because of this rather cumbersome process, it's kind of hard to believe it all actually works!

2.4GHz (802.11g)

The 802.11g standard was ratified in June 2003 and is backward compatible with 802.11b. The 802.11g standard delivers the same 54Mbps maximum data rate as 802.11a but runs in the 2.4GHz range—the same as 802.11b.

Because 802.11b/g operates in the same 2.4GHz unlicensed band, migrating to 802.11g is an affordable choice for organizations with existing 802.11b wireless infrastructures. Just keep in mind that 802.11b products can't be "software upgraded" to 802.11g. This limitation is because 802.11g radios use a different chipset in order to deliver the higher data rate.

But still, much like Ethernet and Fast Ethernet, 802.11g products can be commingled with 802.11b products in the same network. Yet, for example, completely unlike Ethernet, if you have four users running 802.11g cards and one user starts using an 802.11b card, everyone connected to the same access point is then forced to run the 802.11b CSMA/CA method—an ugly fact that really makes throughput suffer. So to optimize performance, it's recommended that you disable the 802.11b-only modes on all your access points.

To explain this further, 802.11b uses a modulation technique called *Direct Sequence Spread Spectrum* (DSSS) that's just not as robust as the Orthogonal Frequency DivisionMultiplexing (OFDM) modulation used by both 802.11g and 802.11a. 802.11g clients using OFDM enjoy much better performance at the same ranges as 802.11b clients do, but—and remember this—when 802.11g clients are operating at the 802.11b rates (11Mbps, 5.5Mbps, 2Mbps, and 1Mbps), they're actually using the same modulation 802.11b does.

Figure 9.3 shows the 14 different channels (each 22MHz wide) that the FCC released in the 2.4GHz range.

FIGURE 9.3 ISM 2.4GHz channels

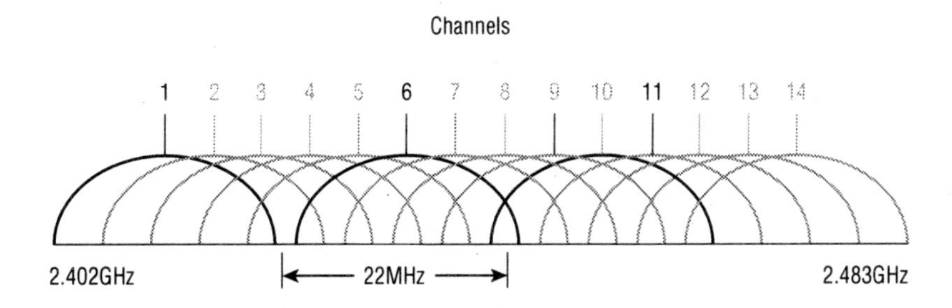

In the United States, only 11 channels are configurable, with channels 1, 6, and 11 being nonoverlapping. This allows you to have three access points in the same area without experiencing interference.

Some potential issues with the 2.4GHz (802.11b/g) range include interference from microwave ovens and cordless phones—even metal file cabinets if you're in a small office! The type of antenna and direction also matters, and if things aren't all good with both, you can experience slow performance and even network drops.

5GHz (802.11a)

The IEEE ratified the 802.11a standard in 1999, but the first 802.11a products didn't begin appearing on the market until late 2001—and, boy, were they pricey! The 802.11a standard delivers a maximum data rate of 54Mbps with 12 nonoverlapping frequency channels. Figure 9.4 shows the UNII bands.

FIGURE 9.4 The UNII 5GHz band has 12 nonoverlapping channels (in the United States).

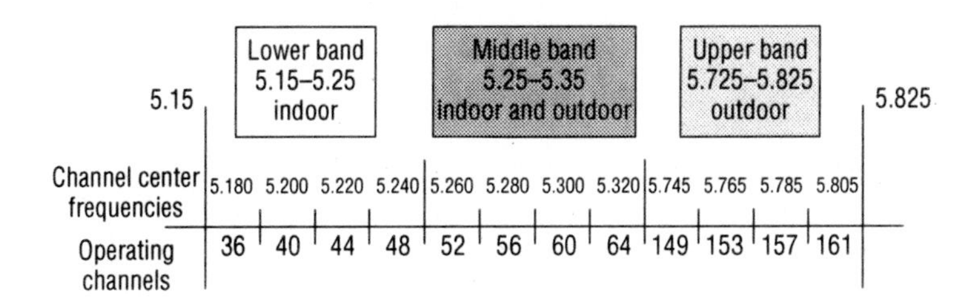

Operating in the 5GHz radio band, 802.11a is also immune to interference from devices that operate in the 2.4GHz band, such as microwave ovens, cordless phones, and Bluetooth devices. 802.11a isn't backward compatible with 802.11b because they are different frequencies, so you don't get to just "upgrade" part of your network and expect everything to work together in perfect harmony. But no worries—plenty of dual-radio devices will work in both types of networks. A definite plus for 802.11a is that it can work in the same physical environment without interference from 802.11b users.

Similar to the 802.11b radios, all 802.11a products also have the ability to data-rate shift while moving. The 802.11a products allow the person operating at 54Mbps to shift to 48Mbps, 36Mbps, 24Mbps, 18Mbps, 12Mbps, and 9Mbps and finally still communicate farthest from the AP at 6Mbps. Roaming capabilities are also supported as long as all access points are configured with the same SSID.

Service Sets

You can typically create two types of wireless networks with wired networks:

- Basic service set (BSS)
- Extended service set (ESS)

Both types of networks define what we call a *service set ID* (SSID) that's used to advertise your wireless network so hosts can connect to the AP. And you can have multiple SSIDs configured on an access point for security reasons. For example, you can designate that one SSID is open access for a public hot spot, while another SSID can use WEP or WPA2 for the employees who work at this public hot spot. The SSID name is broadcast out the AP by default so the clients can find the AP and connect to the wireless network, and of course you can turn this feature off for security reasons.

BSS/IBSS

A BSS involves only a single access point. You create a BSS by bringing up an AP and creating a name for the SSID. Users can then connect to and use this SSID to access the wireless network, which provides connectivity to the wired resources. When the AP connects to a wired network, it then becomes known as an *infrastructure basic service set* (IBSS). Keep in mind that if you have a BSS/IBSS, users won't be able to maintain network connectivity when roaming from AP to AP because each AP is configured with a different SSID name.

BSS wireless networks are also really helpful if you happen to have a couple hosts that need to establish wireless communication directly between just them. You can also make this happen through something we call *ad hoc networking*, but if you have an AP between the hosts, it's just called a BSS.

Figure 9.5 shows a basic service set using one SSID.

ESS

Mobile wireless clients can roam around within the same network if you set all your access points to the same SSID. Doing this creates an ESS. Figure 9.6 shows four APs configured with the same SSID in an office thereby creating the ESS network.

FIGURE 9.5 BSS

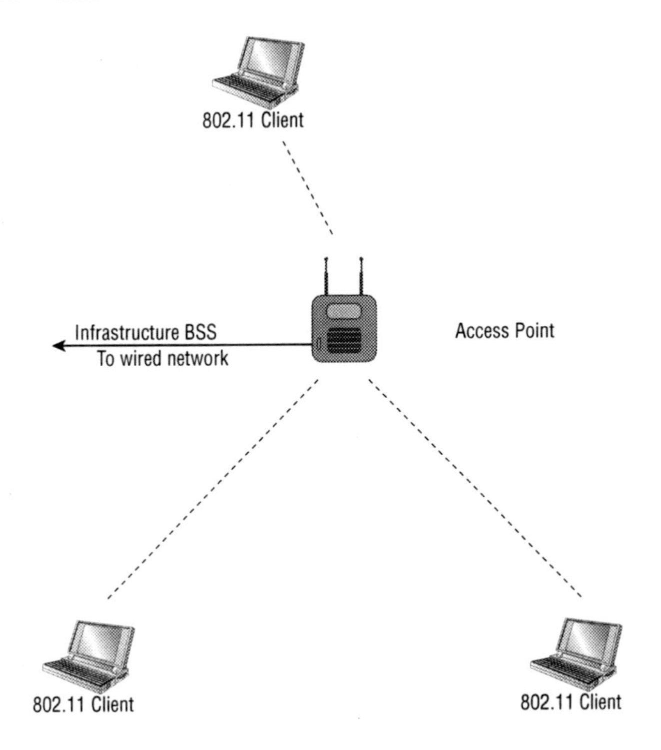

FIGURE 9.6

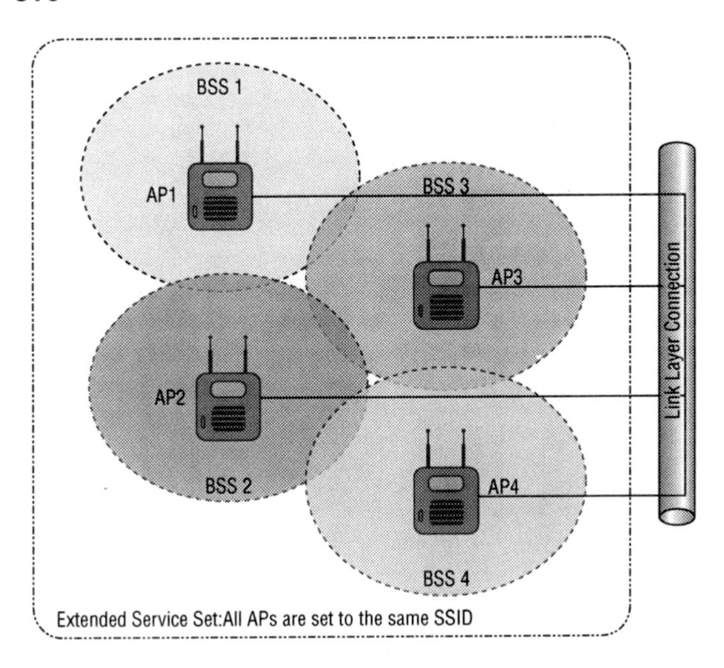

For users to be able to roam throughout the wireless network—from AP to AP without losing their connection to the network—all APs must overlap by at least 10 percent or more, and the channels on each AP shouldn't be set the same either. And remember, in an 802.11b/g network, there are only three nonoverlapping channels (1, 6, 11), so design is really important here!

Wireless Security

A good place to start is by discussing the standard basic security that was added to the original 802.11 standards and why those standards are way too flimsy and incomplete to enable you to create a secure wireless network relevant to today's challenges.

Open Access

All WiFi-certified wireless LAN products are shipped in "open-access" mode, with their security features turned off. Although open access or no security may be appropriate and acceptable for public hot spots such as coffee shops, college campuses, and maybe airports, it's definitely not an option for an enterprise organization, and it's likely not even adequate for your private home network.

Security needs to be enabled on wireless devices during their installation in enterprise environments. It may come as quite a shock, but some companies actually don't enable any WLAN security features. Obviously, the companies that do this are exposing their networks to tremendous risk!

The reason that the products are shipped with open access is so that any person who knows absolutely nothing about computers can just buy an access point, plug it into their cable or DSL modem, and *voilà*—they're up and running. It's marketing, plain and simple, and simplicity sells.

SSIDs, WEP, and MAC Address Authentication

What the original designers of 802.11 did to create basic security was include the use of SSIDs, open or shared-key authentication, static Wired Equivalency Protocol (WEP), and optional Media Access Control (MAC) authentication. It sounds like a lot, but none of these really offers any type of serious security solution—all they may be close to adequate for is use on a common home network. But I'll cover them anyway....

SSID is a common network name for the devices in a WLAN system that create the wireless LAN. An SSID prevents access by any client device that doesn't have the SSID. The thing is, by default, an access point broadcasts its SSID in its beacon many times a second. And even if SSID broadcasting is turned off, a bad guy can discover the SSID by monitoring the network and just waiting for a client response to the access point. Why? Well, believe it or not, that information, as regulated in the original 802.11 specifications, must be sent in the clear—how secure!

If the SSID broadcast from an AP (also called *guest mode*) is disabled, clients can still connect to the AP by setting the SSID value on the client software to the SSID configured on the AP.

The IEEE 802.11 committee specified two types of authentication: open and shared-key authentication. Open authentication involves little more than supplying the correct SSID, but it's the most common method in use today. With shared-key authentication, the access point sends the client device a challenge-text packet that the client must then encrypt with the correct WEP key and return to the access point. Without the correct key, authentication will fail, and the client won't be allowed to associate with the access point. But shared-key authentication is still not considered secure because all an intruder has to do to get around this is detect both the clear-text challenge and the same challenge encrypted with a WEP key and then decipher the WEP key. Surprise—shared key isn't used in today's WLANs because of the clear-text challenge.

With open authentication, even if a client can complete authentication and associate with an access point, using WEP prevents the client from sending and receiving data from the access point unless the client has the correct WEP key. A WEP key is composed of either 40 or 128 bits and, in its basic form, is usually statically defined by the network administrator on the access point and all clients that communicate with that access point. When static WEP keys are used, a network administrator must perform the time-consuming task of entering the same keys on every device in the WLAN. Obviously, we now have fixes for this because this would be administratively impossible in today's huge corporate wireless networks!

Last, client MAC addresses can be statically typed into each access point, and any of them that show up without that MAC address in the filter table would be denied access. That sounds good, but of course all MAC layer information must be sent in the clear—anyone equipped with a free wireless sniffer can just read the client packets sent to the access point and spoof their MAC address.

WEP can actually work if administered correctly. But basic static WEP keys are no longer a viable option in today's corporate networks without some of the proprietary fixes that run on top of WEP. So, I'll talk about some of these now.

You can set some basic security for an AP by changing the default value on an AP (Cisco's default is tsunami) as well as configuring a new administrator password on the AP.

WPA or WPA 2 Pre-Shared Key

Now we're getting somewhere. Although this is another form of basic security that's really just an add-on to the specifications, WPA or WPA2 Pre-Shared Key (PSK) is a better form of wireless security than any other basic wireless security method mentioned so far. I did say "basic."

The PSK verifies users via a password or identifying code (also called a *passphrase*) on both the client machine and the access point. A client gains access to the network only if its password matches the access point's password. The PSK also provides keying material that TKIP or AES uses to generate an encryption key for each packet of transmitted data. Although more secure than static WEP, PSK still has a lot in common with static WEP in that the PSK is stored on the client station and can be compromised if the client station is lost or stolen, even though finding this key isn't all that easy to do. It's a definite recommendation to use a strong PSK passphrase that includes a mixture of letters, numbers, and nonalphanumeric characters.

WPA is preferred over static WEP because the values of WPA keys can change dynamically while the system is used.

Wi-Fi Protected Access (WPA) is a standard developed in 2003 by the Wi-Fi Alliance, formerly known as WECA. WPA provides a standard for the authentication and encryption of WLANs that's intended to solve known security problems existing up to and including the year 2003. This takes into account the well-publicized AirSnort and man-in-the-middle WLAN attacks.

WPA is a step toward the IEEE 802.11i standard and uses many of the same components, with the exception of encryption—802.11i uses AES encryption. WPA's mechanisms are designed to be implementable by current hardware vendors, meaning that users should be able to implement WPA on their systems with only a firmware/software modification.

The IEEE 802.11i standard replaced WEP with a specific mode of the Advanced Encryption Standard (AES) known as the *Counter Mode Cipher Block Chaining-Message Authentication Code (CBC-MAC) Protocol* (CCMP). This allows AES-CCMP to provide both data confidentiality (encryption) and data integrity.

Unlike WEP, which uses a single key for unicast data encryption and can use a separate key for multicast and broadcast data encryption, WPA2 uses four keys for each wireless client/wireless AP pair. The keys are known as the *pairwise temporal keys*. It also uses two different keys—one for multicast and one for broadcast traffic.

OK, let's configure some wireless devices now!

Configuring Cisco Wireless Using the IOS

I'll configure two types of devices in this section using the CLI:

- A Cisco router with a routed wireless radio
- A basic Cisco wireless access point

The router and the AP configuration through the CLI are not much different. Here, in Table 9.3, are some of the minimum commands needed for configuring a wireless card in a router:

TABLE 9.3 Command and Meaning

Command	Meaning
`hostname`	Sets the name for the device
`interface` *interface*	Takes you to interface mode
`ip address`	Sets an IP address on an interface
`no shutdown`	Enables an interface
`ssid` *ssid*	Sets an SSID on a radio
`guest-mode`	Broadcasts the SSID on the BSS
`authentication-open`	Sets the authentication to open
`infrastructuire-ssid`	Tells the BSS clients that the wired network can be reached through this SSID
`line con 0`	Chooses the console line
`password` *password*	Sets a password on a line
`logging synchronous`	Stops the console messages from overwriting what you are typing
`line vty` *first_line_number last_line _number*	Chooses the Telnet or SSH line numbers
`ip dhcp pool` *pool_name*	Creates a DHCP pool
`network` *network mask*	Creates a pool of addresses used by the DHCP pool
`default-router`	Sets the default gateway for the DHCP service to advertise
`ip dhcp excluded-address` *ip_address*	Lists addresses that the DHCP will not hand out to DHCP clients
`copy running-config startup-config`	Saves the running-config to NVRAM

I'll start by showing how to configure an 871W router with an 802.11b/g radio:

```
Router>en
Router#config t
Router(config)#hostname 871W
871W(config)#int vlan 1
871W(config-if)#ip address 10.1.11.2 255.255.255.0
871W(config-if)#no shut
871W(config-if)#int dot11radio 0
871W(config-if)#ip address 10.1.12.1 255.255.255.0
871W(config-if)#no shut
871W(config-if)#ssid R3WLAN
871W(config-if-ssid)#guest-mode
871W(config-if-ssid)#authentication open
871W(config-if-ssid)#infrastructure-ssid
871W(config-if-ssid)#line con 0
871W(config-line)#password console
871W(config-line)#login
871W(config-line)#logging sync
871W(config-line)#exec-timeout 0 0
871W(config-line)#exit
871W(config)#line vty 0 ?
  <1-4>  Last Line number
  <cr>
871W(config)#line vty 0 4
871W(config-line)#password telnet
871W(config-line)#login
871W(config-line)#ip dhcp pool R3WLAN
871W(dhcp-config)#network 10.1.12.0 255.255.255.0
871W(dhcp-config)#default-router 10.1.12.1
871W(dhcp-config)#exit
871W(config)#ip dhcp excluded-address 10.1.12.1
871W(config)#exit
871W#copy run start
Destination filename [startup-config]?[enter]
Building configuration...
[OK]
871W#
```

The 871W I configured has a four-port switch, which means you have to place the IP address under the management VLAN interface. You just can't get away with simply putting IP addresses on layer-2 switch interfaces.

To be honest, I think this was a faster configuration than using SDM. But I guess, in production, the SDM with HTTPS would really be a more secure way to administer the router.

AP Configuration

Configuring the AP is a bit different because it's an access point (again, think hub), not a router. I'll configure this device from the CLI, but you can use an HTTP interface as well. But you can't use SDM. The HTTP interface will be easier to use when you start adding security and when you get into some more complex configurations.

Check out the output:

```
ap>en
Password:
ap#config t
ap(config)#hostname 1242AP
1242AP(config)#enable secret todd
242AP(config)#int dot11Radio 0
1242AP(config-if)#description CORPWLAN
1242AP(config-if)#no shutdown
1242AP(config-if)#ssid CORPWLAN
1242AP(config-if-ssid)#guest-mode
1242AP(config-if-ssid)#authentication open
1242AP(config-if-ssid)#infrastructure-ssid
1242AP(config-if-ssid)#exit
1242AP(config-if)#exit
1242AP(config)#line con 0
1242AP(config-line)#password console
1242AP(config-line)#login
1242AP(config-line)#logging synchronous
1242AP(config-line)#exec-timeout 0 0
1242AP(config-line)#exit
1242AP(config)#line vty 0 ?
  <1-15>  Last Line number
  <cr>
1242AP(config)#line vty 0 15
1242AP(config-line)#password telnet
```

```
1242AP(config-line)#login
1242AP(config-line)#int bvi 1
1242AP(config-if)#ip address 10.1.1.2 255.255.255.0
1242AP(config-if)#no shut
1242AP(config-if)#exit
1242AP(config)#ip default-gateway 10.1.1.1
1242AP(config)#ip dhcp pool CORPWLAN
1242AP(dhcp-config)#network 10.1.1.0 255.255.255.0
1242AP(dhcp-config)#default-router 10.1.1.1
1242AP(dhcp-config)#exit
1242AP(config)#ip dhcp excluded-address 10.1.1.1
1242AP(config)#ip dhcp excluded-address 10.1.1.2
1242AP(config)#no ip domain-lookup
1242AP(config)#^Z
1242AP#copy run start
Destination filename [startup-config]?[enter]
Building configuration...
[OK]
1242AP#
```

Even though the SSID configuration is the same as it is for the R2 routed radio interface, notice there's no IP address under the Dot11radio 0 interface. Why? It's not a routed port, so the IP address is instead placed under the bridge virtual interface (BVI). I also set a default gateway so this device can be managed from outside the LAN.

You need to know that, just as with a switch, you don't need to add an IP address to the AP for it to function. I could just as easily have added the DHCP pool to the Corp router for the wireless LAN and not added an IP address or pool to the AP at all, and it still would have worked just the same.

Configuring Cisco Wireless Using the SDM/HTTP

Configuring through the SDM is definitely the easiest way to go for wireless configurations. Basically, all you need to do to bring up an access point is to just turn it on. But if you do have a wireless card in your router, you'll need to configure it just as I showed you in the previous section.

This is my router showing that I can configure the wireless card I have installed in slot 3:

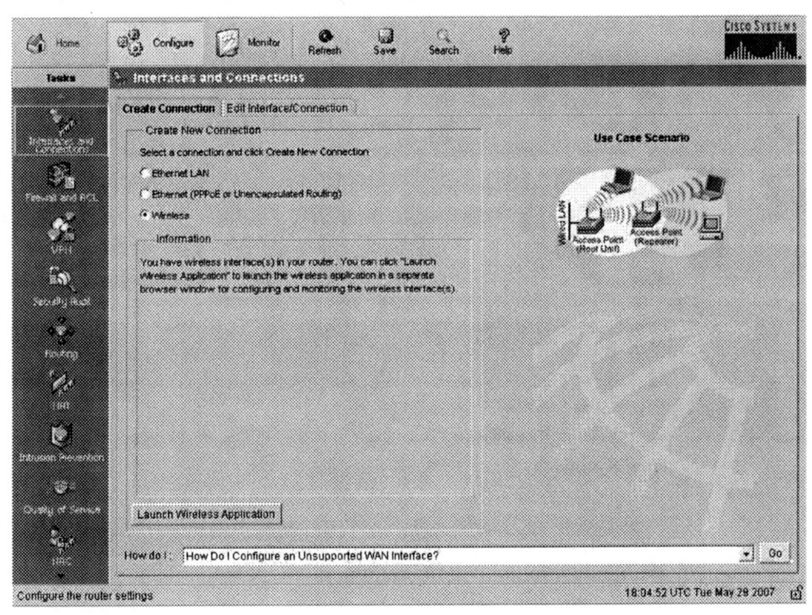

There really isn't too much you can do from within SDM itself, but if I were to click the Edit Interface/Connection tab and then click Summary, I could enable and disable the interface, as well as click the Edit button, which would allow me to add NAT, access lists, and so on, to the interface:

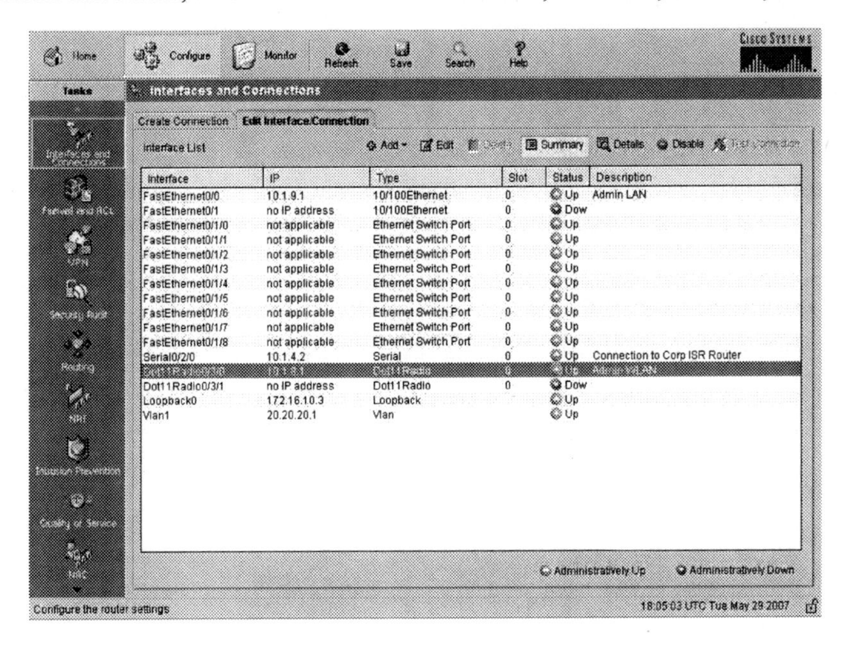

From either the Create Connection screen shown earlier or the screen that appears when you click the Edit button of the second screen, you can click Launch Wireless Application. This will open a new HTTP screen that your wireless device is configured from called the Express Set-up screen.

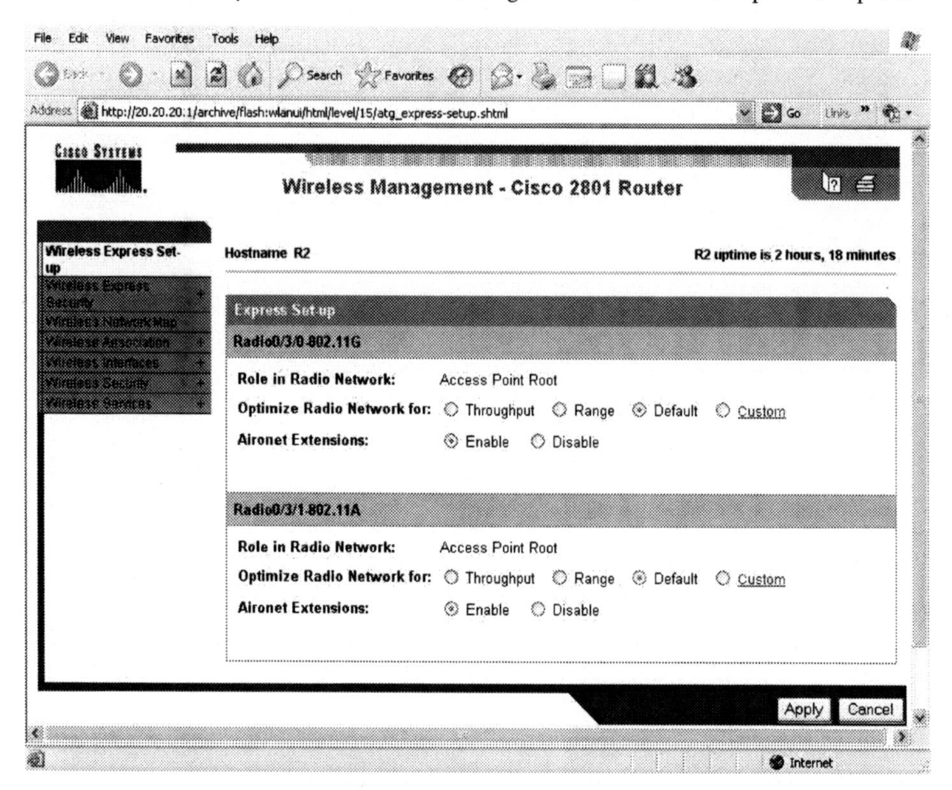

This is the same screen you would see if you just typed **HTTP** into an access point—one like my 1242AP. The SDM will be used with wireless interfaces for monitoring, for providing statistics, and for gaining access into the wireless configuration mode on a router that has wireless interfaces. This is so we don't have to use the CLI for the hard configurations.

Again, you can configure only some basic information from here. But from the next screen, Wireless Express Security, you can configure the wireless AP in either bridging mode or routing mode—a really cool feature!

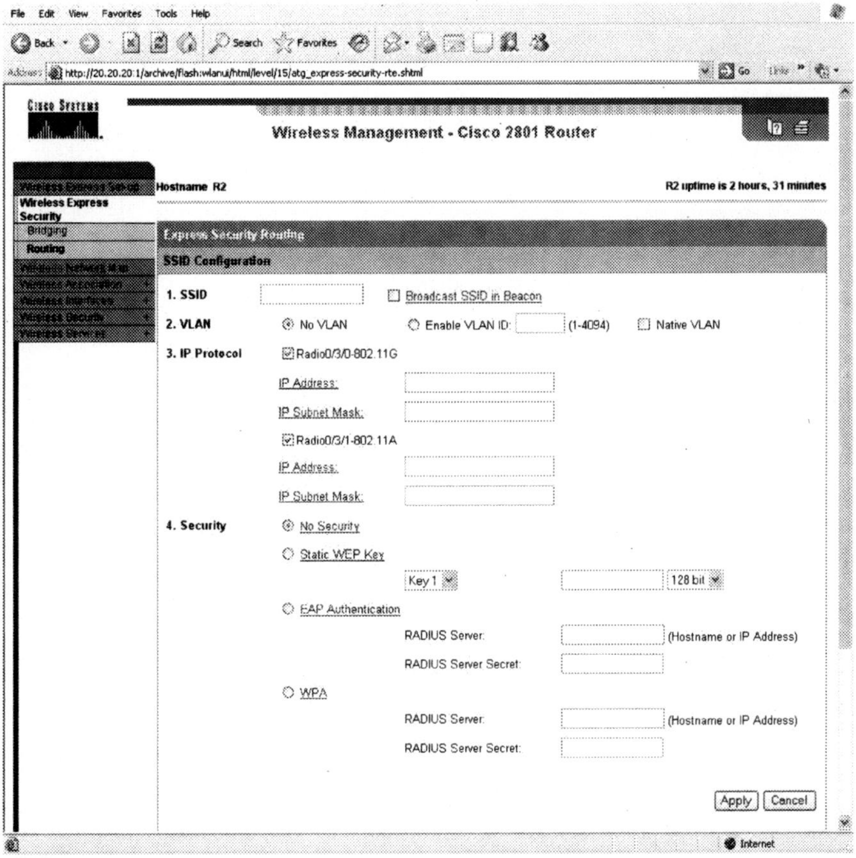

File Edit View Favorites Tools Help

Back Search Favorites

Address http://20.20.20.1/archive/flash:wlanui/html/level/15/atg_express-security-rte.shtml Go Links

Cisco Systems

Wireless Management - Cisco 2801 Router

Wireless Express Setup
Wireless Express Security
Bridging
Routing
Wireless Network Map
Wireless Association
Wireless Interfaces
Wireless Security
Wireless Services

Hostname R2

R2 uptime is 2 hours, 31 minutes

Express Security Routing

SSID Configuration

1. SSID

Broadcast SSID in Beacon

2. VLAN

No VLAN

Enable VLAN ID: (1-4094)

Native VLAN

3. IP Protocol

Radio0/3/0-802.11G

IP Address:

IP Subnet Mask:

Radio0/3/1-802.11A

IP Address:

IP Subnet Mask:

4. Security

No Security

Static WEP Key

Key 1

128 bit

EAP Authentication

RADIUS Server: (Hostname or IP Address)

RADIUS Server Secret:

WPA

RADIUS Server: (Hostname or IP Address)

RADIUS Server Secret:

Apply Cancel

Internet

The next screen shows the wireless interfaces and the basic settings:

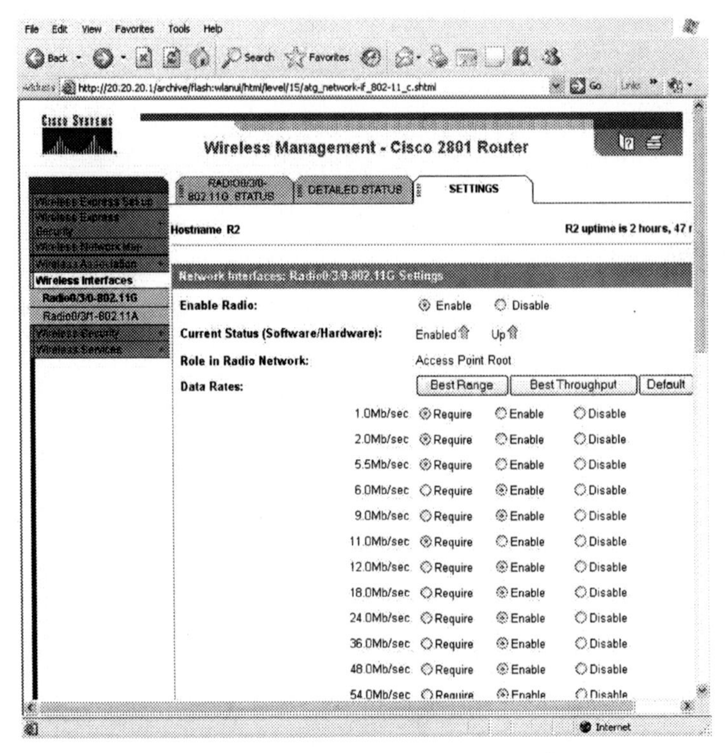

This is the second part of the Wireless Interfaces screen:

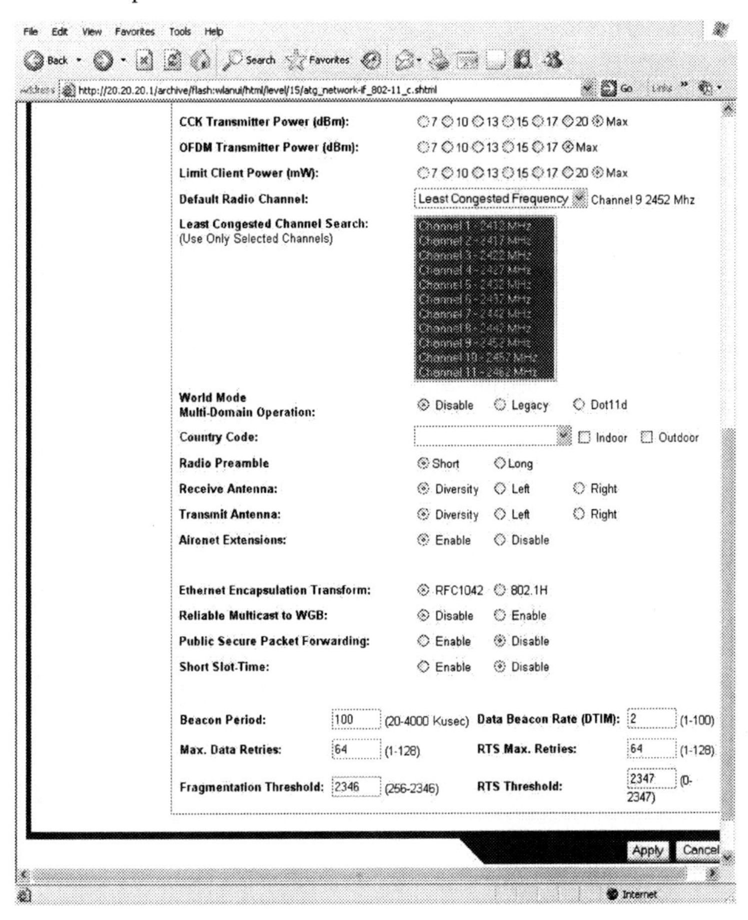

Under the Wireless Security heading is really where HTTP management shines! You can configure encryption, add SSIDs, and configure your RADIUS server settings.

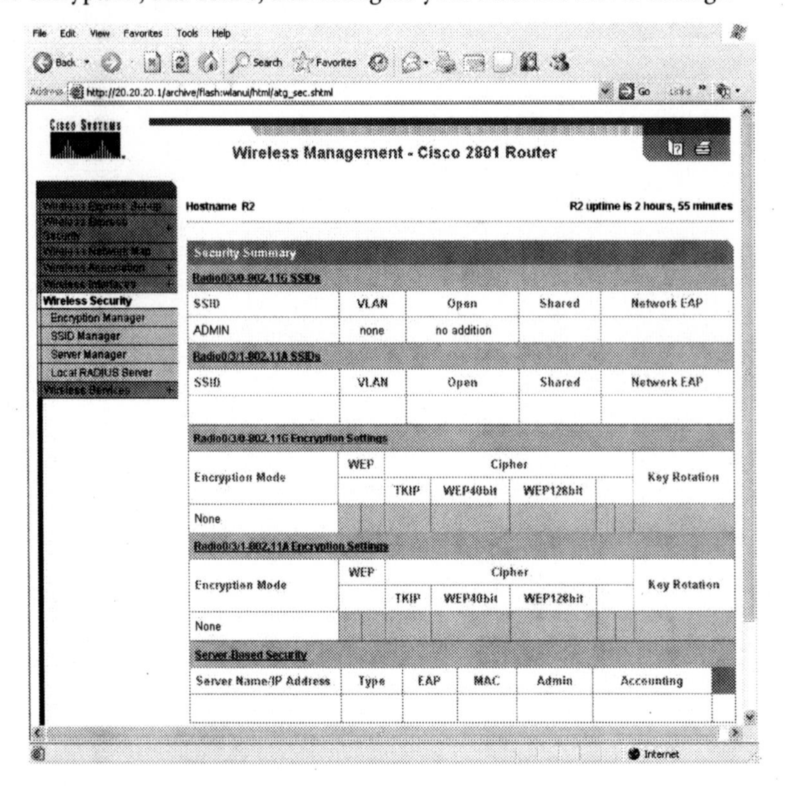

Now, if you were to just HTTP in to the 1242AG AP, you'll see this screen:

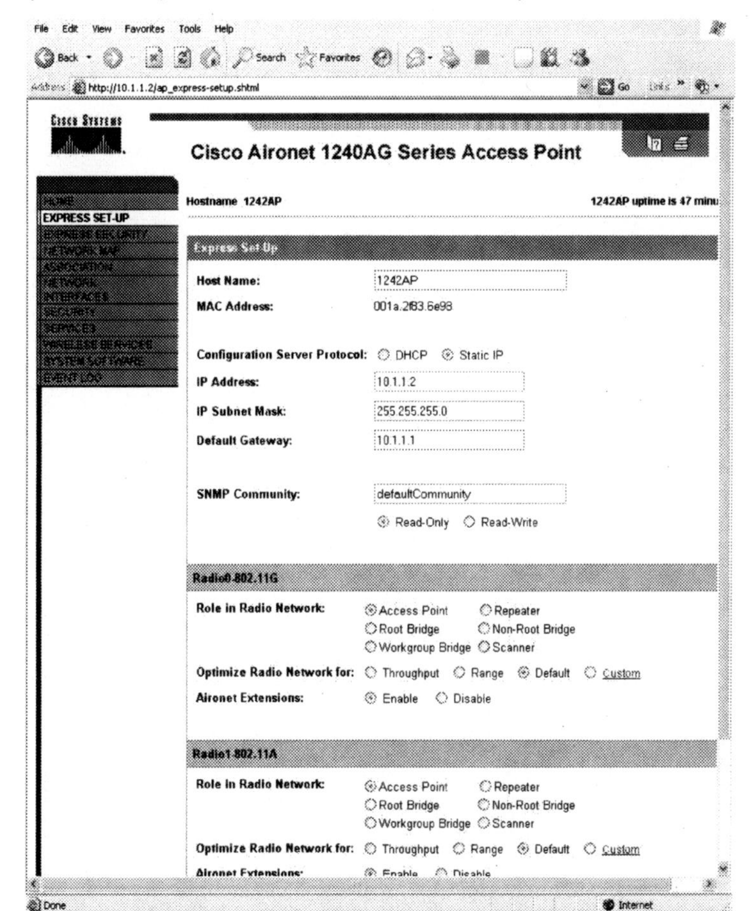

This looks amazingly like the APs you'll find in your ISR routers, and you can configure the same devices and security too.

Chapter 10

Internet Protocol Version 6 (IPv6)

People refer to IPv6 as the "next-generation Internet protocol," and it was originally created as the answer to IPv4's inevitable, looming address-exhaustion crisis. Though you've probably heard a thing or two about IPv6 already, it has been improved even further in the quest to bring you the flexibility, efficiency, capability, and optimized functionality that can truly meet your ever-increasing needs. The capacity of its predecessor, IPv4, pales in comparison—and that's the reason it will eventually fade into history completely.

The IPv6 header and address structure has been completely overhauled, and many of the features that were basically just afterthoughts and addendums in IPv4 are now included as full-blown standards in IPv6. It's seriously well equipped, poised, and ready to manage the mind-blowing demands of the Internet to come.

For up-to-the-minute updates for this chapter, please see `www.lammle.com` or `www.sybex.com/go/IOS`

Why Do We Need IPv6?

Well, the short answer is, we need to communicate, and our current system isn't really cutting it anymore—kind of like how the Pony Express can't compete with airmail. Just look at how much time and effort we've invested in coming up with slick new ways to conserve bandwidth and IP addresses. We've even come up with variable-length subnet masks (VLSMs) in our struggle to overcome the worsening address drought.

It's reality—the amount of people and devices that connect to networks increases every day. That's not a bad thing at all—we're finding new and exciting ways to communicate to more people all the time, and that's a good thing. In fact, it's a basic human need. But the forecast isn't exactly blue skies and sunshine because IPv4, upon which our ability to communicate is currently dependent, is going to run out of addresses for us to use. IPv4 has only about 4.3 billion addresses available—that's in theory, and we know that we don't even get to use all of those. There really are only about 250 million addresses that can be assigned to devices. Sure, Classless Inter-Domain Routing (CIDR) and Network Address Translation (NAT) have helped to extend the inevitable dearth of addresses, but we will run out of them, and it's going to happen within a few years. China is barely online, and we know there's a huge population of people and corporations there that surely want to be. Many reports give us all kinds of numbers, but all you really need to think about to convince yourself that I'm not just being an alarmist is the fact that there are about 6.5 billion people in the world today, and it's estimated that just more than 10 percent of that population is connected to the Internet—wow!

That statistic is basically screaming at us the ugly truth that, based on IPv4's capacity, every person can't even have a computer—let alone all the other devices we use with them. I have more than one computer, and it's pretty likely you do too. And I'm not even including in the mix phones, laptops, game consoles, fax machines, routers, switches, and a mother lode of other devices we use every day! So I think I've made it pretty clear that we have to do something before we run out of addresses and lose the ability to connect with each other as we know it. And that "something" just happens to be implementing IPv6.

IPv6 Addressing and Expressions

Just as understanding how IP addresses are structured and used is critical with IPv4 addressing, it's also vital when it comes to IPv6. You already know that at 128 bits, an IPv6 address is much larger than an IPv4 address. Because of this, as well as the new ways the addresses can be used, you've probably guessed that IPv6 will be more complicated to manage. But no worries! As I said, I'll break down the basics and show you what the address looks like, how you can write it, and what many of its common uses are. It's going to be a little weird at first, but before you know it, you'll have it nailed!

So let's take a look at Figure 10.1, which has a sample IPv6 address broken down into sections.

FIGURE 10.1 IPv6 address example

```
2001:0db8:3c4d:0012:0000:0000:1234:56ab
_____________|____|_________________
Global prefix   Subnet        Interface ID
```

So as you can now see, the address is truly much larger—but what else is different? Well, first, notice that it has eight groups of numbers instead of four and also that those groups are separated by colons instead of periods. And, hey, wait a second...there are letters in that address! Yep, the address is expressed in hexadecimal just like a MAC address is, so you could say this address has eight 16-bit hexadecimal colon-delimited blocks. That's already quite a mouthful, and you probably haven't even tried to say the address out loud yet!

When you use a web browser to make an HTTP connection to an IPv6 device, you have to type the address into the browser with brackets around the literal address. Why? Well, the browser is already using a colon for specifying a port number. So basically, if you don't enclose the address in brackets, the browser will have no way to identify the information.

Here's an example of how this looks:

```
http://[2001:0db8:3c4d:0012:0000:0000:1234:56ab]/default.html
```

Now obviously, if you can, you would rather use names to specify a destination (such as `www.lammle.com`). However, even though it's definitely going to be a pain in the rear, we just have to accept the fact that sometimes we have to type the address number. So, it should be pretty clear that DNS is going to become extremely important when implementing IPv6.

Shortened Expression

The good news is there are a few tricks to help rescue us when writing these monster addresses. For one thing, you can actually omit parts of the address to abbreviate it, but to get away with doing that you have to follow a couple of rules. First, you can drop any leading zeros in each of the individual blocks. After you do that, the sample address from earlier would then look like this:

```
2001:db8:3c4d:12:0:0:1234:56ab
```

OK, that's a definite improvement—at least we don't have to write all of those extra zeros! But what about whole blocks that don't have anything in them except zeros? Well, we can kind of lose those too—at least some of them. Again referring to our sample address, we can remove the two blocks of zeros by replacing them with double colons, like this:

```
2001:db8:3c4d:12::1234:56ab
```

Cool—we replaced the blocks of all zeros with double colons. The rule you have to follow to get away with this is that you can replace only one contiguous block of zeros in an address. So if my address has four blocks of zeros and each of them were separated, I just don't get to replace them all. Check out this example:

```
2001:0000:0000:0012:0000:0000:1234:56ab
```

And just know that you *can't* do this:

```
2001::12::1234:56ab
```

Instead, this is the best you can do:

```
2001::12:0:0:1234:56ab
```

The reason why the previous example is your best shot is that if you remove two sets of zeros, the device looking at the address will have no way of knowing where the zeros go back in. Basically, the router would look at the incorrect address and say, "Well, do I place two blocks into the first set of double colons and two into the second set, or do I place three blocks into the first set and one block into the second set?" And on and on it would go because the information the router needs just isn't there.

Configuring Cisco Routers with IPv6

Look at Table 10.1.

TABLE 10.1 Basic IPv6 Cisco Router Commands

Command	Meaning
(config)#**ipv6 unicast-routing**	Starts the IPv6 routing on a router
(config-if)#**ipv6 address mask**	Configures a router interface with the IPv6 routed protocol
(config-if)#**ipv6 enable**	Enables IPv6 on a LAN link only

To enable IPv6 on a router, you have to use the ipv6 unicast-routing global configuration command:

```
Corp(config)#ipv6 unicast-routing
```

By default, IPv6 traffic forwarding is disabled, so using this command enables it. Also, as you've probably guessed, IPv6 isn't enabled by default on any interfaces either, so we have to go to each interface individually and enable it.

You can do this in a few different ways, but a really easy way is to just add an address to the interface. You use the interface configuration command ipv6 address <ipv6prefix>/<prefix-length> [eui-64]to get this done.

Here's an example:

```
Corp(config-if)#ipv6 address 2001:db8:3c4d:1:0260.d6FF.FE73.1987/64
```

You can specify the entire 128-bit global IPv6 address, or you can use the eui-64 option. Remember, the eui-64 format allows the device to use its MAC address and pad it to make the interface ID. Check it out:

```
Corp(config-if)#ipv6 address 2001:db8:3c4d:1::/64 eui-64
```

As an alternative to typing an IPv6 address on a router, you can enable the interface instead to permit the application of an automatic link-local address.

To configure a router so that it uses only link-local addresses, use the ipv6 enable interface configuration command:

```
Corp(config-if)#ipv6 enable
```

OK, now let's dive into stateful IPv6 by configuring a DHCP server for IPv6 use. Take a look at Table 10.2.

DHCPv6

TABLE 10.2 IPv6 DHCP Commands

Command	Meaning
(config)#**ipv6 dhcp pool**	Creates a pool of address on the router
(config-dhcp)#**dns-server**	Sets IPv6 address of the DNS server
(config-dhcp)#**domain-name**	Company domain name used for DNS lookups
(config-dhcp)#**Prefix-delegation**	Sets the IPv6 subnet mask for the pool and the registered lifetime
(config-if)#**ipv6 dhcp server pool-name**	Assigns the pool to an interface on the router

DHCPv6 works pretty much the same way DHCP does in version 4, with the obvious difference that it supports the new addressing scheme for IPv6. It might come as a surprise, but there are a couple of other options that DHCP still provides for us that autoconfiguration doesn't. I'm serious—there's absolutely no mention of DNS servers, domain names, or many of the other options that DHCP has always provided via IPv4 with autoconfiguration. This is a big reason why it's likely we'll still be using DHCP in IPv6 most of the time.

Upon booting up in IPv4, a client sends out a DHCP discover message looking for a server to give it the information it needs. But remember, in IPv6, the Router Solicitation and Router Advertisements process happens first. If there's a DHCPv6 server on the network, the RA that comes back to the client will tell it whether DHCP is available for use. If a router isn't found, the client will respond by sending out a DHCP solicit message—a solicit message that's actually a multicast message addressed with a source of ff02::1:2, meaning all DHCP agents, including both servers and relays.

It's good to know that there's some support for DHCPv6 in the Cisco IOS. But it's limited to a stateless DHCP server, meaning it doesn't offer any address management of the pool, plus the options available for configuring that address pool are limited to the DNS, domain name, and SIP servers only.

This means you're definitely going to need some other server around that can supply and dispense all the additional, required information, as well as manage the address assignment.

Anyway, here's how the configuration looks for the stateless DHCP server in the router IOS—it's really close to what you'd configure with IPv4:

```
Router1(config)#ipv6 dhcp pool ?
WORD  DHCP pool name
Router1(config)#ipv6 dhcp pool test
Router1(config-dhcp)#?
```

```
IPv6 DHCP configuration commands:
  default             Set a command to its defaults
  dns-server          DNS servers
  domain-name         Domain name to complete unqualified host names
  exit                Exit from DHCPv6 configuration mode
  no                  Negate a command or set its defaults
  prefix-delegation   IPv6 prefix delegation
  sip                 SIP Servers options
Router1(config-dhcp)#dns-server ?
  Hostname or X:X:X:X::X  Server's name or IPv6 address
Router1(config-dhcp)#domain-name lammle.com
Router1(config-dhcp)#prefix-delegation ?
  X:X:X:X::X/<0-128>  IPv6  x:x::y/<z>
  aaa                 Acquire prefix from AAA
  pool                IPv6 prefix pool
Router1(config-dhcp)#prefix-delegation pool ?
  WORD  IPv6 prefix pool
Router1(config-dhcp)#prefix-delegation pool test ?
  lifetime  Configure prefix lifetimes
  <cr>
Router1(config-dhcp)#prefix-delegation pool test lifetime ?
  <60-4294967295>  Valid lifetime (seconds)
  at               Expire prefix at a specific time/date
  infinite         Infinite valid lifetime
Router1(config-dhcp)#prefix-delegation pool test lifetime 3600 ?
  <60-4294967295>  Preferred lifetime (seconds)
  infinite         Infinite preferred lifetime
Router1(config-dhcp)#prefix-delegation pool test lifetime 3600 3600 ?
  <cr>
Router1(config-dhcp)#prefix-delegation pool test lifetime 3600 3600
```

Notice that just like in DHCP with IPv4, you don't need to set a lifetime.

Now that I have the pool configured, I just have to assign it to an interface, which is a departure from IPv4:

```
Router1(config)#int fa 0/0
Router1(config-if)#ipv6 dhcp server ?
  WORD  Name of IPv6 DHCP pool
Router1(config-if)#ipv6 dhcp server test
```

Sweet—I now have a fully configured DHCPv6 server applied to the interface fa0/0!

IPv6 Routing Protocols

Most of the routing protocols I've already discussed have been upgraded for use in IPv6 networks. Also, many of the functions and configurations you've already learned will be used in almost the same way as they're used now. Knowing that broadcasts have been eliminated in IPv6, it follows that any protocols that use entirely broadcast traffic will go the way of the dodo—but unlike the dodo, it'll be good to say goodbye to these bandwidth-hogging, performance-annihilating little gremlins!

The routing protocols you'll still use in v6 have gotten a new name and a facelift. I'll talk about a few of them now.

First on the list is *RIPng* (next generation). If you've been in IT for a while, you know that RIP has worked well on smaller networks, which happens to be the reason it didn't get whacked and will still be around in IPv6. And you still have EIGRPv6 because it already had protocol-dependent modules, and all you have to do was add a new one to it for the IPv6 protocol. Rounding out the group of protocol survivors is OSPFv3—that's not a typo; it really is v3. OSPF for IPv4 was actually v2, so when it got its upgrade to IPv6, it became OSPFv3.

RIPng

TABLE 10.3 IPv6 RIP Commands

Command	Meaning
(config-if)#**ipv6 rip 1 enable**	Enables RIP on the router interface
(config)#**ipv6 router rip 1**	Enters router configuration mode

Table 10.3 lists IPv6 RIP Commands. To be honest, the primary features of RIPng are the same as they were with RIPv2. It is still a distance-vector protocol; has a max hop count of 15; and uses split horizon, poison reverse, and other loop avoidance mechanisms. However, it now uses UDP port 521.

It still uses multicast to send its updates too, but in IPv6, it uses FF02::9 for the transport address. This is actually kind of cool since in RIPv2, the multicast address was 224.0.0.9, so the address still has a 9 at the end in the new IPv6 multicast range. In fact, most routing protocols got to keep a little bit of their IPv4 identities like that.

But of course there are differences in the new version, or it wouldn't be a new version, would it? We know that routers keep the next-hop addresses of their neighbor routers for every destination network in their routing table. The difference is that with RIPng, the router keeps track of this next-hop address using the link-local address, not a global address.

Probably one of the biggest changes with RIPng (and all of the IPv6 routing protocols for that matter) is that you configure or enable the advertisement of a network from interface configuration mode instead of with a network command in router configuration mode. So in

RIPng's case, if you enable it directly on an interface without going into router configuration mode and starting a RIPng process, a new RIPng process will simply be started for you. It will look something like this:

```
Router1(config-if)#ipv6 rip 1 enable
```

That 1 you see in this command is a tag that identifies the process of RIPng that's running, and as I said, this will start a process of RIPng so you don't have to go into router configuration mode.

But if you need to go to router configuration mode to configure something else like redistribution, you still can. If you do that, it will look like this on your router:

```
Router1(config)#ipv6 router rip 1
Router1(config-rtr)#
```

So, just remember that RIPng will pretty much work the same way as with IPv4, with the biggest difference being that it uses the network itself instead of using the network command you used to use to enable the interface to route the connected network.

EIGRPv6

TABLE 10.4 IPv6 EIGRP Commands

Command	Meaning
(config)#**ipv6 router eigrp AS**	Enables EIGRP on the router
(config-rtr)#**no shutdown**	Is required for EIGRP to be enabled on the router
(config-if)#**ipv6 eigrp 10**	Enables EIGRP on each interface you want to use

As with RIPng, EIGRPv6 works much the same as its IPv4 predecessor does (see Table 10.4)—most of the features that EIGRP provided before EIGRPv6 will still be available.

EIGRPv6 is still an advanced distance-vector protocol that has some link-state features. The neighbor discovery process using hellos still happens, and it still provides reliable communication with reliable transport protocol that gives you loop-free fast convergence using the Diffusing Update Algorithm (DUAL).

Hello packets and updates are sent using multicast transmission, and as with RIPng, EIGRPv6's multicast address stayed almost the same. In IPv4 it was 224.0.0.10; in IPv6, it's FF02::A (A = 10 in hexadecimal notation).

But obviously, there are differences between the two versions. Most notably, and just as with RIPng, the use of the network command is gone, and the network and interface to be advertised must be enabled from interface configuration mode. But you still have to use the router configuration mode to enable the routing protocol in EIGRPv6 because the routing process must be turned on like an interface with the `no shutdown` command—interesting!

The configuration for EIGRPv6 is going to look like this:

```
Router1(config)#ipv6 router eigrp 10
```

The 10 in this case is still the autonomous system (AS) number. The prompt changes to `(config-rtr)`, and from here you must perform a `no shutdown`:

```
Router1(config-rtr)#no shutdown
```

Other options also can be configured in this mode, such as redistribution.

So now, let's go to the interface and enable IPv6:

```
Router1(config-if)#ipv6 eigrp 10
```

The 10 in the interface command again references the AS number that was enabled in the configuration mode.

Last to check out in this group is what OSPF looks like in the IPv6 routing protocol.

OSPFv3

Take a look at Table 10.5.

TABLE 10.5 IPv6 OSPF Commands

Command	Meaning
`(config)#`**ipv6 router ospf process_id**	Enables the OSPF database on the router
`(config-rtr)#`**router-id a.b.c.d**	Sets the RID of the router
`(config-if)#`**ipv6 ospf process_id area area**	Configures the area for the interface

The new version of OSPF continues the trend of the routing protocols having many similarities with their IPv4 versions.

The foundation of OSPF remains the same—it is still a link-state routing protocol that divides an entire internetwork or autonomous system into areas, making a hierarchy. And just trust me—be really thankful that multiarea OSPF is out of scope for the CCNA objectives—at least, for now!

In OSPF version 2, the router ID (RID) is determined by the highest IP addresses assigned to the router (or you could assign it). In version 3, you assign the RID, area ID, and link-state ID, which are all still 32-bit values but are not found using the IP address anymore because an IPv6 address is 128 bits. Changes regarding how these values are assigned, along with the removal of the IP address information from OSPF packet headers, makes the new version of OSPF capable of being routed over almost any Network layer protocol—cool!

Adjacencies and next-hop attributes now use link-local addresses, and OSPFv3 still uses multicast traffic to send its updates and acknowledgments, with the addresses FF02::5 for OSPF routers and FF02::6 for OSPF-designated routers. These new addresses are the replacements for 224.0.0.5 and 224.0.0.6, respectively.

Other, less flexible IPv4 protocols don't give you the ability that OSPFv2 does to assign specific networks and interfaces into the OSPF process—however, this is something that is still configured under the router configuration process. And with OSPFv3, just as with the other IPv6 routing protocols we've talked about, the interfaces and therefore the networks attached to them are configured directly on the interface in interface configuration mode.

The configuration of OSPFv3 is going to look like this:

```
Router1(config)#ipv6 router osfp 10
Router1(config-rtr)#router-id 1.1.1.1
```

You get to perform some configurations from router configuration mode such as summarization and redistribution, but you don't even need to configure OSPFv3 from this prompt if you configure OSPFv3 from the interface.

When the interface configuration is completed, the router configuration process is added automatically. and the interface configuration looks like this:

```
Router1(config-if)#ipv6 ospf 10 area 0.0.0.0
```

So, if you just go to each interface and assign a process ID and area, poof, you're done!

With all that behind you, it's now time to move on and learn about how to migrate to IPv6 from IPv4.

Migrating to IPv6

Table 10.6 lists IPv6 Tunnel Commands and their meaning.

TABLE 10.6 IPv6 Tunnel Commands

Command	Meaning
(config)#**ipv6 unicast-routing**	Enables IPv6 on the router
(config)#**interface interface**	Chooses your first interface
(config-if)#**ipv6 address ipv6_address mask**	Sets the IPv6 address on the interface
(config-if)#**ip address ip_address mask**	Sets the IP address on the interface
(config)#**int tunnel 0**	Chooses the tunnel interface
(config-if)#**ipv6 address ipv6_address**	Sets the IPv6 address on the tunnel
(config-if)#**tunnel source ip address**	Sets the source IP address
(config-if)#**tunnel destination ip_address**	Sets the destination IP address
(config-if)#**tunnel mode ipv6ip**	Configures the tunnel mode to be used

I certainly have talked a lot about how IPv6 works and how you can configure it to work on your networks, but what is doing that going to cost you? And how much work is it really going to take? These are good questions for sure, but the answers to them won't be the same for everyone. This is because how much you end up having to pony up is highly dependent upon what you have going on already in terms of your infrastructure. Obviously, if you've been making your really old routers and switches "last" and therefore have to upgrade every one of them so that they're IPv6 compliant, that could very well turn out to be a good-sized chunk of change! Oh, and that sum doesn't even include server and computer operating systems (OSs) and the blood, sweat, and maybe even tears spent on making all your applications compliant. So, my friend, it could cost you quite a bit! The good news is that unless you've really let things go, many OSs and network devices have been IPv6 compliant for a few years—we just haven't been using all their features until now.

Then there's that other question about the amount of work and time. Straight up—this one could still be pretty intense. No matter what, it's going to take you some time to get all your systems moved over and make sure things are working correctly. And if you're talking about a huge network with tons of devices, well, it could take a really long time! But don't panic—that's why migration strategies have been created to allow for a slower integration. I'm going to show you three of the primary transition strategies available to you:

- The first is called *dual stacking*, which allows a device to have both the IPv4 and IPv6 protocol stack running so it's capable of continuing with its existing communications and simultaneously run newer IPv6 communications as they're implemented.
- The next strategy is the 6to4 tunneling approach; this is your choice if you have an all-IPv6 network that must communicate over an IPv4 network to reach another IPv6 network.

Dual Stacking

Dual stacking is the most common type of migration strategy because, well, it's the easiest on you—it allows your devices to communicate using either IPv4 or IPv6. Dual stacking lets you upgrade your devices and applications on the network one at a time. As more and more hosts and devices on the network are upgraded, more of your communication will happen over IPv6, and after you've arrived, everything is running on IPv6, and you get to remove all the old IPv4 protocol stacks you no longer need.

Plus, configuring dual stacking on a Cisco router is amazingly easy—all you have to do is enable IPv6 forwarding and apply an address to the interfaces already configured with IPv4. It'll look something like this:

```
Corp(config)#ipv6 unicast-routing
Corp(config)#interface fastethernet 0/0
Corp(config-if)#ipv6 address 2001:db8:3c4d:1::/64 eui-64
Corp(config-if)#ip address 192.168.255.1 255.255.255.0
```

But to be honest, it's really a good idea to understand the various tunneling techniques because it'll probably be a while before we all start running IPv6 as a solo routed protocol.

6to4 Tunneling

6to4 tunneling is really useful for carrying IPv6 data over a network that's still IPv4. It's quite possible that you'll have IPv6 subnets or other portions of your network that are all IPv6, and those networks will have to communicate with each other. That's not so complicated, but when you consider that you might find this happening over a WAN or some other network that you don't control, well, that could be a bit ugly. So what do you do about this if you don't control the whole tamale? Create a tunnel that will carry the IPv6 traffic for you across the IPv4 network, that's what.

The whole idea of tunneling isn't a difficult concept, and creating tunnels really isn't as hard as you might think. All it really comes down to is snatching the IPv6 packet that's happily traveling across the network and sticking an IPv4 header onto the front of it. It's kind of like catch-and-release fishing, except the fish doesn't get something plastered on its face before being thrown back into the stream.

To get a picture of this, take a look at Figure 10.2.

FIGURE 10.2 Creating a 6to4 tunnel

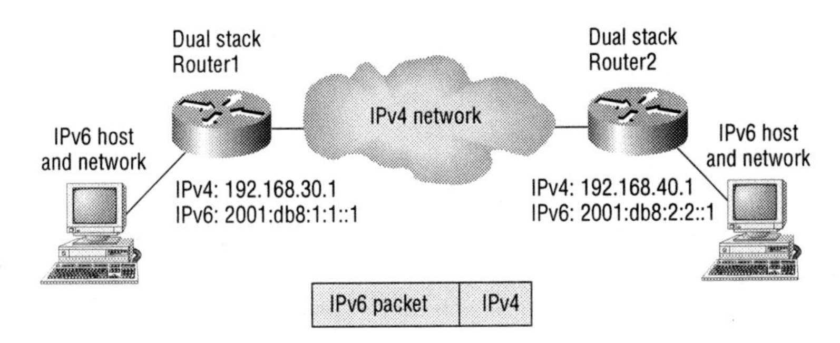

Nice—but to make this happen, you'll need a couple of dual-stacked devices, which I just demonstrated for you, so you should be good to go. Now you have to add a little configuration to place a tunnel between those routers. Tunnels are pretty simple—you just have to tell each router where the tunnel begins and where you want it to end. Here's an example:

```
Router1(config)#int tunnel 0
Router1(config-if)#ipv6 address 2001:db8:1:1::1/64
Router1(config-if)#tunnel source 192.168.30.1
Router1(config-if)#tunnel destination 192.168.40.1
Router1(config-if)#tunnel mode ipv6ip
```

```
Router2(config)#int tunnel 0
Router2(config-if)#ipv6 address 2001:db8:2:2::1/64
Router2(config-if)#tunnel source 192.168.40.1
Router2(config-if)#tunnel destination 192.168.30.1
Router2(config-if)#tunnel mode ipv6ip
```

With this in place, your IPv6 networks can now communicate over the IPv4 network. Now, I have to tell you that this is not meant to be a permanent configuration; your end goal should still be to run a total, complete IPv6 network end to end.

One important note here—if the IPv4 network that you're traversing in this situation has a NAT translation point, it would absolutely break the tunnel encapsulation you've just created! Over the years, NAT has been upgraded a lot so that it can handle specific protocols and dynamic connections, and without one of these upgrades, NAT likes to demolish most connections. And since this transition strategy isn't present in most NAT implementations, that means trouble.

There is a way around this little problem, and it's called *Teredo*, which allows all your tunnel traffic to be placed in UDP packets. NAT doesn't blast away at UDP packets, so they won't get broken as other protocols packets do. So with Teredo in place and your packets disguised under their UDP cloak, the packets will easily slip by NAT alive and well!

Verifying RIPng

Now take a look at Table 10.7.

TABLE 10.7 Verifying IPv6 RIP

Command	Meaning
`show ipv6 route`	Displays the IPv6 routing table on a router
`show ipv6 protocols`	Doesn't display much, but it does show up the IPv6 routing protocols that are enabled
`Show ipv6 rip`	Displays the administrative distance, plus the multicast group, maximum paths, and timers
`show ipv6 interface interface`	Displays the IPv6 address, unicast address, and other interface information regarding IPv6
`debug ipv6 rip`	Displays the IPv6 RIP updates sent and received on a router

I'll start with the usual `show ipv6 route` command. Here's the output from the R3 router:

```
R3#sh ipv6 route
R    2001:DB8:3C4D:11::/64 [120/2]
      via FE80::21A:2FFF:FE55:C9E8, Serial0/0/1
R    2001:DB8:3C4D:12::/64 [120/2]
      via FE80::21A:2FFF:FE55:C9E8, Serial0/0/1
R    2001:DB8:3C4D:13::/64 [120/2]
      via FE80::21A:2FFF:FE55:C9E8, Serial0/0/1
R    2001:DB8:3C4D:14::/64 [120/2]
      via FE80::21A:2FFF:FE55:C9E8, Serial0/0/1
C    2001:DB8:3C4D:15::/64 [0/0]
      via ::, Serial0/0/1
L    2001:DB8:3C4D:15:21A:6DFF:FE37:A44E/128 [0/0]
      via ::, Serial0/0/1
L    FE80::/10 [0/0]
      via ::, Null0
L    FF00::/8 [0/0]
      via ::, Null0
R3#
```

Wow, it looks just like the regular IPv4 RIP table, including the administrative distance and hop count. I can see subnets 11, 12, 13, 14, and 15.

Let's take a look at a few more verification commands:

```
R3#sh ipv6 protocols
IPv6 Routing Protocol is "connected"
IPv6 Routing Protocol is "static"
IPv6 Routing Protocol is "rip 1"
  Interfaces:
    Serial0/0/1
  Redistribution:
    None
R3#
```

Not too much information is provided with the `show ipv6 protocols` command. Let's try the `show ipv6 rip` command:

```
R3#sh ipv6 rip
RIP process "1", port 521, multicast-group FF02::9, pid 60
     Administrative distance is 120. Maximum paths is 16
     Updates every 30 seconds, expire after 180
     Holddown lasts 0 seconds, garbage collect after 120
```

```
    Split horizon is on; poison reverse is off
    Default routes are not generated
    Periodic updates 44, trigger updates 19
  Interfaces:
    Serial0/0/1
  Redistribution:
    None
```

Now we're talking! You can see that the administrative distance is still 120, plus the multicast group, maximum paths, and timers. So, let's try two more verification commands, beginning with the `show ipv6 interface s0/0/1` command:

```
R3#sh ipv6 interface serial 0/0/1
Serial0/0/1 is up, line protocol is up
  IPv6 is enabled, link-local address is FE80::21A:6DFF:FE37:A44E
  Global unicast address(es):
    2001:DB8:3C4D:1:21A:6DFF:FE37:A44E, subnet is 2001:DB8:3C4D:1::/64 [EUI]
  Joined group address(es):
    FF02::1
    FF02::2
    FF02::9
    FF02::1:FF37:A44E
  MTU is 1500 bytes
  ICMP error messages limited to one every 100 milliseconds
  ICMP redirects are enabled
  ND DAD is enabled, number of DAD attempts: 1
  ND reachable time is 30000 milliseconds
  Hosts use stateless autoconfig for addresses.
```

This got us some pretty good information too. But wait, the best is yet to come: the `debug ipv6 rip` command. This should be good:

```
R3#debug ipv6 rip
*May 24 18:31:11.959: RIPng: Sending multicast update on Serial0/0/1 for 1
*May 24 18:31:11.959:        src=FE80::21A:6DFF:FE37:A44E
*May 24 18:31:11.959:        dst=FF02::9 (Serial0/0/1)
*May 24 18:31:11.959:        sport=521, dport=521, length=32
*May 24 18:31:11.959:        command=2, version=1, mbz=0, #rte=1
*May 24 18:31:11.959:        tag=0, metric=1, prefix=2001:DB8:3C4D:1::/64
*May 24 18:40:44.079: %LINEPROTO-5-UPDOWN: Line protocol on Interface
   Serial0/0/0, changed state to down
*May 24 18:31:24.959: RIPng: response received from
   FE80::21A:2FFF:FE55:C9E8 on Serial0/0/1 for 1
```

```
*May 24 18:31:24.959:       src=FE80::21A:2FFF:FE55:C9E8 (Serial0/0/1)
*May 24 18:31:24.959:       dst=FF02::9
*May 24 18:31:24.959:       sport=521, dport=521, length=32
*May 24 18:31:24.959:       command=2, version=1, mbz=0, #rte=1
*May 24 18:31:24.959:       tag=0, metric=16,
   prefix=2001:DB8:3C4D:12::/64
*May 24 18:31:24.959: RIPng: 2001:DB8:3C4D:12::/64, path
   FE80::21A:2FFF:FE55:C9E8/Serial0/0/1 unreachable
*May 24 18:31:24.959: RIPng: 2001:DB8:3C4D:12::/64, expired, ttg is 120
*May 24 18:31:24.959: RIPng: Triggered update requested
*May 24 18:31:25.959: RIPng: generating triggered update for 1
*May 24 18:31:25.959: RIPng: Suppressed null multicast update on
   Serial0/0/1 for 1
```

Now this is interesting. You can see that the source and destination ports used are 521 (yes, I'm still using UDP) and that network/subnet 12 is unreachable. This is because the s0/0/0 interface of my Corp router has just decided to go bad. (I swear, writing this book is just like being at work!) Either way, you can see that RIPng still has some basic IPv4 RIP characteristics. Let's add OSPFv3 to the routers.

Verifying OSPFv3

Note the information in Table 10.8.

TABLE 10.8 Verifying IPv6 OSPF

Command	Meaning
`show ipv6 route`	Displays the IPv6 routing table on the router
`show ipv6 protocols`	Displays minimal routing protocol information
`show ipv6 ospf neighbor`	Displays the OSPF "neighborship" table
`debug ipv6 ospf packet`	Displays the events that occur if an update takes place
`debug ipv6 ospf hello`	Displays the updates between neighbor routers

I'll start as usual with the `show ipv6 route` command:

```
R3#sh ipv6 route
IPv6 Routing Table - 7 entries
```

```
O    2001:DB8:3C4D:11::/64 [110/65]
      via FE80::21A:2FFF:FE55:C9E8, Serial0/0/1
O    2001:DB8:3C4D:13::/64 [110/128]
      via FE80::21A:2FFF:FE55:C9E8, Serial0/0/1
O    2001:DB8:3C4D:14::/64 [110/128]
      via FE80::21A:2FFF:FE55:C9E8, Serial0/0/1
C    2001:DB8:3C4D:15::/64 [0/0]
      via ::, Serial0/0/1
L    2001:DB8:3C4D:15:21A:6DFF:FE37:A44E/128 [0/0]
      via ::, Serial0/0/1
L    FE80::/10 [0/0]
      via ::, Null0
L    FF00::/8 [0/0]
      via ::, Null0
R3#
```

Perfect. I see all the subnets (except 12, which is down because of that bad interface). Let's take a look at the `show ipv6 protocols` command:

```
R3#sh ipv6 protocols
IPv6 Routing Protocol is "connected"
IPv6 Routing Protocol is "static"
IPv6 Routing Protocol is "rip 1"
  Interfaces:
    Serial0/0/1
  Redistribution:
    None
IPv6 Routing Protocol is "ospf 1"
  Interfaces (Area 0):
    Serial0/0/1
  Redistribution:
    None
```

For the next command, I want to go back to the Corp router so can I see more connections: `show ipv6 ospf neighbor`:

```
Corp#sh ipv6 ospf neighbor
Neighbor ID     Pri   State    Dead Time   Interface ID  Interface
172.16.10.4       1   FULL/  - 00:00:36     6            Serial0/2/0
172.16.10.3       1   FULL/  - 00:00:33     16           Serial0/1/0
172.16.10.2       1   FULL/  - 00:00:30     6            Serial0/0/1
Corp#
```

Wait! I need to do the debugging commands. I'll use two of them: `debug ipv6 ospf packet` and `debug ipv6 ospf hello` (almost the same commands I used with IPv4):

```
Corp#debug ipv6 ospf packet
  OSPFv3 packet debugging is on
Corp#
*May 24 19:38:12.283: OSPFv3: rcv. v:3 t:1 l:40 rid:172.16.10.3
      aid:0.0.0.0 chk:E1D2 inst:0 from Serial0/1/0
Corp#
*May 24 19:38:15.103: OSPFv3: rcv. v:3 t:1 l:40 rid:172.16.10.4
      aid:0.0.0.0 chk:7EBB inst:0 from Serial0/2/0
Corp#
*May 24 19:38:18.875: OSPFv3: rcv. v:3 t:1 l:40 rid:172.16.10.2
      aid:0.0.0.0 chk:192D inst:0 from Serial0/0/1
Corp#
*May 24 19:38:22.283: OSPFv3: rcv. v:3 t:1 l:40 rid:172.16.10.3
      aid:0.0.0.0 chk:E1D2 inst:0 from Serial0/1/0
Corp#un all
All possible debugging has been turned off
Corp#debug ipv6 ospf hello
  OSPFv3 hello events debugging is on
Corp#
*May 24 19:38:32.283: OSPFv3: Rcv hello from 172.16.10.3 area 0 from
   Serial0/1/0 FE80::213:60FF:FE20:4E4C interface ID 16
*May 24 19:38:32.283: OSPFv3: End of hello processing
Corp#
*May 24 19:38:35.103: OSPFv3: Rcv hello from 172.16.10.4 area 0 from
   Serial0/2/0 FE80::21A:6DFF:FE37:A44E interface ID 6
*May 24 19:38:35.103: OSPFv3: End of hello processing
Corp#
*May 24 19:38:38.875: OSPFv3: Rcv hello from 172.16.10.2 area 0 from
   Serial0/0/1 FE80::21A:6DFF:FE64:9B2 interface ID 6
*May 24 19:38:38.875: OSPFv3: End of hello processing
Corp#un all
All possible debugging has been turned off
Corp#
```

Chapter 11

Wide Area Networks (WANs)

The Cisco IOS supports a ton of different wide area network (WAN) protocols that help you extend your local LANs to other LANs at remote sites. And I don't think I have to tell you how positively essential information exchange between disparate sites is these days—it's vital! But even so, it wouldn't exactly be cost effective or efficient to install your own cable and connect all of your company's remote locations yourself, now would it? A much better way to go about doing this is to simply lease the existing installations that service providers already have in place—and then save big time.

So it follows that I'm going to discuss the various types of connections, technologies, and devices used in accordance with WANs in this chapter. I'll also get into how to implement and configure High-Level Data-Link Control (HDLC), Point-to-Point Protocol (PPP), Point-to-Point Protocol over Ethernet (PPPoE), cable, DSL, and Frame Relay. I'll also introduce you to WAN security concepts, tunneling, and virtual private network basics.

Just so you know, I'm not going to cover every type of Cisco WAN support here—again, the focus of this book is to equip you with everything you need to successfully meet the CCNA objectives.

But first things first—let's begin with an exploration into WAN basics.

For up-to-the-minute updates for this chapter, check out `www.lammle.com` or `www.sybex.com/go/IOS`

Introduction to Wide Area Networks

So what, exactly, is it that makes something a *wide area network (WAN)* instead of a local area network (LAN)? Well, there's obviously the distance thing, but these days, wireless LANs can cover some serious turf. What about bandwidth? Well, here again, some really big pipes can be had for a price in many places, so that's not it either. So, what the heck is it then?

One of the main ways a WAN differs from a LAN is that while you generally own a LAN infrastructure, you usually lease WAN infrastructure from a service provider. To be honest, modern technologies even blur this definition, but it still fits neatly into the context of Cisco's exam objectives.

Anyway, I've already talked about the data link that you usually own (Ethernet), but now you're going to find out about the kind you usually don't own—the type most often leased from a service provider.

The key to understanding WAN technologies is to be familiar with the different WAN terms and connection types commonly used by service providers to join your networks together.

Defining WAN Terms

Before you run out and order a WAN service type from a provider, it would be a really good idea to understand the following terms that service providers typically use:

Customer premises equipment (CPE) Equipment that's owned by the subscriber and located on the subscriber's premises.

Demarcation point The precise spot where the service provider's responsibility ends and the CPE begins. It's generally a device in a telecommunications closet owned and installed by the telecommunications company (telco). It's your responsibility to add cable (extended demarc) from this box to the CPE, which is usually a connection to a CSU/DSU or ISDN interface.

Local loop Connects the demarc to the closest switching office, which is called a *central office*.

Central office (CO) Connects the customer's network to the provider's switching network. Good to know is that a CO is sometimes referred to as a *point of presence (POP)*.

Toll network A trunk line inside a WAN provider's network. This network is a collection of switches and facilities owned by the ISP.

Definitely familiarize yourself with these terms because they're crucial to understanding WAN technologies.

WAN Support

First, take a look at Table 11.1.

TABLE 11.1 Setting the Encapsulation on an Interface

Command	Meaning
`configure terminal`	Takes you to global configuration mode
`interface` *interface*	Chooses your interface to configure
`encapsulation` *encapsulation*	Sets the WAN encapsulation type

Basically, Cisco just supports HDLC, PPP, and Frame Relay on its serial interfaces, and you can see this with the `encapsulation ?` command from any serial interface (your output may vary depending on the IOS version you are running):

```
Corp#config t
Corp(config)#int s0/0/0
Corp(config-if)#encapsulation ?
  atm-dxi       ATM-DXI encapsulation
  frame-relay   Frame Relay networks
  hdlc          Serial HDLC synchronous
  lapb          LAPB (X.25 Level 2)
  ppp           Point-to-Point protocol
  smds          Switched Megabit Data Service (SMDS)
  x25           X.25
```

Understand that if I had other types of interfaces on my router, I would have other encapsulation options, such as ISDN or ADSL. And remember, you can't configure Ethernet or Token Ring encapsulation on a serial interface.

Next, I'm going to define the most prominently known WAN protocols used today: Frame Relay, ISDN, LAPB, LAPD, HDLC, PPP, PPPoE, cable, DSL, MPLS, and ATM. Just so you know, the only WAN protocols you'll usually find configured on a serial interface are HDLC, PPP, and Frame Relay, but who said we're stuck with using only serial interfaces for wide area connections?

Frame Relay A packet-switched technology that made its debut in the early 1990s, *Frame Relay* is a high-performance Data Link and Physical layer specification. It's pretty much a successor to X.25, except that much of the technology in X.25 that used to compensate for physical errors (noisy lines) has been eliminated. An upside to Frame Relay is that it can be more cost effective than point-to-point links; plus, it typically runs at speeds of 64Kbps up to 45Mbps (T3). Another Frame Relay benefit is that it provides features for dynamic bandwidth allocation and congestion control.

ISDN *Integrated Services Digital Network (ISDN)* is a set of digital services that transmit voice and data over existing phone lines. ISDN offers a cost-effective solution for remote users who need a higher-speed connection than analog dial-up links can give them, and it's also a good choice to use as a backup link for other types of links such as Frame Relay or T1 connections.

LAPB *Link Access Procedure, Balanced (LAPB)* was created to be a connection-oriented protocol at the Data Link layer for use with X.25, but it can also be used as a simple data link transport. A not-so-good characteristic of LAPB is that it tends to create a tremendous amount of overhead because of its strict timeout and windowing techniques.

LAPD *Link Access Procedure, D-Channel (LAPD)* is used with ISDN at the Data Link layer (layer 2) as a protocol for the D (signaling) channel. LAPD was derived from the Link Access Procedure, Balanced (LAPB) protocol and is designed primarily to satisfy the signaling requirements of ISDN basic access.

HDLC *High-Level Data-Link Control (HDLC)* was derived from Synchronous Data Link Control (SDLC), which was created by IBM as a Data Link connection protocol. HDLC works at the Data Link layer and creates very little overhead compared to LAPB.

It wasn't intended to encapsulate multiple Network layer protocols across the same link—the HDLC header doesn't contain any identification about the type of protocol being carried inside the HDLC encapsulation. Because of this, each vendor that uses HDLC has its own way of identifying the Network layer protocol, meaning each vendor's HDLC is proprietary with regard to its specific equipment.

PPP *Point-to-Point Protocol (PPP)* is a pretty famous, industry-standard protocol. Because all multiprotocol versions of HDLC are proprietary, PPP can be used to create point-to-point links between different vendors' equipment. It uses a Network Control Protocol field in the Data Link header to identify the Network layer protocol and allows authentication and multilink connections to be run over asynchronous and synchronous links.

PPPoE Point-to-Point Protocol over Ethernet encapsulates PPP frames in Ethernet frames and is usually used in conjunction with ADSL services. It gives you a lot of the familiar PPP features such as authentication, encryption, and compression, but there's a downside—it has a lower maximum transmission unit (MTU) than standard Ethernet does, and if your firewall isn't solidly configured, this little attribute can really give you some grief!

Still somewhat popular in the United States, PPPoE on Ethernet's main feature is that it adds a direct connection to Ethernet interfaces while providing DSL support as well. It's often used by many hosts on a shared Ethernet interface for opening PPP sessions to various destinations via at least one bridging modem.

Cable In a modern HFC network, typically 500 to 2,000 active data subscribers are connected to a certain cable network segment, all sharing the upstream and downstream bandwidth. (*Hybrid fiber-coaxial*, or HFC, is a telecommunications industry term for a network that incorporates both optical fiber and coaxial cable to create a broadband network.) The actual bandwidth for Internet service over a cable TV (CATV) line can be up to about 27Mbps on the download path to the subscriber, with about 2.5Mbps of bandwidth on the upload path. Typically users get an access speed from 256Kbps to 6Mbps. This data rate varies greatly throughout the United States.

DSL *Digital subscriber line* is a technology used by traditional telephone companies to deliver advanced services (high-speed data and sometimes video) over twisted-pair copper telephone wires. It typically has lower data carrying capacity than HFC networks, and data speeds can range by line lengths and quality. DSL is not a complete end-to-end solution but rather a Physical layer transmission technology like dial-up, cable, or wireless. DSL connections are deployed in the last mile of a local telephone network—the local loop. The connection is set up between a pair of modems on either end of a copper wire that is between the CPE and the DSLAM. A DSLAM is the device located at the provider's CO and concentrates connections from multiple DSL subscribers.

MPLS *MultiProtocol Label Switching (MPLS)* is a data-carrying mechanism that emulates some properties of a circuit-switched network over a packet-switched network. MPLS is a switching mechanism that imposes labels (numbers) to packets and then uses those labels to forward packets. The labels are assigned on the edge of the MPLS of the network, and forwarding inside the MPLS network is done solely based on labels. Labels usually correspond to a path to layer-3 destination addresses (equal to IP destination-based routing). MPLS was designed to support forwarding of protocols other than TCP/IP. Because of this, label switching within the network is performed the same regardless of the layer-3 protocol. In larger networks, the result of MPLS labeling is that only the edge routers perform a routing lookup. All the core routers forward packets based on the labels, which makes forwarding the packets through the service provider network faster. (Most companies are replacing their Frame Relay networks with MPLS today.)

ATM *Asynchronous Transfer Mode* (ATM) was created for time-sensitive traffic, providing simultaneous transmission of voice, video, and data. ATM uses cells that are a fixed 53 bytes long instead of packets. It also can use isochronous clocking (external clocking) to help the data move faster. Typically, if you are running Frame Relay today, you will be running Frame Relay over ATM.

High-Level Data-Link Control (HDLC) Protocol

HDLC is a popular ISO-standard, bit-oriented, Data Link layer protocol. It specifies an encapsulation method for data on synchronous serial data links using frame characters and checksums. HDLC is a point-to-point protocol used on leased lines. No authentication can be used with HDLC.

In *byte-oriented protocols*, control information is encoded using entire bytes. On the other hand, *bit-oriented protocols* use single bits to represent the control information. Some common bit-oriented protocols include SDLC, LLC, HDLC, TCP, and IP.

HDLC is the default encapsulation used by Cisco routers over synchronous serial links. And Cisco's HDLC is proprietary—it won't communicate with any other vendor's HDLC implementation. But don't give Cisco grief for it—*everyone's* HDLC implementation is proprietary. Figure 11.1 shows the Cisco HDLC format.

As shown in the figure, the reason that every vendor has a proprietary HDLC encapsulation method is that each vendor has a different way for the HDLC protocol to encapsulate multiple Network layer protocols. If the vendors didn't have a way for HDLC to communicate the different layer-3 protocols, then HDLC would be able to carry only one protocol. This proprietary header is placed in the data field of the HDLC encapsulation.

FIGURE 11.1 Cisco HDLC frame format

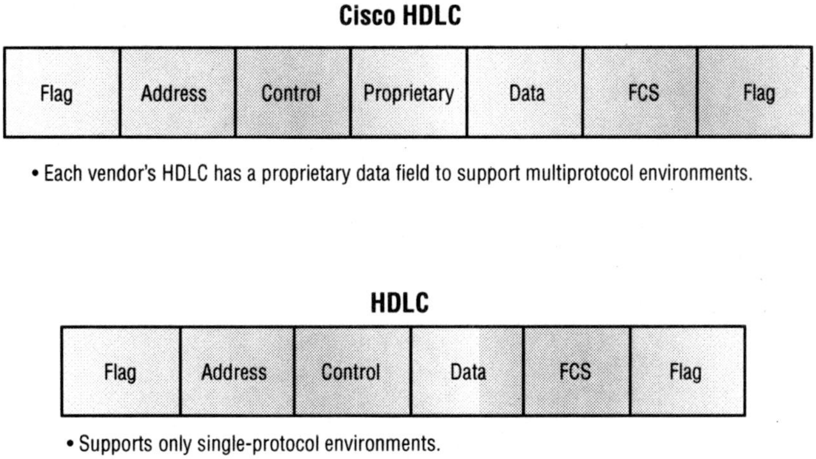

Cisco HDLC

Flag	Address	Control	Proprietary	Data	FCS	Flag

- Each vendor's HDLC has a proprietary data field to support multiprotocol environments.

HDLC

Flag	Address	Control	Data	FCS	Flag

- Supports only single-protocol environments.

Point-to-Point Protocol (PPP)

Let's spend a little time on PPP. Remember that it's a Data Link layer protocol that can be used over either asynchronous serial (dial-up) or synchronous serial (ISDN) media. It uses Link Control Protocol (LCP) to build and maintain data-link connections. Network Control Protocol (NCP) is used to allow multiple Network layer protocols (routed protocols) to be used on a point-to-point connection.

Since HDLC is the default serial encapsulation on Cisco serial links and it works great, why and when would you choose to use PPP? Well, the basic purpose of PPP is to transport layer-3 packets across a Data Link layer point-to-point link, and it's nonproprietary. So unless you have all Cisco routers, you need PPP on your serial interfaces—the HDLC encapsulation is Cisco proprietary, remember? Plus, since PPP can encapsulate several layer-3 routed protocols and provide authentication, dynamic addressing, and callback, PPP could be the best encapsulation solution for you instead of HDLC.

Figure 11.2 shows the protocol stack compared to the OSI reference model.

PPP contains four main components:

EIA/TIA-232-C, V.24, V.35, and ISDN A Physical layer international standard for serial communication.

HDLC A method for encapsulating datagrams over serial links.

FIGURE 11.2 PPP stack

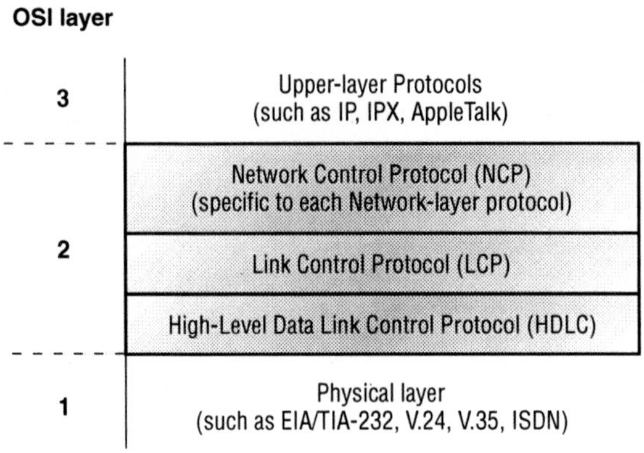

LCP A method of establishing, configuring, maintaining, and terminating the point-to-point connection.

NCP A method of establishing and configuring different Network layer protocols. NCP is designed to allow the simultaneous use of multiple Network layer protocols. Some examples of protocols here are Internet Protocol Control Protocol (IPCP) and Internetwork Packet Exchange Control Protocol (IPXCP).

Burn it into your mind that the PPP protocol stack is specified at the Physical and Data Link layers only. NCP is used to allow communication of multiple Network layer protocols by encapsulating the protocols across a PPP data link.

Configuring PPP on Cisco Routers

TABLE 11.2 Configuring PPP Encapsulation

Command	Meaning
`configure terminal`	Takes you to global configuration mode
`interface` *interface*	Chooses your interface to configure
`encapsulation ppp`	Sets the WAN encapsulation type to `ppp`

Configuring PPP encapsulation (see Table 11.2) on an interface is really pretty straightforward. To configure it from the CLI, follow these simple router commands:

```
Router#config t
Enter configuration commands, one per line. End with CNTL/Z.
```

```
Router(config)#int s0
Router(config-if)#encapsulation ppp
Router(config-if)#^Z
Router#
```

Of course, PPP encapsulation has to be enabled on both interfaces connected to a serial line in order to work, and several additional configuration options are available to you via the `help` command.

Configuring PPP Authentication

TABLE 11.3 PPP Authentication Commands

Command	Meaning
`configure terminal`	Takes you to global configuration mode
`hostname` *hostname*	Configures the hostname of the local router
`username` *username* `password` *password*	Configures the hostname of the remote router that your local router will authenticate with and the password that both routers will use for authentication
`ppp authentication` *chap|pap*	Configures the PPP authentication method under the physical interface to either chap or pap, typically just chap

After you configure your serial interface to support PPP encapsulation, you can configure authentication using PPP between routers (see Table 11.3). First, you need to set the hostname of the router, if it's not already. Then you set the username and password for the remote router that will be connecting to your router:

Here's an example:

```
Router#config t
Enter configuration commands, one per line. End with CNTL/Z.
Router(config)#hostname RouterA
RouterA(config)#username RouterB password cisco
```

When using the `hostname` command, remember that the username is the hostname of the remote router that's connecting to your router. And it's case sensitive too. Also, the password on both routers must be the same. It's a plain-text password that you can see with a `show run` command; you can encrypt the password by using the command `service password-encryption`.

You must have a username and password configured for each remote system to which you plan to connect. The remote routers must also be configured with usernames and passwords.

Now, after you've set the hostname, usernames, and passwords, choose the authentication type, either chap or pap:

```
RouterA#config t
Enter configuration commands, one per line. End with CNTL/Z.
RouterA(config)#int s0
RouterA(config-if)#ppp authentication chap pap
RouterA(config-if)#^Z
RouterA#
```

If both methods are configured on the same line, as shown here, then only the first method will be used during link negotiation—the second acts as a backup just in case the first method fails.

Verifying PPP Encapsulation

TABLE 11.4 Verifying PPP

Command	Meaning
show interface *interface*	Verifies the interface configuration and encapsulation set on each interface
debug ppp authentication	Displays the CHAP authentication process as it occurs between two routers in the network
show cdp neighbors detail	Displays a detailed output of all directly connected Cisco devices, which includes the IP addresses of each device and their hostname

Now that PPP encapsulation is enabled, I'll show you how to verify that it's up and running (see Table 11.4) connected with either a point-to-point serial or ISDN connection.

FIGURE 11.3 PPP authentication example

```
hostname Pod1R1
username Pod1R2 password cisco
 interface serial 0
  ip address 10.0.1.1 255.255.255.0
 encapsulation ppp
 ppp authentication chap
```

```
hostname Pod1R2
username Pod1R1 password cisco
 interface serial 0
  ip address 10.0.1.2 255.255.255.0
 encapsulation ppp
 ppp authentication chap
```

You can start verifying the configuration with the `show interface` command:

```
Pod1R1#sh int s0/0
Serial0/0 is up, line protocol is up
  Hardware is PowerQUICC Serial
  Internet address is 10.0.1.1/24
  MTU 1500 bytes, BW 1544 Kbit, DLY 20000 usec,
     reliability 239/255, txload 1/255, rxload 1/255
  Encapsulation PPP
  loopback not set
  Keepalive set (10 sec)
  LCP Open
  Open: IPCP, CDPCP
[output cut]
```

Notice that the sixth line lists encapsulation as PPP and the eighth line shows that the LCP is open. This means it has negotiated the session establishment and all is good! The ninth line tells you that NCP is listening for the protocols IP and CDP.

But what will you see if everything isn't perfect? I'm going to type in the configuration shown in Figure 11.4 and find out.

FIGURE 11.4 Failed PPP authentication

```
hostname Pod1R1
username Pod1R2 password Cisco
 interface serial 0
  ip address 10.0.1.1 255.255.255.0
 encapsulation ppp
 ppp authentication chap
```

```
hostname Pod1R2
username Pod1R1 password cisco
 interface serial 0
  ip address 10.0.1.2 255.255.255.0
 encapsulation ppp
 ppp authentication chap
```

What's wrong here? Take a look at the usernames and passwords. Do you see the problem now? That's right, the C is capitalized on the Pod1R2 username command found in the configuration of router Pod1R1. This is wrong because the usernames and passwords are case sensitive, remember? Let's take a look at the `show interface` command and see what happens:

```
Pod1R1#sh int s0/0
Serial0/0 is up, line protocol is down
  Hardware is PowerQUICC Serial
  Internet address is 10.0.1.1/24
  MTU 1500 bytes, BW 1544 Kbit, DLY 20000 usec,
     reliability 243/255, txload 1/255, rxload 1/255
```

```
Encapsulation PPP, loopback not set
Keepalive set (10 sec)
LCP Closed
Closed: IPCP, CDPCP
```

First, notice in the first line of output that `Serial0/0 is up, line protocol is down`. This is because there are no keepalives coming from the remote router. Second, notice that the LCP is closed because the authentication failed.

Debugging PPP Authentication

To display the CHAP authentication process as it occurs between two routers in the network, just use the command `debug ppp authentication`.

If your PPP encapsulation and authentication are set up correctly on both routers and if your usernames and passwords are all good, then the `debug ppp authentication` command will display output that looks like this:

```
d16h: Se0/0 PPP: Using default call direction
1d16h: Se0/0 PPP: Treating connection as a dedicated line
1d16h: Se0/0 CHAP: O CHALLENGE id 219 len 27 from "Pod1R1"
1d16h: Se0/0 CHAP: I CHALLENGE id 208 len 27 from "Pod1R2"
1d16h: Se0/0 CHAP: O RESPONSE id 208 len 27 from "Pod1R1"
1d16h: Se0/0 CHAP: I RESPONSE id 219 len 27 from "Pod1R2"
1d16h: Se0/0 CHAP: O SUCCESS id 219 len 4
1d16h: Se0/0 CHAP: I SUCCESS id 208 len 4
```

But if you have the username wrong, as we did previously in the PPP authentication failure example in Figure 11.4, the output would look something like this:

```
1d16h: Se0/0 PPP: Using default call direction
1d16h: Se0/0 PPP: Treating connection as a dedicated line
1d16h: %SYS-5-CONFIG_I: Configured from console by console
1d16h: Se0/0 CHAP: O CHALLENGE id 220 len 27 from "Pod1R1"
1d16h: Se0/0 CHAP: I CHALLENGE id 209 len 27 from "Pod1R2"
1d16h: Se0/0 CHAP: O RESPONSE id 209 len 27 from "Pod1R1"
1d16h: Se0/0 CHAP: I RESPONSE id 220 len 27 from "Pod1R2"
1d16h: Se0/0 CHAP: O FAILURE id 220 len 25 msg is "MD/DES compare failed"
```

PPP with CHAP authentication is a three-way authentication, and if the username and passwords are not configured exactly the way they should be, then the authentication will fail and the link will be down.

Mismatched WAN Encapsulations

If you have a point-to-point link but the encapsulations aren't the same, the link will never come up. Figure 11.5 shows one link with PPP and one with HDLC.

FIGURE 11.5 Mismatched WAN encapsulations

```
hostname Pod1R1
username Pod1R2 password Cisco
 interface serial 0
  ip address 10.0.1.1 255.255.255.0
  encapsulation ppp
```

```
hostname Pod1R2
username Pod1R1 password cisco
 interface serial 0
  ip address 10.0.1.2 255.255.255.0
  encapsulation HDLC
```

Look at router Pod1R1 in this output:

```
Pod1R1#sh int s0/0
Serial0/0 is up, line protocol is down
  Hardware is PowerQUICC Serial
  Internet address is 10.0.1.1/24
  MTU 1500 bytes, BW 1544 Kbit, DLY 20000 usec,
     reliability 254/255, txload 1/255, rxload 1/255
  Encapsulation PPP, loopback not set
  Keepalive set (10 sec)
  LCP REQsent
Closed: IPCP, CDPCP
```

The serial interface is down, and LCP is sending requests but will never receive any responses because router Pod1R2 is using the HDLC encapsulation. To fix this problem, you would have to go to router Pod1R2 and configure the PPP encapsulation on the serial interface. One more thing—even though the usernames are configured and they're wrong, it doesn't matter because the command `ppp authentication chap` isn't used under the serial interface configuration and the username command isn't relevant in this example.

Mismatched IP Addresses

A tricky problem to spot is if you have HDLC or PPP configured on your serial interface but your IP addresses are wrong. Things seem to be just fine because the interfaces will show that they are up. Take a look at Figure 11.6, and see whether you can see what I mean; the two routers are connected with different subnets—router Pod1R1 with 10.0.1.1/24 and router Pod1R2 with 10.2.1.2/24.

FIGURE 11.6 Mismatched IP addresses

```
hostname Pod1R1
username Pod1R2 password cisco
 interface serial 0
  ip address 10.0.1.1 255.255.255.0
  encapsulation ppp
  ppp authentication chap
```

```
hostname Pod1R2
username Pod1R1 password cisco
 interface serial 0
  ip address 10.2.1.2 255.255.255.0
  encapsulation ppp
  ppp authentication chap
```

This will never work. But as I said, take a look at the output:

```
Pod1R1#sh int s0/0
Serial0/0 is up, line protocol is up
  Hardware is PowerQUICC Serial
  Internet address is 10.0.1.1/24
  MTU 1500 bytes, BW 1544 Kbit, DLY 20000 usec,
     reliability 255/255, txload 1/255, rxload 1/255
  Encapsulation PPP, loopback not set
  Keepalive set (10 sec)
  LCP Open
  Open: IPCP, CDPCP
```

See that? The IP addresses between the routers are wrong, but the link looks like it's working fine. This is because PPP, like HDLC and Frame Relay, is a layer-2 WAN encapsulation and doesn't care about IP addresses at all. So yes, the link is up, but you can't use IP across this link since it's misconfigured.

To find and fix this problem, you can use the `show running-config` or `show interfaces` command on each router, or you can the `show cdp neighbors detail` command:

```
Pod1R1#sh cdp neighbors detail
-------------------------
Device ID: Pod1R2
Entry address(es):
  IP address: 10.2.1.2
```

You can view and verify the directly connected neighbor's IP address and then solve your problem.

Before we move onto Frame Relay, let's take a look at PPPoE.

PPPoE Configuration

Take a look at Table 11.5.

TABLE 11.5 PPPoE Configuration Commands

Command	Meaning
`interface` *interface*	Chooses your interface
`pppoe enable group`	Configures pppoe under a physical interface and allows you to enable a pppoe and group
`pppoe max-sessions`	Configures the amount of sessions allows on the interface at one time
`pppoe-client dial-pool-number` *number*	Uses a `dial-pool` number to attach the physical interface to a dialer interface

If you have a router with an interface that supports PPPoE and the router is connected to a DSL modem, you can configure the router to be a PPPoE client—well, assuming your ISP has provided you with the authentication information, that is.

Let's take a look at configuring a PPPoE client on a router. Here's what it looks like under the physical interface:

```
R1(config)#int f0/0
R1(config-if)#p?
pppoe  pppoe-client  priority-group
R1(config-if)#pppoe ?
  enable        Enable pppoe
  max-sessions  Maximum PPPOE sessions
R1(config-if)#pppoe enable ?
  group  attach a BBA group
  <cr>
R1(config-if)#pppoe enable group ?
  WORD    BBA Group name
  global  Attach global PPPoE group
R1(config-if)#pppoe enable group global
R1(config-if)#pppoe-client dial-pool-number ?
  <1-255>  Dialer pool number
R1(config-if)#pppoe-client dial-pool-number 1

!
interface FastEthernet4
```

```
 description $ETH-WAN$
 no ip address
 duplex auto
 speed auto
 pppoe enable group global
 pppoe-client dial-pool-number 1
!
```

After all that, there really are only two commands needed under the physical interface—the `pppoe enable` command and the `pppoe-client` command. And both of them reference the logical interface we haven't created yet.

To add a PPPoE connection to your router, you need to also create a dialer interface. This is a logical interface, and under it, I'm going to add the `ip address negotiated` command so a DHCP address can be received and configured on the interface. And by the way, if you're using private IP addresses between the DSL modem and your router, you can easily add a static IP address on this interface. Take a look:

```
!
interface Dialer0
 ip address negotiated
 ip mtu 1452
 encapsulation ppp
 dialer pool 1
 dialer-group 1
 ppp authentication chap callin
 ppp chap hostname Todd
 ppp chap password 0 lammle
!
```

Take special notice of how the logical interface associates itself to the physical interface with both the `dial pool 1` command and the `dialer-group 1` command.

Last, under the dialer interface, the PPP authentication is set using the `ppp authentication` and `ppp chap` commands. Using the CLI, I provided these commands at global configuration mode, but in this setup, I'll configure the command directly under the logical interface instead.

Although this is a pretty simple configuration, it works really well! Still, I'll show you how to configure PPPoE using the SDM in a bit.

Introduction to Frame Relay Technology

As a CCNA, you'll need to understand the basics of the Frame Relay technology and be able to configure it in simple scenarios. First, understand that Frame Relay is a packet-switched technology. From everything you've learned so far, just telling you this should make you immediately realize several things about it:

- You won't be using the `encapsulation hdlc` or `encapsulation ppp` command to configure it.
- Frame Relay doesn't work like a point-to-point leased line (although it can be made to look and act like one).
- Frame Relay is usually less expensive than leased lines are, but there are some sacrifices to make to get that savings.

So, why would you even consider using Frame Relay? Take a look at Figure 11.7 to get an idea of what a network looked like before Frame Relay.

FIGURE 11.7 Before Frame Relay

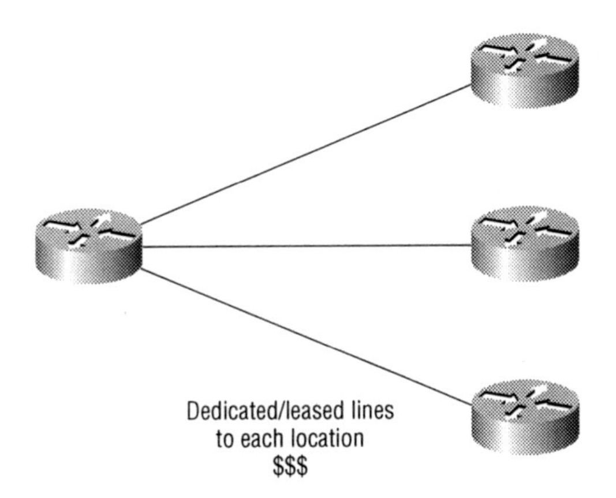

Now check out Figure 11.8. You can see that there's now only one connection between the Corporate router and the Frame Relay switch. That saves some major cash!

If, for example, you had to add seven remote sites to the corporate office and had only one free serial port on your router, it's Frame Relay to the rescue! Of course, I should probably mention that you now also have one single point of failure, which is not so good. But Frame Relay is used to save money, not to make a network more resilient.

Coming up, I'm going to cover the Frame Relay technology information you need to know about when studying the CCNA objectives.

FIGURE 11.8 After Frame Relay

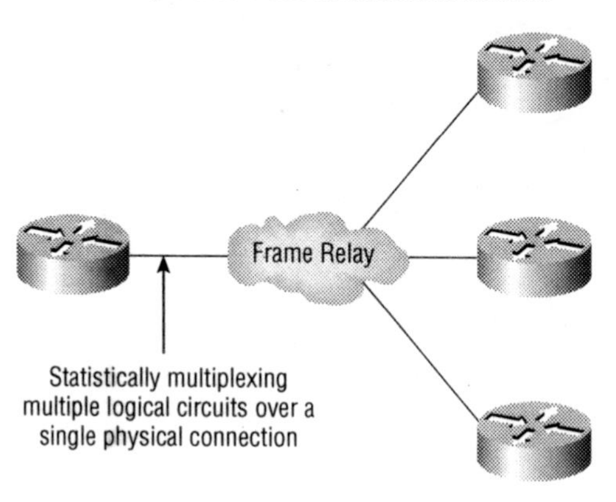

Frame Relay Encapsulation Types

Note the Frame-Relay encapsulation commands in Table 11.6.

TABLE 11.6 Frame-Relay Encapsulation Commands

Command	Meaning
`interface` *interface*	Chooses your interface
`encapsulation frame-relay`	Sets the Frame Relay encapsulation to Cisco
`encapsulation frame-relay ietf`	Sets the Frame Relay encapsulation to IETF

When configuring Frame Relay on Cisco routers, you need to specify it as an encapsulation on serial interfaces. As I said earlier, you can't use HDLC or PPP with Frame Relay. When you configure Frame Relay, you specify an encapsulation of Frame Relay (as shown in the following output). But unlike HDLC or PPP, with Frame Relay there are two encapsulation types: Cisco and Internet Engineering Task Force (IETF). The following router output shows these two different encapsulation methods when Frame Relay is chosen on your Cisco router:

```
RouterA(config)#int s0
RouterA(config-if)#encapsulation frame-relay ?
  ietf  Use RFC1490 encapsulation
  <cr>
```

The default encapsulation is Cisco unless you manually type in `ietf`, and Cisco is the type to use when connecting two Cisco devices. You'd opt for the IETF-type encapsulation if you needed to connect a Cisco device to a non-Cisco device with Frame Relay. Whichever you choose, make sure the Frame Relay encapsulation is the same on both ends.

Data Link Connection Identifiers (DLCIs)

Table 11.7 lists the command for configuring and verifying DLCI's.

TABLE 11.7 Configuring and Verifying Your DLCI's

Command	Meaning
`show frame-relay map`	Displays the Network layer–to–DLCI mappings.
`show frame-relay pvc`	Provides you with a list of all configured PVCs and DLCI numbers. It provides the status of each PVC connection and traffic statistics too.
`frame-relay interface-dlci` *dlci-number*	Configures the DLCI number for the interface.

Frame Relay PVCs are identified to DTE end devices by *Data Link Connection Identifiers (DLCIs)*. A Frame Relay service provider typically assigns DLCI values, which are used on Frame Relay interfaces to distinguish between different virtual circuits. Because many virtual circuits can be terminated on one multipoint Frame Relay interface, many DLCIs are often affiliated with it.

Let me explain—suppose you have a central HQ with three branch offices. If you were to connect each branch office to HQ using a T1, you would need three serial interfaces on your router at HQ, one for each T1. Simple, right? Well, suppose you use Frame Relay PVCs instead. You could have a T1 at each branch connected to a service provider and only a *single* T1 at HQ. There would be three PVCs on the single T1 at HQ, one going to each branch. And even though there's only a single interface and a single CSU/DSU, the three PVCs function as three separate circuits.

Before I continue, I want to define Inverse ARP (IARP) and discuss how it's used with DLCIs in a Frame Relay network. Yes, it is somewhat similar to ARP in that it maps a DLCI to an IP address—kind of like ARP does with MAC addresses to IP addresses. And even though you can't configure IARP, you can disable it. It runs on a Frame Relay router and maps the DLCI to an IP address for Frame Relay so it knows how to get to the Frame Relay switch. You can see IP-to-DLCI mappings with the `show frame-relay map` command.

But if you have a non-Cisco router living in your network and it doesn't support IARP, then you're stuck with having to statically provide IP-to-DLCI mappings with the `frame-relay map` command—something I'll demonstrate in a bit.

Let's talk about DLCIs a bit more. They're locally significant—global significance requires the entire network to use the LMI extensions that offer global significance. This is why you'll mostly find global DLCIs only in private networks.

To discover why DLCIs are considered locally significant, take a look at Figure 11.9. In the figure, DLCI 100 is considered locally significant to RouterA and identifies the circuit between RouterA and its ingress Frame Relay switch. DLCI 200 would identify the circuit between RouterB and its ingress Frame Relay switch.

FIGURE 11.9 DLCIs are local to your router

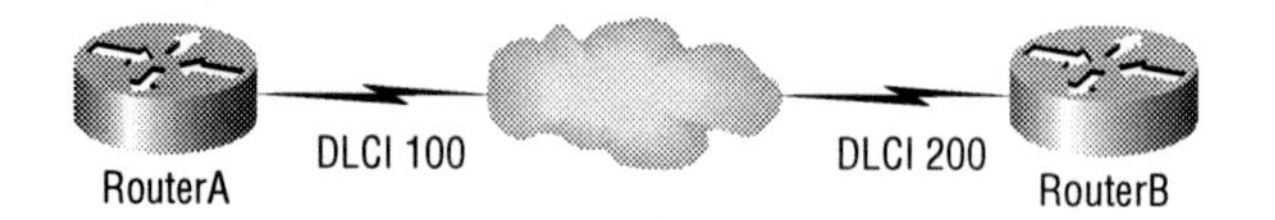

DLCI numbers that are used to identify a PVC are typically assigned by the provider and start at 16.

You configure a DLCI number to be applied to an interface like this:

```
RouterA(config-if)#frame-relay interface-dlci ?
  <16-1007> Define a DLCI as part of the current
            subinterface
RouterA(config-if)#frame-relay interface-dlci 16
```

DLCIs identify the logical circuit between the local router and a Frame Relay switch.

Local Management Interface (LMI)

Take a look at Table 11.8.

TABLE 11.8 Configuring the LMI

Command	Meaning
`frame-relay lmi-type` *type*	Sets the LMI type on the Frame Relay interface

Local Management Interface (LMI) is a signaling standard used between your router and the first Frame Relay switch to which it's connected. It allows for passing information about the operation and status of the virtual circuit between the provider's network and the DTE (your router). It communicates information about the following:

Keepalives These verify that data is flowing.

Multicasting This is an optional extension of the LMI specification that allows, for example, the efficient distribution of routing information and ARP requests over a Frame Relay network. Multicasting uses the reserved DLCIs from 1019 through 1022.

Global addressing This provides global significance to DLCIs, allowing the Frame Relay cloud to work exactly like a LAN.

Status of virtual circuits This provides DLCI status. The status inquiries and messages are used as keepalives when there is no regular LMI traffic to send.

But remember, LMI is not communication between your routers; it's communication between your router and the nearest Frame Relay switch. So, it's entirely possible that the router on one end of a PVC is actively receiving LMI while the router on the other end of the PVC is not. And of course, PVCs won't work with one end down. (I say this to clarify the local nature of LMI communications.)

There are three different types of LMI message formats: Cisco, ANSI, and Q.933A. The different kinds in use depend on both the type and the configuration of the telco's switching gear, so it's imperative that you configure your router for the correct format, which should be provided by the telco.

On Cisco equipment, the default type is, surprise, Cisco, but you still might have to change to ANSI or Q.933A depending on what your service provider tells you. The three different LMI types are shown in the following router output:

```
RouterA(config-if)#frame-relay lmi-type ?
  cisco
  ansi
  q933a
```

As shown in the output, all three standard LMI signaling formats are supported. Here's a description of each:

Cisco LMI was defined by the Gang of Four (default). The Local Management Interface (LMI) was developed in 1990 by Cisco Systems, StrataCom, Northern Telecom, and Digital Equipment Corporation and became known as the Gang-of-Four LMI, or Cisco LMI.

ANSI Annex D is included with ANSI standard T1.617.

ITU-T (Q.933A) Annex A is included in the ITU-T standard and defined by using the Q.933a command keyword.

Routers receive LMI information from the service provider's Frame Relay switch on a frame-encapsulated interface and update the virtual circuit status to one of three different states:

Active state Everything is up, and routers can exchange information.

Inactive state The router's interface is up and working with a connection to the switching office, but the remote router isn't up.

Deleted state No LMI information is being received on the interface from the switch, which could be because of a mapping problem or a line failure.

Troubleshooting Using Frame Relay Congestion Control

TABLE 11.9 Verifying your PVC

Command	Meaning
show frame-relay pvc	Provides you with a list of all configured PVCs and DLCI numbers. It provides the status of each PVC connection and traffic statistics too.

Now let's say all your users are whining that their Frame Relay connection to the corporate site is super slow. Because you strongly suspect that the link is overloaded, you verify (see Table 11.9) the Frame Relay congestion control information with the `show frame-relay pvc` command and get this:

```
RouterA#sh frame-relay pvc

PVC Statistics for interface Serial0/0 (Frame Relay DTE)

              Active     Inactive      Deleted       Static
  Local          1           0            0             0
  Switched       0           0            0             0
  Unused         0           0            0             0

DLCI = 100, DLCI USAGE = LOCAL, PVC STATUS = ACTIVE, INTERFACE = Serial0/0
  input pkts 1300          output pkts 1270        in bytes 21212000
  out bytes 21802000       dropped pkts 4          in pkts dropped 147
  out pkts dropped 0       out bytes dropped 0       in FECN pkts 147
   in BECN pkts 192        out FECN pkts 147
  out BECN pkts 259        in DE pkts 0              out DE pkts 214
  out bcast pkts 0         out bcast bytes 0
  pvc create time 00:00:06, last time pvc status changed 00:00:06
Pod1R1#
```

What you want to look for is the `in BECN pkts 192` output because this is what's telling the local router that traffic sent to the corporate site is experiencing congestion. BECN means that the path that a frame took to "return" to you is congested.

Frame Relay Implementation and Monitoring

TABLE 11.10 Implementing Frame-Relay

Command	Meaning
`configure terminal`	Takes you to global configuration mode
`interface` *interface*	Chooses your interface
`encapsulation frame-relay`	Sets the Frame Relay encapsulation to Cisco
`encapsulation frame-relay ietf`	Sets the Frame Relay encapsulation to IETF
`ip address` *address* `mask`	Sets the IP address and mask for the Frame Relay interface
`frame-relay lmi-type` *type*	Sets the LMI type for the Frame Relay interface
`frame-relay interferface-dlci` *dlci-number*	Configures the DLCI number for the interface

As I've said, there are a ton of Frame Relay commands and configuration options (see Table 11.10), but I'm going to zero in on the ones you really need to know when studying for the CCNA exam objectives. I'm going to start with one of the simplest configuration options—two routers with a single PVC between them. Next, I'll show you a more complex configuration using subinterfaces and demonstrate some of the monitoring commands available to verify the configuration.

Single Interface

Let's get started by looking at a simple example. Say that you just want to connect two routers with a single PVC. Here's how that configuration would look:

```
RouterA#config t
Enter configuration commands, one per line.  End with CNTL/Z.
RouterA(config)#int s0/0
RouterA(config-if)#encapsulation frame-relay
RouterA(config-if)#ip address 172.16.20.1 255.255.255.0
RouterA(config-if)#frame-relay lmi-type ansi
RouterA(config-if)#frame-relay interface-dlci 101
RouterA(config-if)#^Z
RouterA#
```

The first step is to specify the encapsulation as Frame Relay. Notice that since I didn't specify a particular encapsulation type—either Cisco or IETF—the Cisco default type was used. If the other router were non-Cisco, I would've specified IETF. Next, I assigned an IP address to the interface and then specified the LMI type of ANSI (the default being Cisco) based on information provided by the telecommunications provider. Finally, I added the DLCI of 101, which indicates the PVC I want to use (again, given to me by my ISP) and assumes there's only one PVC on this physical interface.

That's all there is to it—if both sides are configured correctly, the circuit will come up.

Check out Hands-on Lab 14.3 in the *Sybex CCNA 640-802 Study Guide* for a complete example of this type of configuration, including instructions on creating your own Frame Relay switch from a router.

Subinterfaces

TABLE 11.11 Subinterface Commands

Command	Meaning
`interface` *interface*	Chooses the interface you are connecting Frame Relay to
`encapsulation frame-relay`	Sets the Frame Relay encapsulation to Cisco
`encapsulation frame-relay ietf`	Sets the Frame Relay encapsulation to IETF
`interface` *interface.subinterface_number* `point-to-point`	Creates a point-to-point subinterface
`interface` *interface.subinteface_number* `multipoint`	Creates a multipoint subinterface

You probably know by now that you can have multiple virtual circuits on a single serial interface and yet treat each as a separate interface—I mentioned this earlier. You can make this happen by creating *subinterfaces* (see Table 11.11). Think of a subinterface as a logical interface defined by the IOS software. Several subinterfaces will share a single hardware interface, yet for configuration purposes they operate as if they were separate physical interfaces, something known as *multiplexing*.

To configure a router in a Frame Relay network so it will avoid split horizon issues by not permitting routing updates, just configure a separate subinterface for each PVC with a unique DLCI and subnet assigned to the subinterface.

You define subinterfaces using a command like `int s0.subinterface number`. First, you have to set the encapsulation on the physical serial interface, and then you can define the subinterfaces—generally one subinterface per PVC. Here's an example:

```
RouterA(config)#int s0
RouterA(config-if)#encapsulation frame-relay
RouterA(config-if)#int s0.?
  <0-4294967295>  Serial interface number
RouterA(config-if)#int s0.16 ?
  multipoint      Treat as a multipoint link
  point-to-point  Treat as a point-to-point link
RouterA(config-if)#int s0.16 point-to-point
```

You can define a serious amount of subinterfaces on any given physical interface, but keep in mind that there are only about 1,000 available DLCIs. In the preceding example, I chose to use subinterface 16 because that represents the DLCI number assigned to that PVC by the carrier. There are two types of subinterfaces:

Point-to-point Used when a single virtual circuit connects one router to another. Each point-to-point subinterface requires its own subnet.

Multipoint This is when the router is the center of a star of virtual circuits that are using a single subnet for all routers' serial interfaces connected to the frame switch. You'll usually find this implemented with the hub router in this mode and the spoke routers in physical interface (always point-to-point) or point-to-point subinterface mode.

Monitoring Frame Relay

Take a look at Table 11.12.

TABLE 11.12 Frame-Relay Verification Commands

Command	Meaning
`show frame-relay ?`	Displays all Frame Relay show commands.
`show frame-relay lmi`	Provides the LMI traffic statistics exchanged between the local router and the Frame Relay switch.
`show frame-relay pvc`	Provides you with a list of all configured PVCs and DLCI numbers. It provides the status of each PVC connection and traffic statistics too.
`show interface interface`	Displays interface information about the encapsulation, as well as layer-2 and layer-3 information. It also displays line, protocol, DLCI, and LMI information.
`show frame-relay map`	Displays the Network layer–to–DLCI mappings.
`debug frame-relay lmi`	Provides information to help you determine whether the router and switch are exchanging the correct LMI information.

Several commands are used frequently to check the status of your interfaces and PVCs once you have Frame Relay encapsulation set up and running. To list them, use the `show frame ?` command, as shown here:

```
RouterA>sho frame ?
end-to-end      Frame-relay end-to-end VC information
fragment        show frame relay fragmentation information
ip              show frame relay IP statistics
lapf            show frame relay lapf status/statistics
lmi             show frame relay lmi statistics
map             Frame-Relay map table
pvc             show frame relay pvc statistics
qos-autosense   show frame relay qos-autosense information
route           show frame relay route
svc             show frame relay SVC stuff
traffic         Frame-Relay protocol statistics
vofr            Show frame-relay VoFR statistics
```

The most common parameters that you view with the `show frame-relay` command are `lmi`, `pvc`, and `map`.

Now, let's take a look at the most frequently used commands and the information they provide.

The *show frame-relay lmi* Command

The `show frame-relay lmi` command will give you the LMI traffic statistics exchanged between the local router and the Frame Relay switch. Here's an example:

```
Router#sh frame lmi

LMI Statistics for interface Serial0 (Frame Relay DTE)
LMI TYPE = CISCO
  Invalid Unnumbered info 0       Invalid Prot Disc 0
  Invalid dummy Call Ref 0        Invalid Msg Type 0
  Invalid Status Message 0        Invalid Lock Shift 0
  Invalid Information ID 0        Invalid Report IE Len 0
  Invalid Report Request 0        Invalid Keep IE Len 0
  Num Status Enq. Sent 0          Num Status msgs Rcvd 0
  Num Update Status Rcvd 0        Num Status Timeouts 0
Router#
```

The router output from the `show frame-relay lmi` command shows you any LMI errors, plus the LMI type.

The *show frame pvc* Command

The show frame pvc command will present you with a list of all configured PVCs and DLCI numbers. It provides the status of each PVC connection and traffic statistics too. It will also give you the number of BECN and FECN packets received on the router per PVC.

Here is an example:

```
RouterA#sho frame pvc

PVC Statistics for interface Serial0 (Frame Relay DTE)

DLCI = 16,DLCI USAGE = LOCAL,PVC STATUS =ACTIVE,
INTERFACE = Serial0.1
 input pkts 50977876    output pkts 41822892
  in bytes 3137403144
 out bytes 3408047602   dropped pkts 5
  in FECN pkts 0
 in BECN pkts 0      out FECN pkts 0      out BECN pkts 0
 in DE pkts 9393     out DE pkts 0
 pvc create time 7w3d, last time pvc status changed 7w3d

DLCI = 18,DLCI USAGE =LOCAL,PVC STATUS =ACTIVE,
INTERFACE = Serial0.3
 input pkts 30572401   output pkts 31139837
  in bytes 1797291100
 out bytes 3227181474   dropped pkts 5
  in FECN pkts 0
 in BECN pkts 0      out FECN pkts 0      out BECN pkts 0
 in DE pkts 28      out DE pkts 0
 pvc create time 7w3d, last time pvc status changed 7w3d
```

If you want to see information only about PVC 16, you can type the command **show frame-relay pvc 16**.

The *show interface* Command

You can use the show interface command to check for LMI traffic. The show interface command displays information about the encapsulation, as well as layer-2 and layer-3 information. It also displays line, protocol, DLCI, and LMI information. Check it out:

```
RouterA#sho int s0
Serial0 is up, line protocol is up
 Hardware is HD64570
 MTU 1500 bytes, BW 1544 Kbit, DLY 20000 usec, rely
  255/255, load 2/255
```

```
Encapsulation FRAME-RELAY, loopback not set, keepalive
 set (10 sec)
LMI enq sent 451751,LMI stat recvd 451750,LMI upd recvd
 164,DTE LMI up
LMI enq recvd 0, LMI stat sent 0, LMI upd sent 0
LMI DLCI 1023 LMI type is CISCO frame relay DTE
Broadcast queue 0/64, broadcasts sent/dropped 0/0,
 interface broadcasts 839294
```

The previous `LMI DLCI` is used to define the type of LMI being used. If it happens to be 1023, it's the default LMI type of Cisco. If `LMI DLCI` is zero, then it's the ANSI LMI type (Q.933A uses 0 as well). If `LMI DLCI` is anything other than 0 or 1023, it's a 911—call your provider; they've got major issues!

The *show frame map* Command

The `show frame map` command displays the Network layer–to–DLCI mappings. Here's how that looks:

```
RouterB#show frame map
Serial0 (up): ipx 20.0007.7842.3575 dlci 16(0x10,0x400),
              dynamic, broadcast,, status defined, active
Serial0 (up): ip 172.16.20.1 dlci 16(0x10,0x400),
              dynamic, broadcast,, status defined, active
Serial1 (up): ipx 40.0007.7842.153a dlci 17(0x11,0x410),
              dynamic, broadcast,, status defined, active
Serial1 (up): ip 172.16.40.2 dlci 17(0x11,0x410),
              dynamic, broadcast,, status defined, active
```

Notice that the serial interfaces have two mappings—one for IP and one for IPX. Also important is that the Network layer addresses were resolved with the dynamic protocol Inverse ARP (IARP). After the DLCI number is listed, you can see some numbers in parentheses. The first one is 0x10, which is the hex equivalent for the DLCI number 16, used on serial 0. And the 0x11 is the hex for DLCI 17 used on serial 1. The second numbers, 0x400 and 0x410, are the DLCI numbers configured in the Frame Relay frame. They're different because of the way the bits are spread out in the frame.

The *debug frame lmi* Command

The `debug frame lmi` command will show output on the router consoles by default (as with any `debug` command). The information this command gives you will enable you to verify and troubleshoot the Frame Relay connection by helping you determine whether the router and switch are exchanging the correct LMI information. Here's an example:

```
Router#debug frame-relay lmi
Serial3/1(in): Status, myseq 214
RT IE 1, length 1, type 0
```

```
KA IE 3, length 2, yourseq 214, myseq 214
PVC IE 0x7 , length 0x6 , dlci 130, status 0x2 , bw 0
Serial3/1(out): StEnq, myseq 215, yourseen 214, DTE up
datagramstart = 0x1959DF4, datagramsize = 13
FR encap = 0xFCF10309
00 75 01 01 01 03 02 D7 D6

Serial3/1(in): Status, myseq 215
RT IE 1, length 1, type 1
KA IE 3, length 2, yourseq 215, myseq 215
Serial3/1(out): StEnq, myseq 216, yourseen 215, DTE up
datagramstart = 0x1959DF4, datagramsize = 13
FR encap = 0xFCF10309
00 75 01 01 01 03 02 D8 D7
```

Troubleshooting Frame Relay Networks

Note the commands listed in Table 11.13.

TABLE 11.13 Verifying the Frame-Relay Encapsulation

Command	Meaning
`configure terminal`	Takes you to global configuration mode
`encapsulation frame-relay`	Sets your Frame Relay interface encapsulation to Cisco
`encapsulation frame-relay ietf`	Sets your Frame Relay interface encapsulation to IETF

Troubleshooting Frame Relay networks isn't any harder than troubleshooting any other type of network as long as you know what to look for, which is what I'm going to cover now. We'll go over some basic problems that commonly occur in Frame Relay configuration and how to solve them.

First on the list are serial encapsulation problems. As you learned recently, there are two Frame Relay encapsulations: Cisco and IETF. Cisco is the default, and it means you have a Cisco router on each end of the Frame Relay network. If you don't have a Cisco router on the remote end of your Frame Relay network, then you need to run the IETF encapsulation, as shown here:

```
RouterA(config)#int s0
RouterA(config-if)#encapsulation frame-relay ?
  ietf  Use RFC1490 encapsulation
  <cr>
RouterA(config-if)#encapsulation frame-relay ietf
```

Once you verify that you're using the correct encapsulation, you then need to check out your Frame Relay mappings. For example, take a look at Figure 11.10.

FIGURE 11.10 Frame Relay mappings

```
RouterA#show running-config
interface s0/0
ip address 172.16.100.2 255.255.0.0
encapsulation frame-relay
frame-relay map ip 172.16.100.1 200 broadcast
```

So why can't RouterA talk to RouterB across the Frame Relay network? To find that out, take a close look at the `frame-relay map` statement. See the problem now? You cannot use a remote DLCI to communicate to the Frame Relay switch; you must use *your* DLCI number! The mapping should have included DLCI 100 instead of DLCI 200.

Now that you know how to ensure that you have the correct Frame Relay encapsulation and that DLCIs are only locally significant, let's look into some routing protocol problems typically associated with Frame Relay. See whether you can find a problem with the two configurations in Figure 11.11.

FIGURE 11.11 Frame Relay routing problems

```
RouterA#show running-config
interface s0/0
ip address 172.16.100.2 255.255.0.0
encapsulation frame-relay
frame-relay map ip 172.16.100.1 100
router rip
        network 172.16.0.0
```

```
RouterB#show running-config
interface s0/0
ip address 172.16.100.1 255.255.0.0
encapsulation frame-relay
frame-relay map ip 172.16.100.2 200
router rip
        network 172.16.0.0
```

Hmmmm, well, the configs look pretty good. Actually, they look great, so what's the problem? Well, remember that Frame Relay is a nonbroadcast multiaccess (NBMA) network by default, meaning that it doesn't send any broadcasts across the PVC. So, because the mapping statements do not have the `broadcast` argument at the end of the line, broadcasts, like RIP updates, won't be sent across the PVC.

Chapter 12

Cisco's Security Device Manager (SDM)

In this chapter, I'll first show you how to log in using SDM by configuring the router through the CLI. I'll then show you how to set the router's hostname, banner, and enable secret password and then assign a DHCP pool on a router and an IP address to an interface.

And if it all goes well, after this chapter, you'll find that SDM will turn out to be much more of a good thing because it will prove to be so much more helpful to you when you're reading the rest of this chapter about managing the IOS; basic IP routing; and configuring RIP, RIPv2, EIGRP, and OSPF.

Configuring Your Router to Be Set Up Through the SDM

All you need in order to follow along in this chapter is a supported ISR router (1800/2800, and so on); you can download the latest version of SDM complete with instructions for installing it on your computer and your router from `www.cisco.com/pcgi-bin/tablebuild.pl/sdm`.

To download this software, you need a Cisco Connection Online (CCO) login. However, this is free and takes only a minute or less to set up. Go to `www.cisco.com`, and click Register in the top-right corner. Fill in the short form, and add the username and password you want to use; then you'll be able to download the SDM and the SDM demo.

From this site, not only can you install the SDM on your computer to help the SDM pages load faster when connecting to your router, but you can also enable the use of the Cisco SDM demo.

You need to know this before you start, though—to set up your host to log in using the SDM, you have to make sure your router is configured first. If you have deleted your configurations and reloaded the router, you'll have to start from scratch. But doing that really isn't all that hard (see Table 12.1 for the commands you'll need). You can just choose a LAN interface of the router and then connect a host directly to the router using a crossover cable—not so bad!

TABLE 12.1 Configuring Your Router for SDM

Command	Meaning
`enable`	Places your console connection into privileged mode

TABLE 12.1 Configuring Your Router for SDM *(continued)*

Command	Meaning
`configure terminal`	Places your connection into global configuration mode
`interface` *interface*	Chooses an interface to configure
`no shutdown`	Enables an interface
`ping`	Tests connectivity from one host to another

Here is what the CLI would look like if you connected to a router through the console port after a router had been erased and rebooted:

```
Would you like to enter the initial configuration dialog? [yes/no]: n
Press RETURN to get started!
Router>en
Router#config t
Enter configuration commands, one per line.  End with CNTL/Z.
Router(config)#int f0/0
Router(config-if)#ip address 1.1.1.1 255.255.255.0
Router(config-if)#no shut
Router(config-if)#do ping 1.1.1.2
Type escape sequence to abort.
Sending 5, 100-byte ICMP Echos to 1.1.1.2, timeout is 2 seconds:
!!!!!
Success rate is 100 percent (5/5), round-trip min/avg/max = 1/1/4 ms
```

So, what's this all about? In the preceding configuration, I configured the FastEthernet interface with an IP address and enabled it with the `no shutdown` command. I then tested my connection by pinging my directly connected host from the router prompt. (This would be a minimum configuration and allow you to connect via SDM.) From here, you just open a browser (with pop-ups enabled), type **http://1.1.1.1**, and follow the easy prompts once connected.

It's different if you want to set the router to use HTTPS, which allows you access into privileged mode upon connection (meaning we're setting the router to the original default configuration). And you need to add a few more commands (see Table 12.2).

TABLE 12.2 Router SDM Configuration Options

Command	Meaning
`(config)#ip http server`	Allows an HTTP host to connect to your router
`(config)#ip http secure-server`	Generates the secure keysD

TABLE 12.2 Router SDM Configuration Options *(continued)*

Command	Meaning
(config)#ip http authentication local	Tells the router the keys and password will be found locally on the router
(config)#username name privilege 0-15password password	Sets the username, privilege level (15 is highest), and password
(config)#Line console 0	Chooses the console line
(config-line)#Login local	Tells the router to use the local information for login found under the console line
(config-line)#Exit	Goes back one level
(config)#Line vty first_line_number last_line_number	Chooses the VTY lines to configure
(config-line)#Privledge level 0-15	Sets the privilege level
(config-line)#Login local	Tells the router to use the local information for login found under the VTY lines
(config-line)#Transport input telnet ssh	Tells the router that it can use both Telnet and SSH for connectivity

First, enable the HTTP/HTTPS server (your router won't support HTTPS if it doesn't have the advanced services IOS):

```
Router(config)#ip http server
Router(config)#ip http secure-server
% Generating 1024 bit RSA keys, keys will be non-exportable...[OK]
Router(config)#ip http authentication local
```

Second, create a user account using privilege level 15 (the highest level):

```
Router(config)#username cisco privilege ?
  <0-15>  User privilege level

Router(config)#username cisco privilege 15 password ?
  0      Specifies an UNENCRYPTED password will follow
  7      Specifies a HIDDEN password will follow
  LINE   The UNENCRYPTED (cleartext) user password
Router(config)#username cisco privilege 15 password 0 cisco
```

Last, configure the console, SSH, and Telnet to provide local login authentication at privilege level access:

```
Router(config)#line console 0
Router(config-line)#login local
Router(config-line)#exit
Router(config)#line vty 0 ?
  <1-1180>  Last Line number
  <cr>
Router(config)#line vty 0 1180
Router(config-line)#privilege level 15
Router(config-line)#login local
Router(config-line)#transport input telnet ssh
Router(config-line)#^Z
```

Voilà! Now let's connect to my 2811 using HTTPS!

As soon as I connected via `https://1.1.1.1`, I received a security alert message.

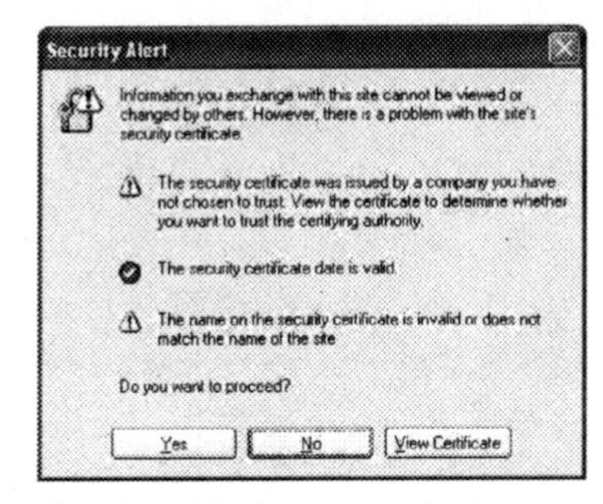

I was then prompted to log in with the username/password I created. SDM started loading and told me to hold on, which means it needs a bit of time to load another window. *Do not* close this window.

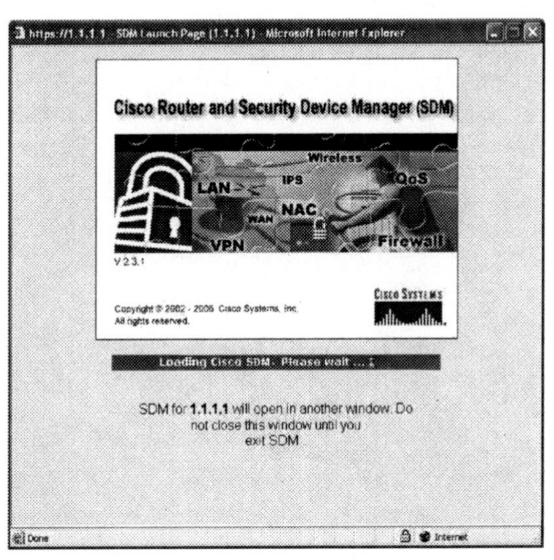

The certificate I created with the `ip http-secure-server` command was loaded onto the router. I chose to click Always Trust Content from this Publisher and then clicked Yes.

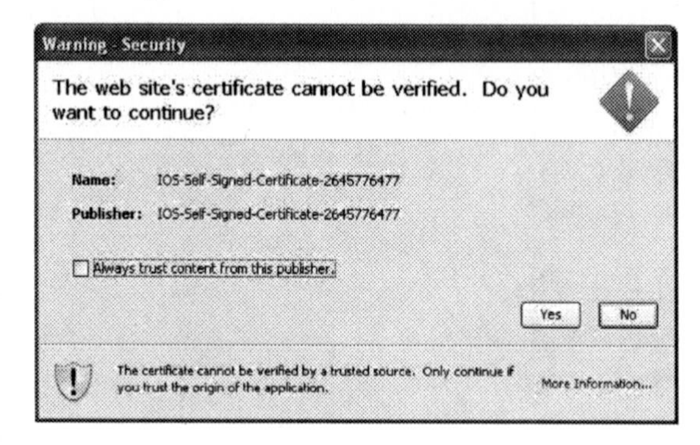

Of course, the certificate would not match any site name, so I then had to verify that I wanted to run it.

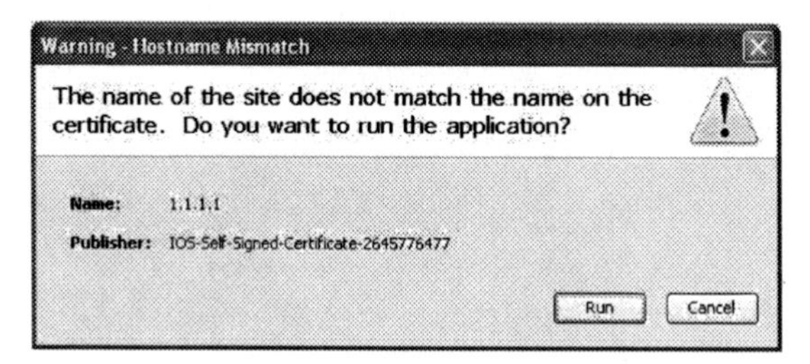

I then had to log in again and then wait for SDM to load, during which time the router had me change my default username and password.

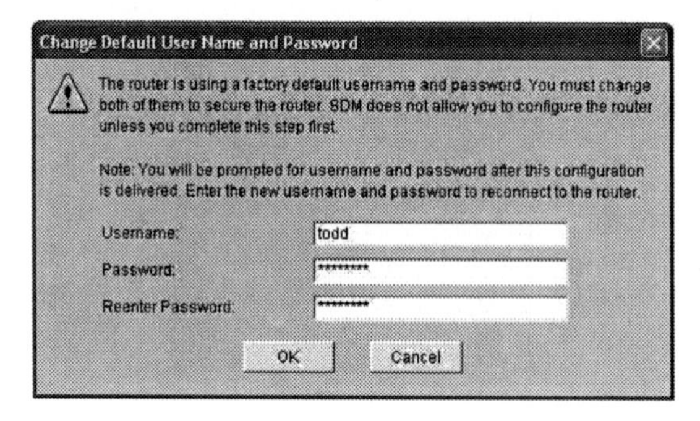

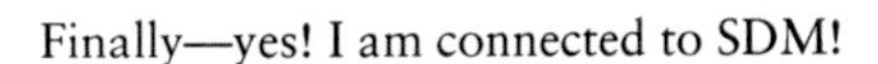

Finally—yes! I am connected to SDM!

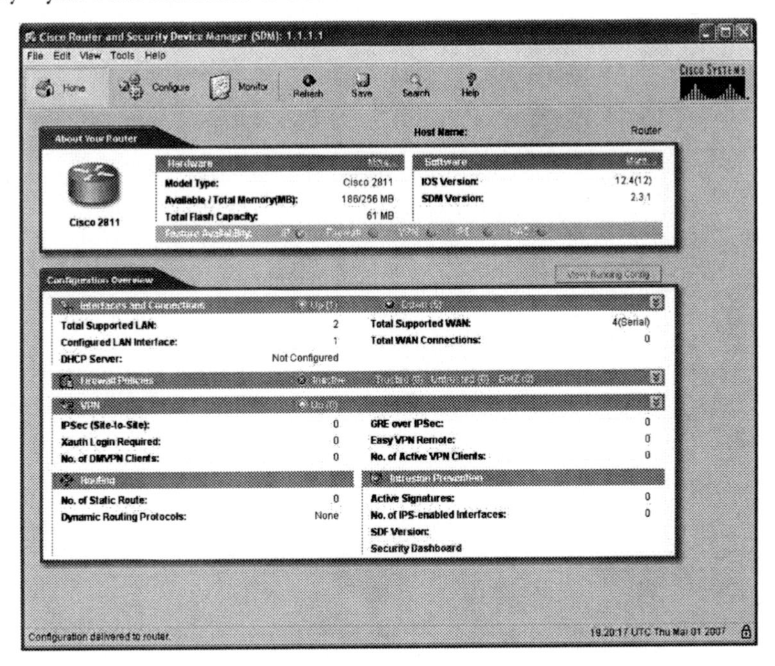

After clicking the Configure button at the top of the page, I chose to go step by step through interface configuration by first choosing the type of interface I wanted to configure and then clicking the Create New Connection button at the bottom of the page. This opens the LAN Wizard or WAN Wizard, depending on which interface you choose to configure.

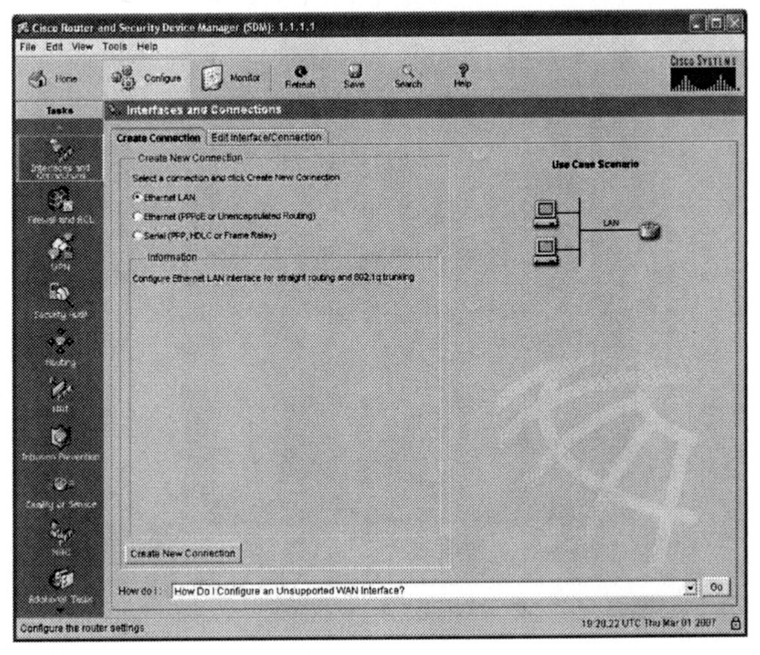

By clicking the Edit Interface/Connection tab, you get to see your interface status.

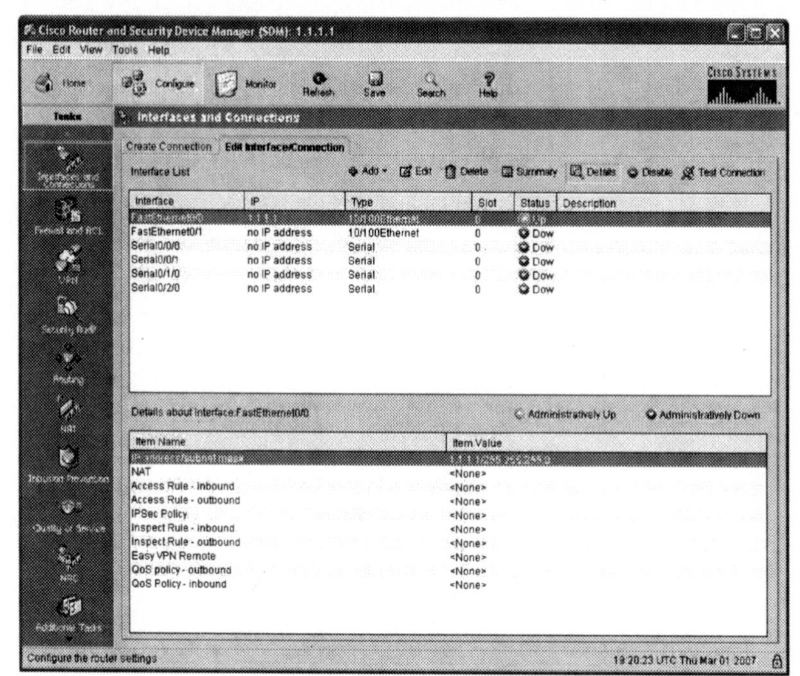

That's not all—just double-click an interface to edit it. (You can do this only after you've gone through the LAN Wizard or WAN Wizard and configured the interface.)

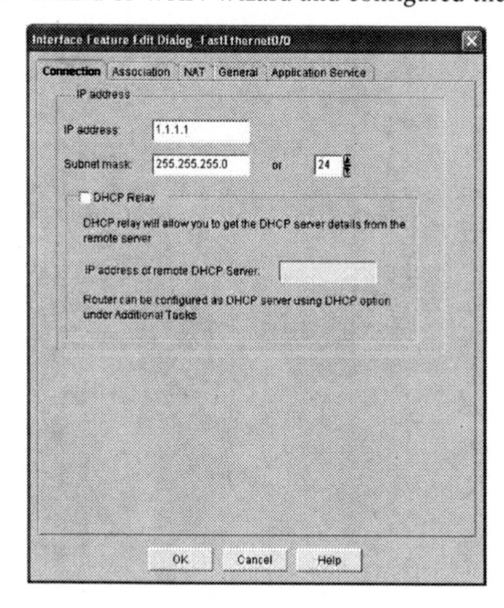

Look down at the bottom-left portion of the wizard page, and click the Additional Tasks button. From there, just click the Router Properties icon.

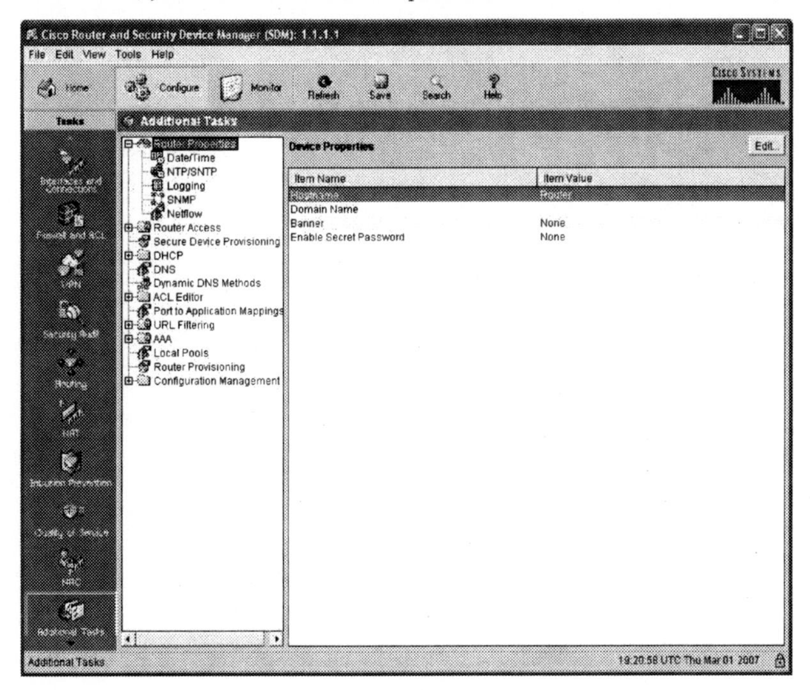

Here, you can set the hostname, MOTD banner, and enable secret password. Last, I clicked the DHCP folder and then the DHCP pool icon. I then clicked Add and created a DHCP pool on my router.

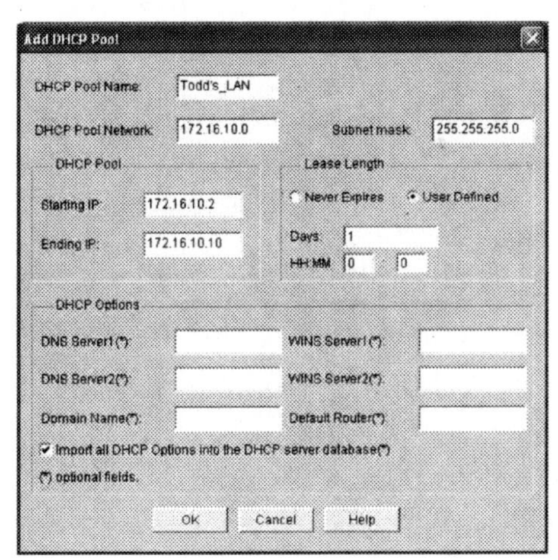

Now, let's take a look at the configuration on the router:

```
Todd#sh run
Building configuration...
[output cut]
hostname Todd
!
ip domain name lammle.com
[output cut]
ip dhcp excluded-address 172.16.10.1
ip dhcp excluded-address 172.16.10.11 172.16.10.254
!
ip dhcp pool Todd's_LAN
   import all
   network 172.16.10.0 255.255.255.0
!
crypto pki trustpoint TP-self-signed-2645776477
 enrollment selfsigned
 subject-name cn=IOS-Self-Signed-Certificate-2645776477
 revocation-check none
 rsakeypair TP-self-signed-2645776477
!
crypto pki certificate chain TP-self-signed-2645776477
 certificate self-signed 01
  3082023E 308201A7 A0030201 02020101 300D0609 2A864886 F70D0101
   04050030 31312F30 2D060355 04031326 494F532D 53656C66 2D536967
   6E65642D 43657274 69666963 6174652D 32363435 37373634 3737301E
   170D3037 30333031 3139313 33335A17 0D323030 31303130 30303030
   305A3031 312F302D 06035504 03132649 4F532D53 656C662D 5369676E
   65642D43 65727469 66696361 74652D32 36343537 37363437 3730819F
   300D0609 2A864886 F70D0101 01050003 818D0030 81890281 8100BB24
   [output cut]
  quit
username todd privilege 15 secret 5 $1$nvgs$QRNCWKJ7rfmtNNkD2xvGq/
[output cut]
!
line con 0
 login local
line aux 0
line vty 0 4
 privilege level 15
 login local
 transport input telnet ssh
```

```
line vty 5 1180
 privilege level 15
 login local
 transport input telnet ssh
!
```

You can see here that the router created the hostname, DHCP pool, and certificate. We went through a lot of setup because we were using HTTPS—it's so much easier and unencumbered with less setup to just use HTTP. But remember, what we used was an ISR default configuration to connect using SDM. I seriously encourage you to get SDM for yourself and start getting familiar with it!

Using the SDM to Manage the Flash Memory

I was going to call this section "Using the SDM to Upgrade, Restore, and Back Up the IOS on Your Router," but the SDM allows management of *all* the files in flash memory (as well as NVRAM), not just the IOS. It can be an easier method of flash file management, but for what it's worth, you won't find it safer to do it this way. It *is* a way to manage your files, though. Let's check it out.

I'm going to connect to an 1841 router (named R3) and upgrade that IOS using the SDM. Let's connect and see what's in flash. Looking at the first screen, we can see that IP is the only feature available and that Firewall, VPN, IPS, and NAC are "X'd" out. Let's fix that!

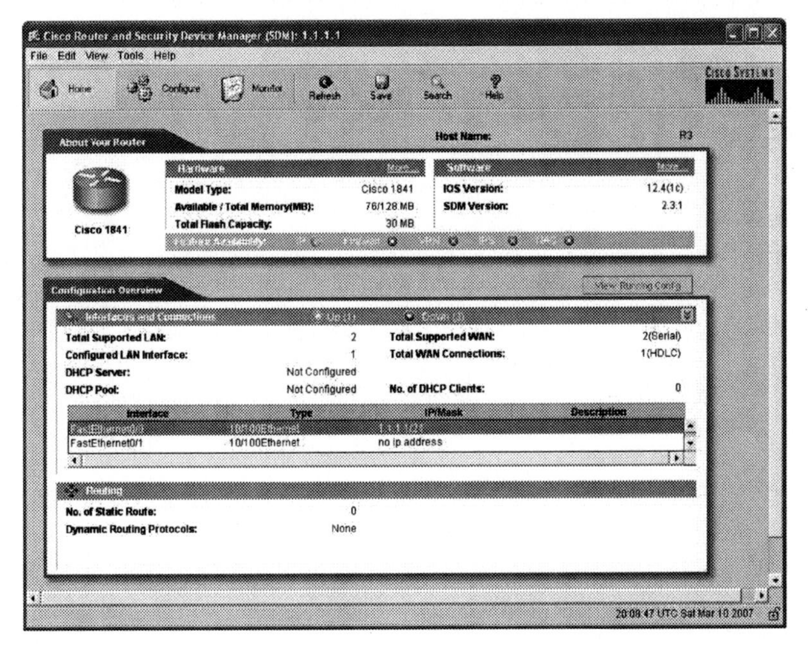

The next screen shows how to open the file management for flash. Chose File ➤ File Management.

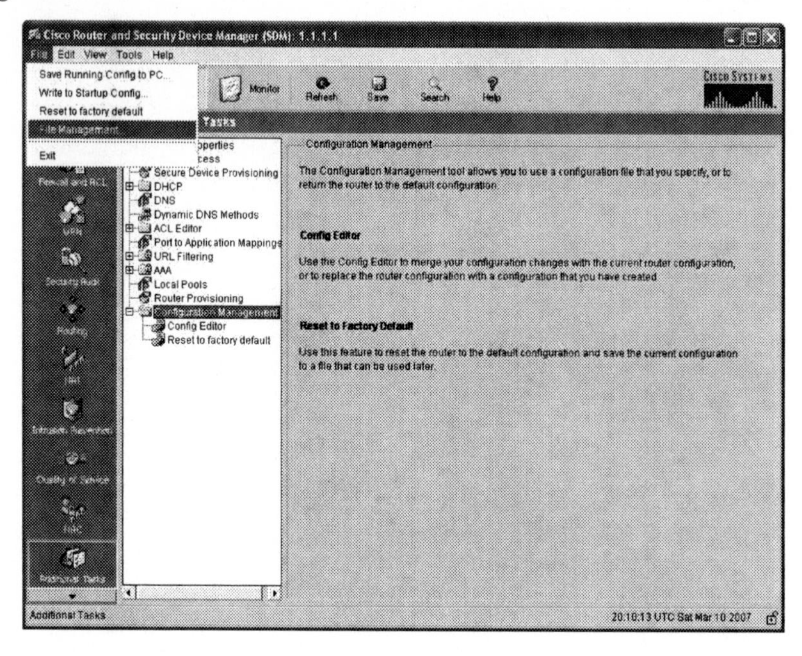

At this point, the screen shows all the files in flash, and we can see that we have the "ipbase" IOS.

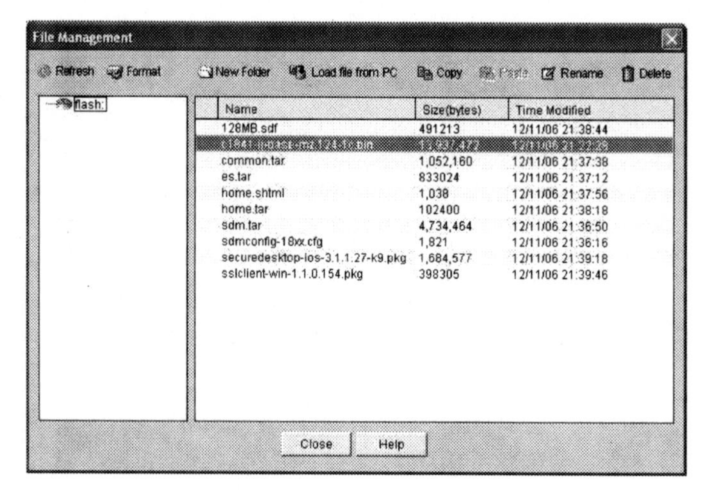

Click Load file from PC on the top of the screen to add a new file. When I tried to load the new IOS, I received the message shown next.

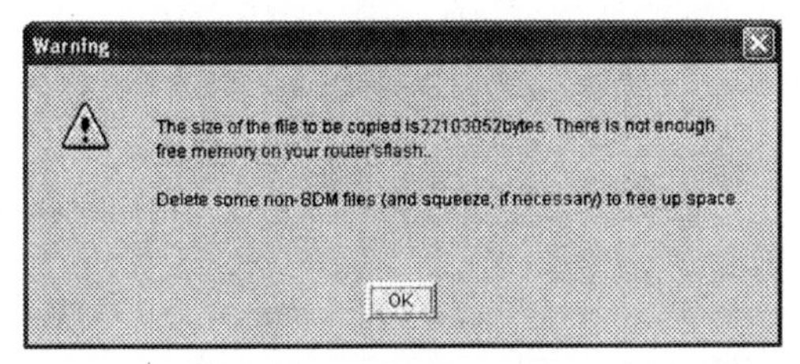

I clicked OK, tried to delete the existing file, and then received this message.

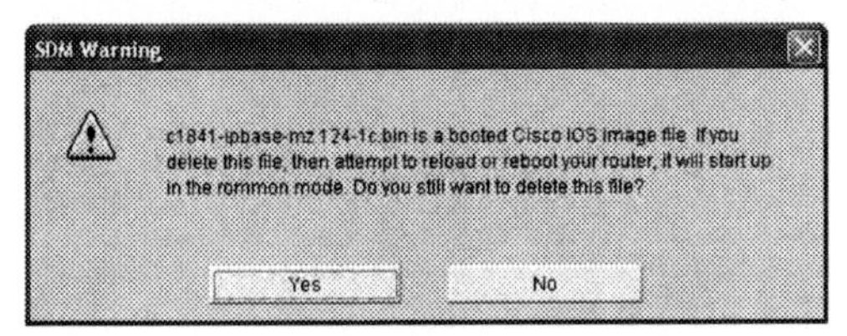

I chose Yes and then looked at the File Management window again to verify that the file was deleted.

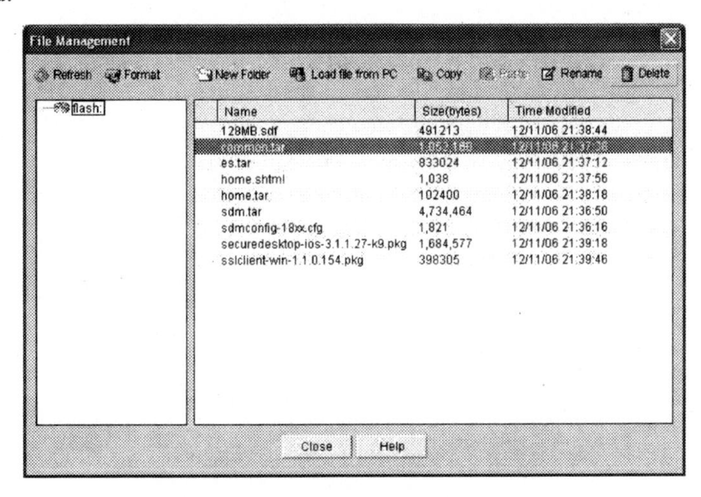

I then chose Load File from PC again, and the file started uploading into flash memory.

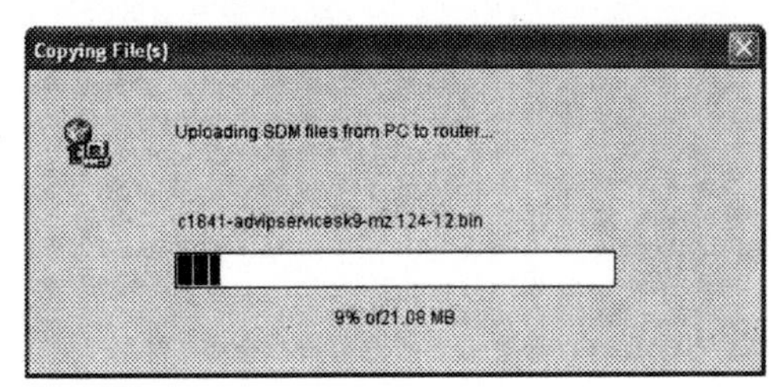

Finally, success!

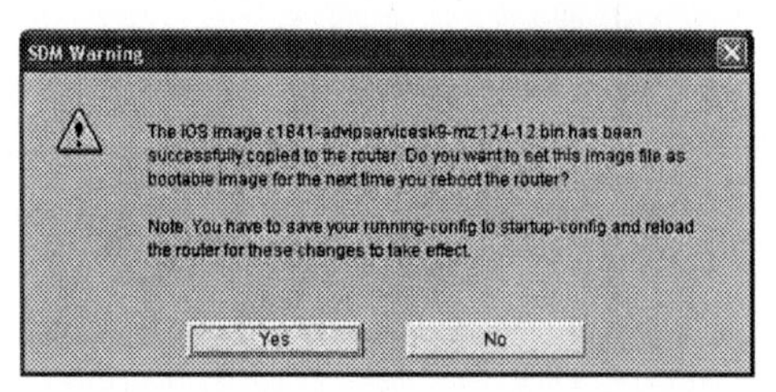

After rebooting, we can see that IP, Firewall, VPN, IPS, and NAC are all available with this new IOS!

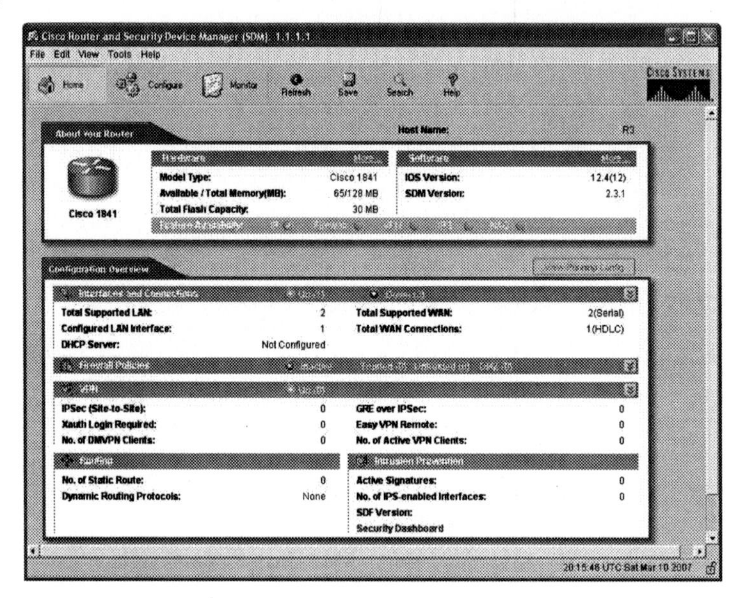

Using the SDM to Back Up, Restore, and Edit the Router's Configuration

Honestly, there really isn't anything special about how the SDM handles configurations on a router. Basically, if you were to telnet to a router, perform a `show run`, and copy this output to a text file on your PC, you've just performed (more or less) what SDM and its configuration management tools can do. But this is still a less confusing way to manage files than doing so through the Cisco IFS.

Why? Well, what's easier about using the SDM rather than the `copy` command we covered earlier in this chapter is that no TFTP host is needed. By using the SDM, you can connect via HTTP or HTTPS to a router and keep all files local on your PC instead of having to configure a TFTP host.

Let's take a quick look at how the SDM can back up and restore your configuration from your host. From the main menu, choose File ➤ Write to Startup Config to back up your configuration to NVRAM.

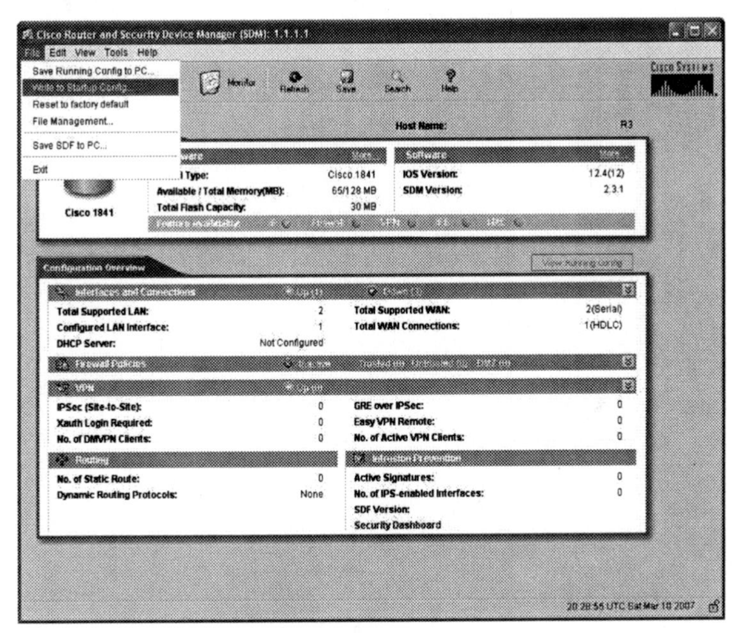

Then choose File ➤ Save Running Config to PC.

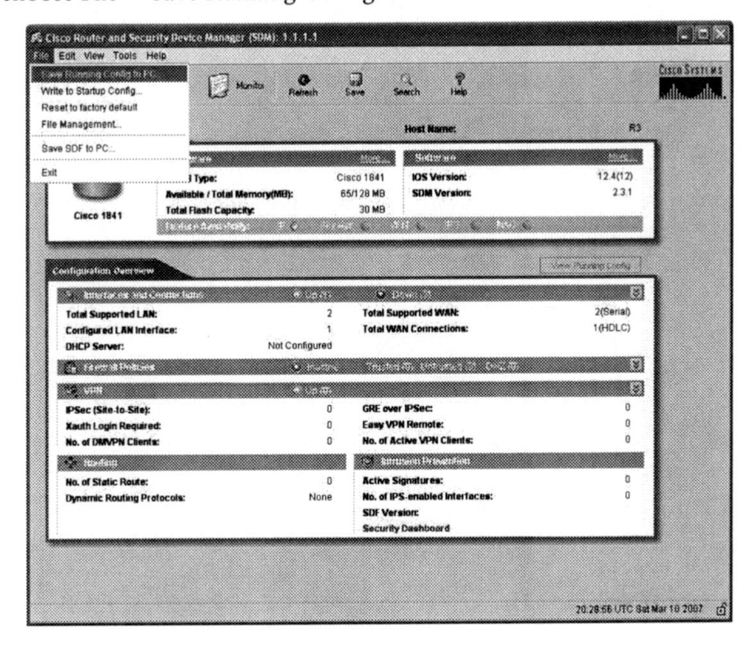

One last option for managing your files is to use the Configuration Management screens under Additional Tasks.

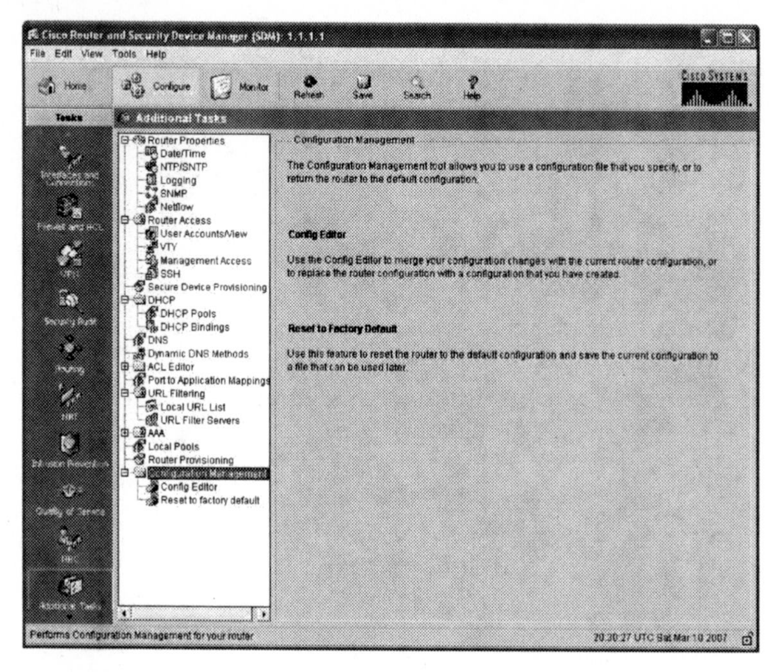

The Config Editor allows you to change the running-config, but before it will let you do that, you have to agree that you can screw up your router's configuration and that this is OK with you!

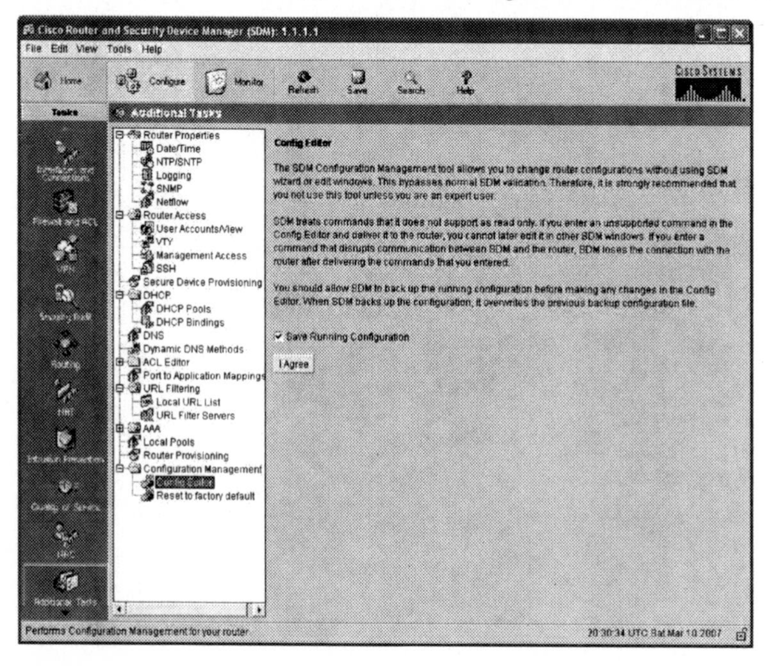

It's best to click the Save Running Configuration button. You can then choose to import the file from RAM or from your PC.

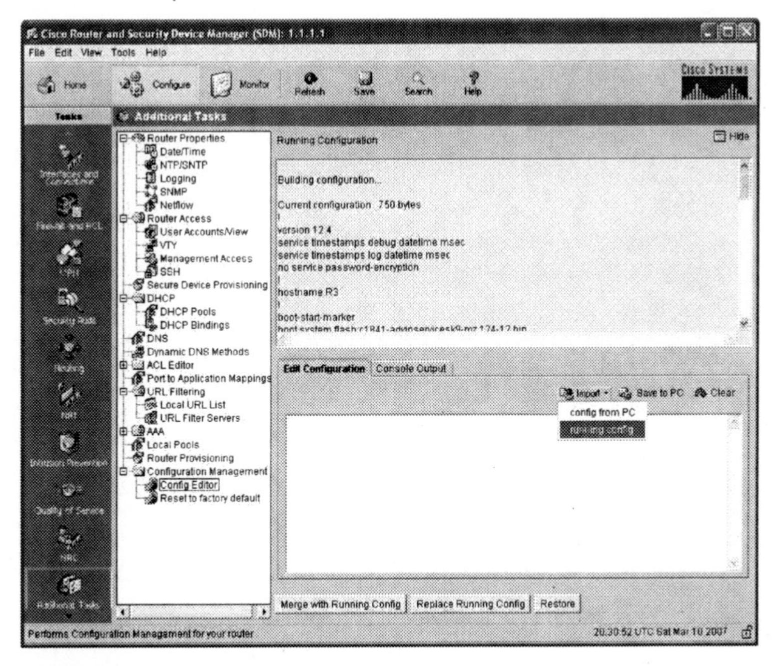

Last, from Configuration Management, you can choose Reset to Factory Default. This will place the HTTPS management back on the router.

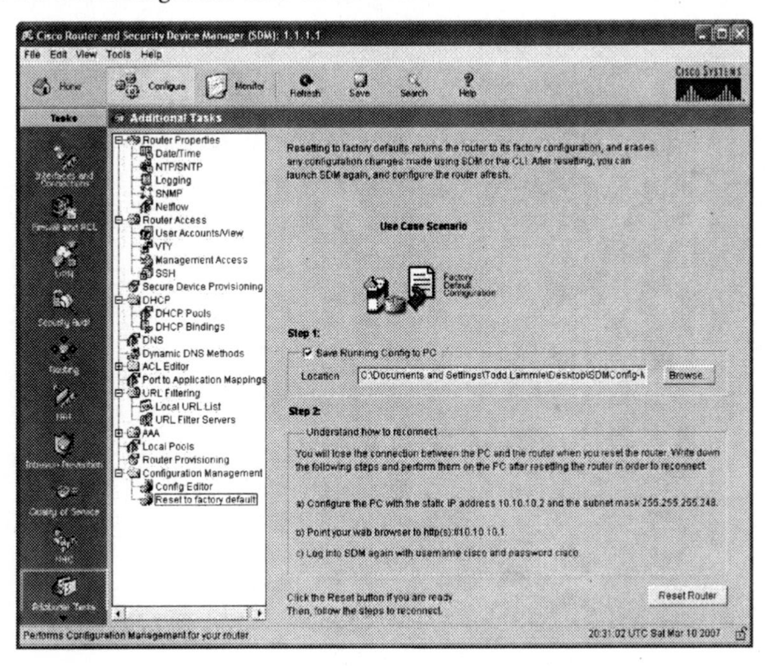

As you can see, there are many different ways to screw up, umm, I mean, change the files in flash, NVRAM, and even RAM.

Configuring LAN and WAN Interfaces and Verifying a Router Using SDM

The first step is to set an IP address on the F0/0 interface of the router I am using (named R3). I used a crossover cable to connect my PC directly to the f0/0 port.

Now since I want to set up the router with security, I have to configure the router back to the factory defaults. I can do this via the CLI just as I showed you back at the beginning of this chapter, but it's actually a whole lot easier to do this using SDM!

Using HTTP, I am able to access the R3 router, go to the Configure page, and choose Additional Tasks. Then, I just clicked Configuration Management and Reset to Factory Default.

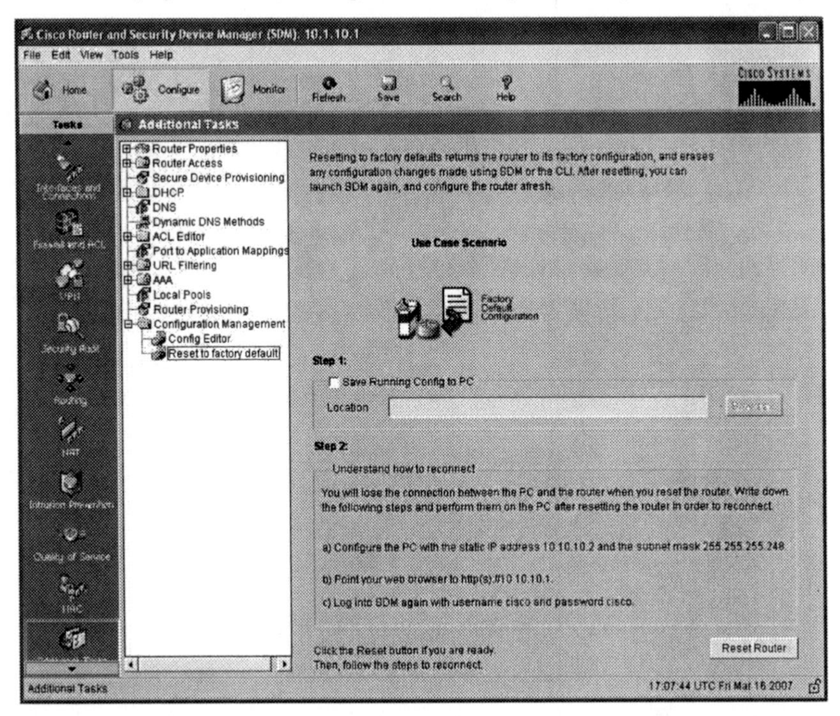

I clicked the Reset Router button in the bottom-right corner and then configured my PC using the directions shown on the screen just shown.

Again, using HTTPS, I connected to SDM using the 10.10.10.1 address that was provided in the directions. SDM had me log in twice with the username *cisco* as well as a password of *cisco*. I then had to accept the certificate from the router, and I'm good to go with a secure connection.

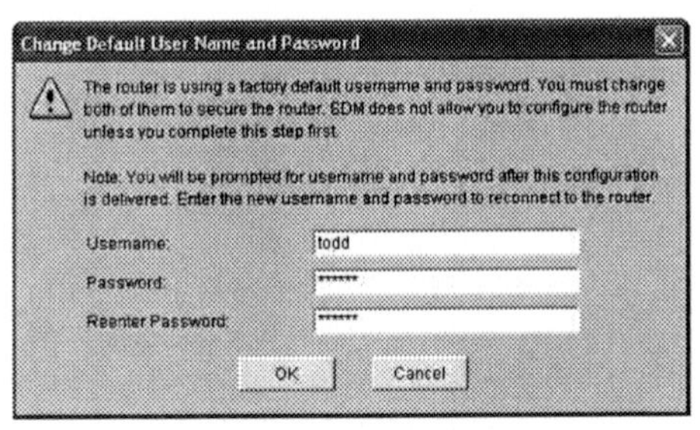

The Create New Connection button took me to the WAN Wizard.

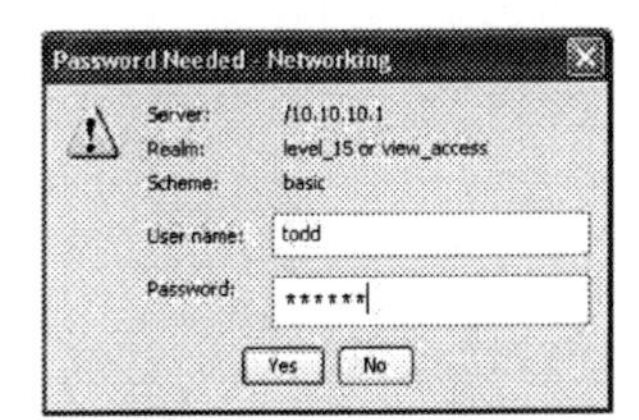

I was then able to choose my interface; then I clicked Next.

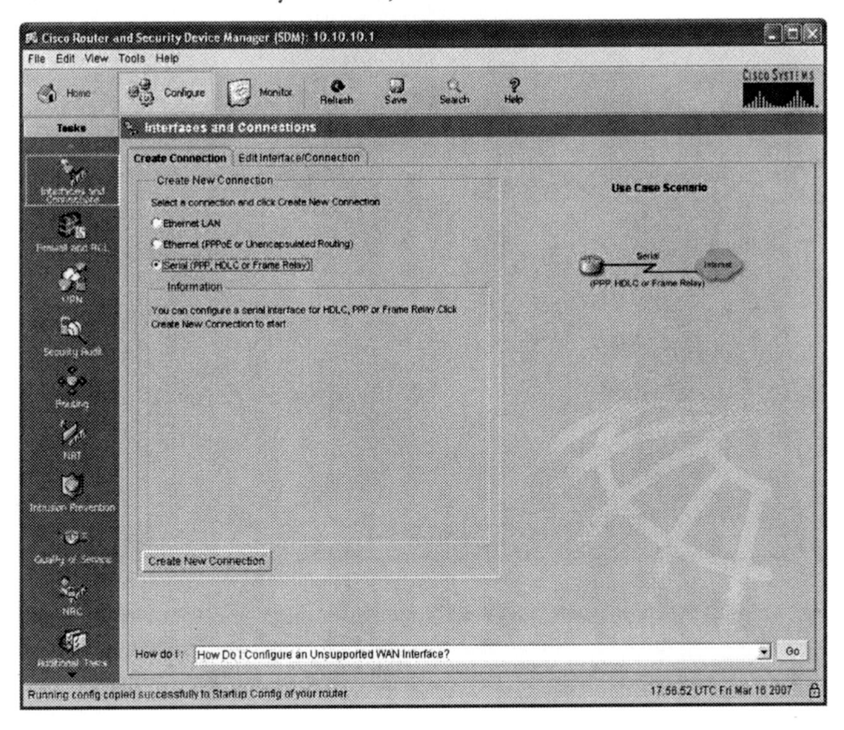

I then chose High-Level Data Link Control and clicked Next.

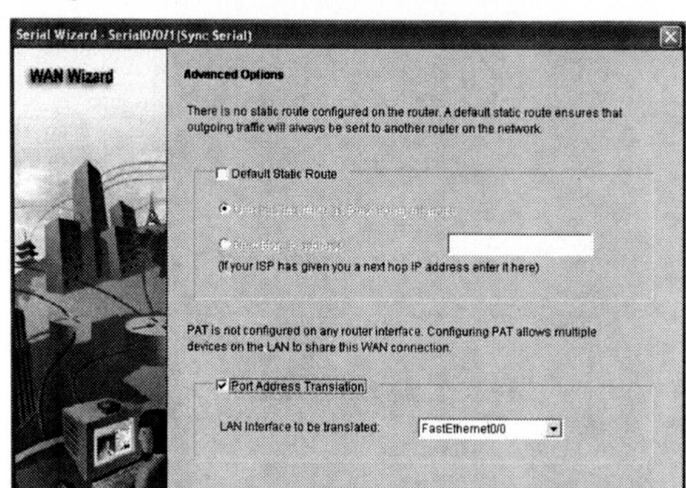

I was then able to add my IP address and mask.

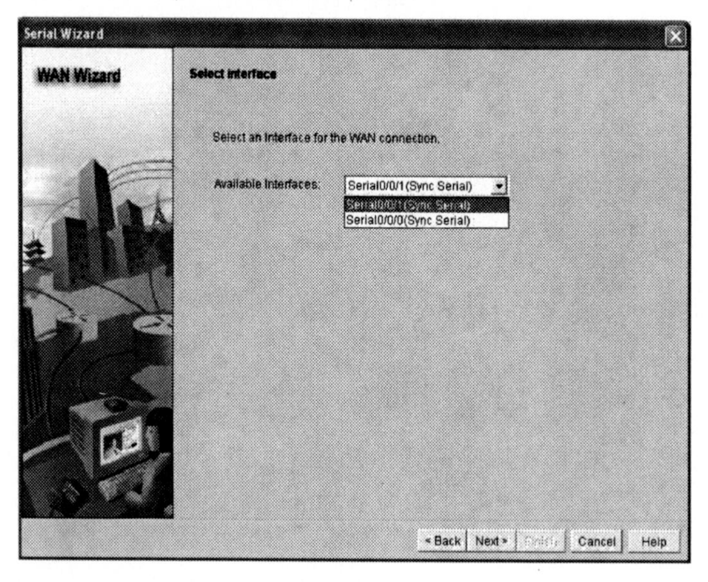

IP Unnumbered is truly an interesting configuration because it lets you set up a network connection without using an IP address. Instead, you "borrow" an IP address from another active interface. This comes in handy if you happen to be a bit short on subnets!

Anyway, the next screen asked whether I wanted to set up static routing and NAT. Again, this is something I'll get into more later, so we're not going to configure it just yet.

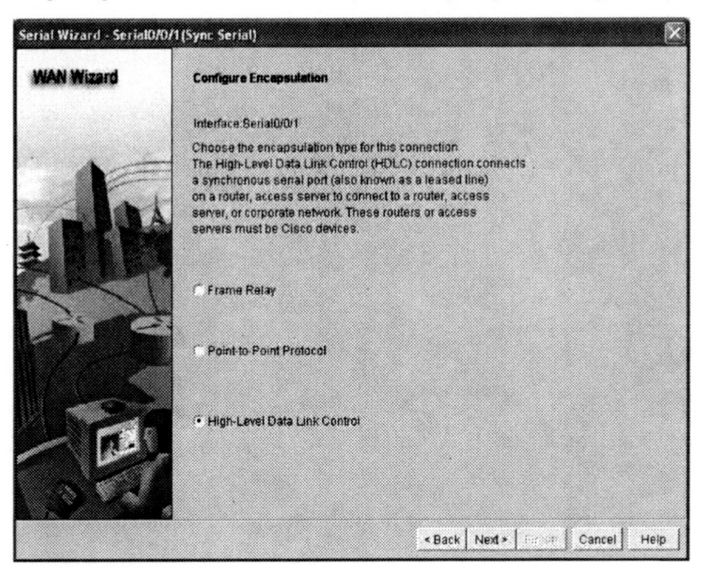

Moving on, I clicked Next and received a summary of my serial 0/0/1 configuration.

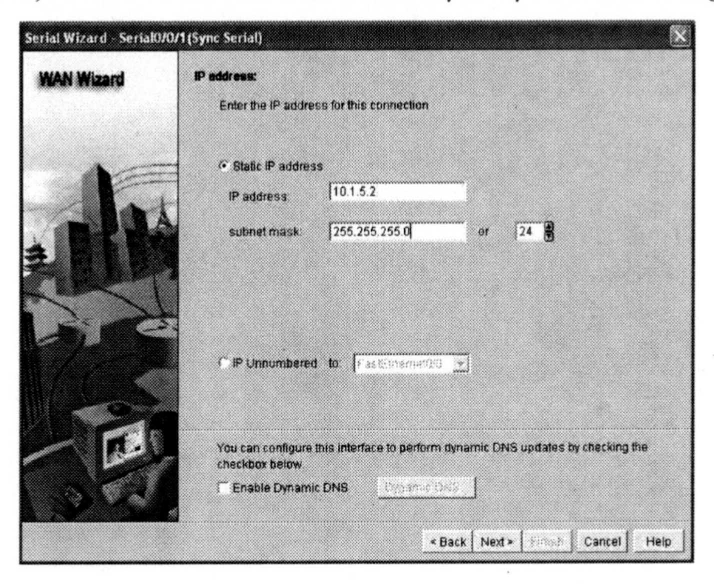

I clicked Finish, and the commands were uploaded to my R3 router. (I'm going to configure both the F0/0 and F0/1 interfaces the same way.)

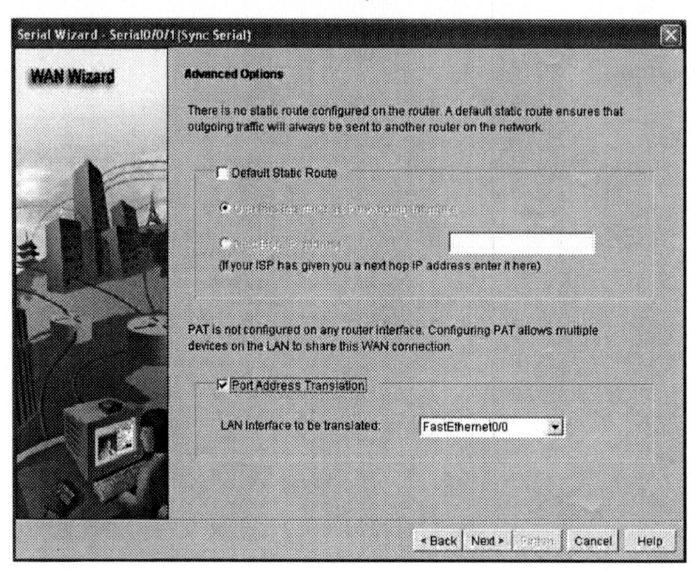

After choosing the FastEthernet 0/1 interface from the same location from where I started to configure the s0/0/1 interface. I chose Create New Connection and was taken to the LAN Wizard.

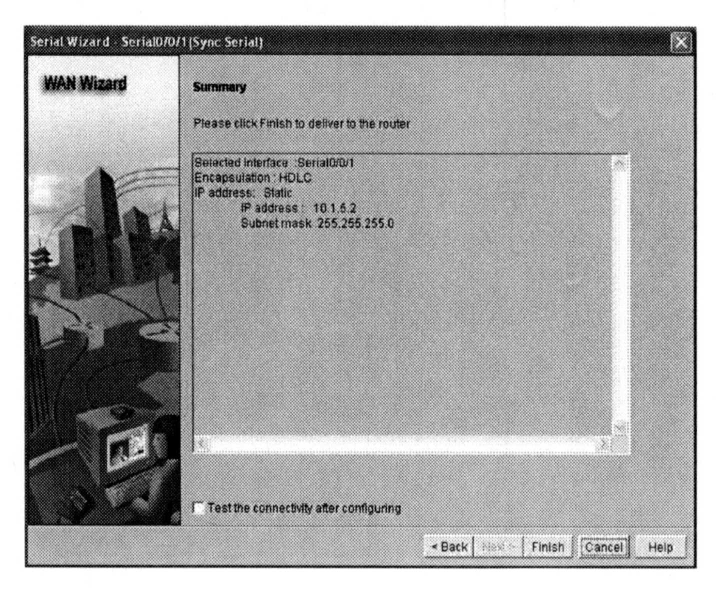

The LAN Wizard allows you to either choose straight routing (which is what we want to do here) or configure 802.1Q trunking. I configured the IP address and mask and then clicked Next.

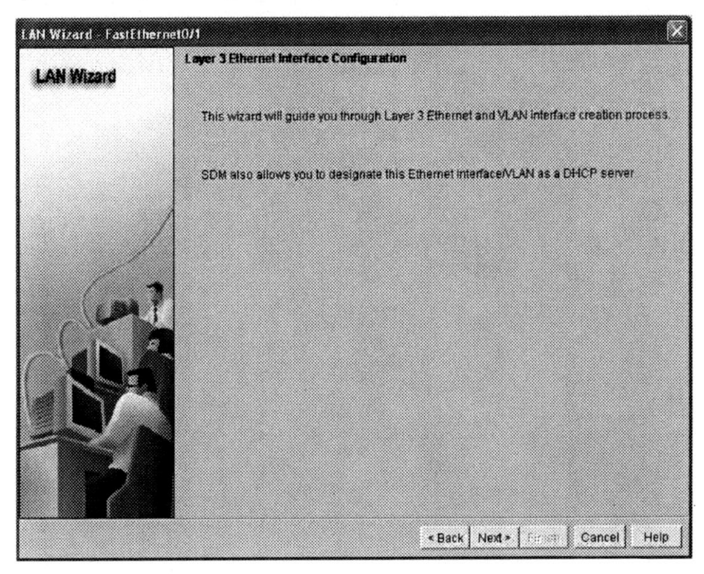

What's cool about the SDM at this point is that it would build a DHCP server for this LAN if I wanted it too. Man, this is easy.

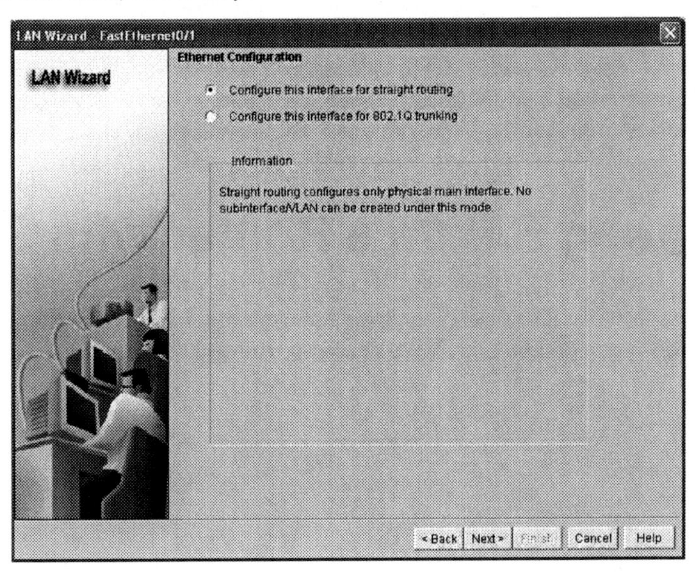

Since I accidentally entered the wrong IP address for F0/1, the only way to change it now is to choose Configure and Edit Interface/Connection in the SDM or use the CLI.

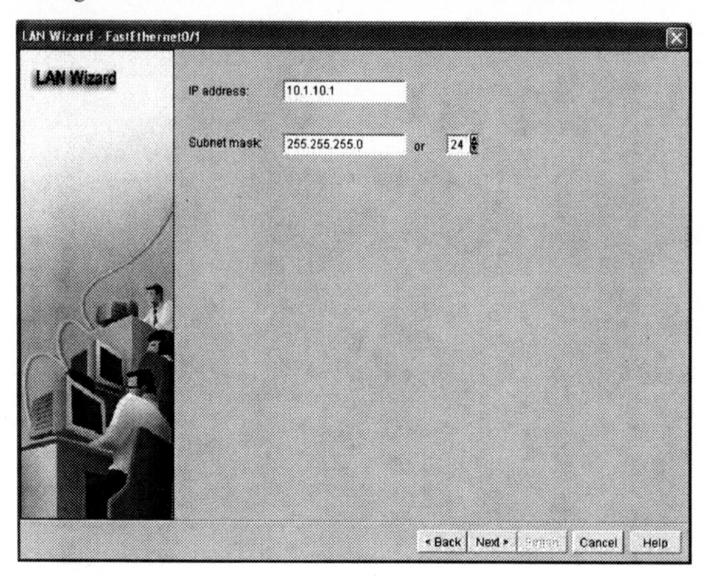

From here, I can double-click the FastEthernet 0/1 interface and change the IP address.

After using the LAN Wizard to set up F0/0, I had to save the configuration and then reconfigure my PC into the right network and reconnect to SDM to verify my configuration.

We're good—R3 is now configured! Even though my console and VTY password get configured automatically when I set up the user todd, I still had to choose Configure and then Additional Tasks and then Router Properties to set the hostname and enable secret password.

Configuring RIP on a Router with SDM

Continuing to use the same R3 router, from the routing screen, I clicked the Edit button to the right of Dynamic Routing. I then was able to configure RIP and the network number and then clicked the interfaces I didn't want RIP to be broadcast out. The interfaces that RIP will broadcast out will be unchecked.

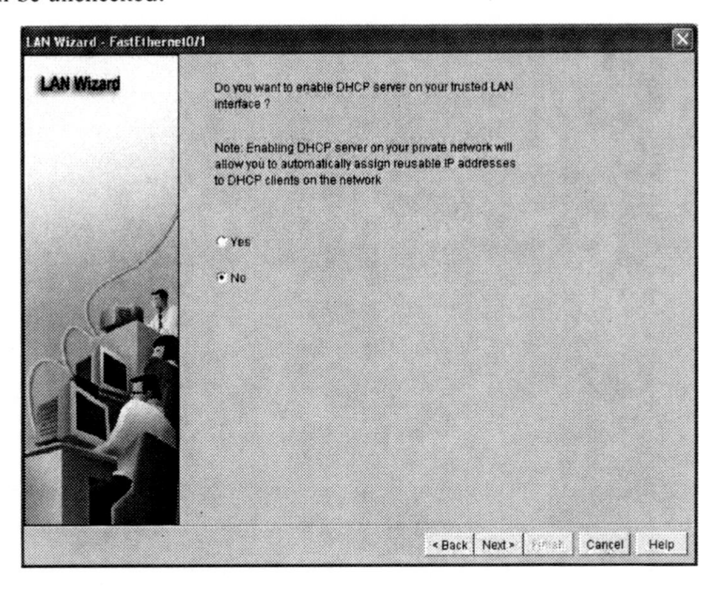

These are called *passive interfaces*, and I'll talk about them more in a minute. No reason to broadcast RIP out an interface where no routers will be.

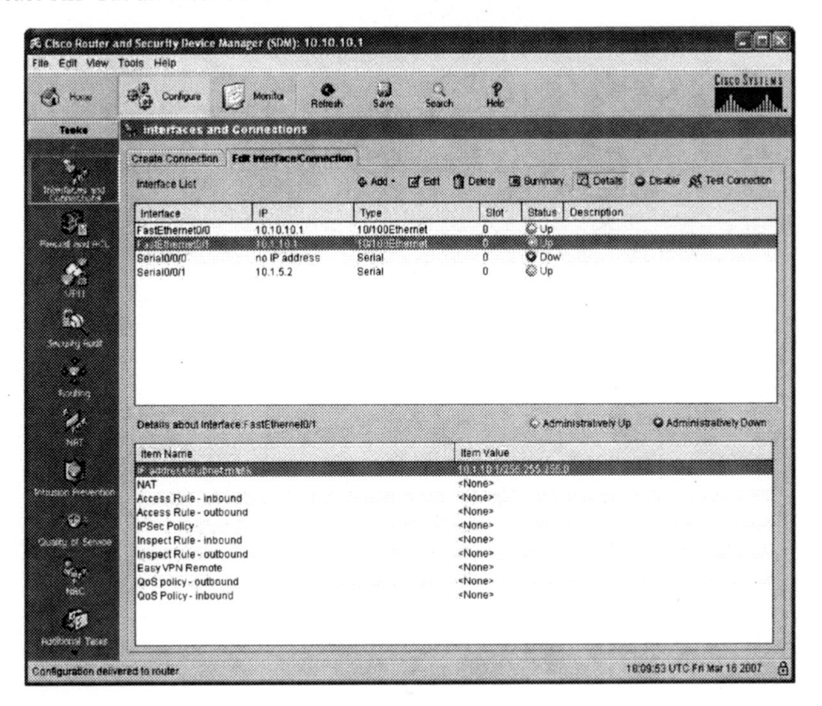

From the SDM screen, you can see that I'm already done configuring RIP on R3.

EIGRP

Let's use the SDM to configure EIGRP just as we've done throughout the previous few sections of this chapter. The configuration process itself won't take long at all—it's the logging in part that I'm going to do first that's going to really eat up some of my time!

Looking at this screen, you can see that we have both static routes and RIPv2 running on the router.

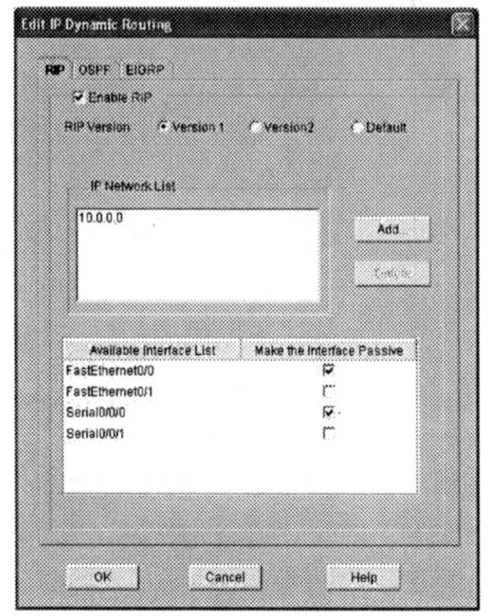

Let's enable EIGRP by adding AS 10 and also choosing to set our passive interfaces—only because it is so easy to do so!

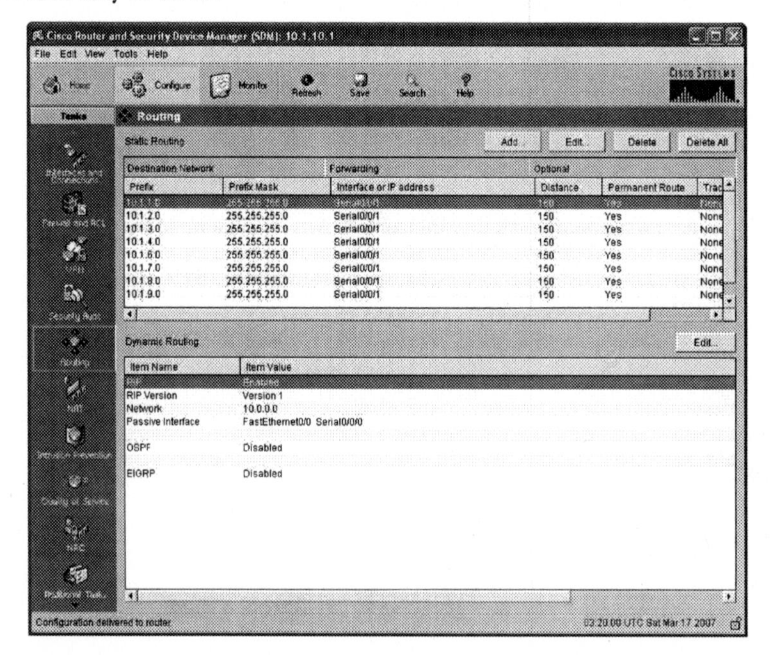

Last, you can see that EIGRP is now running with AS 10.

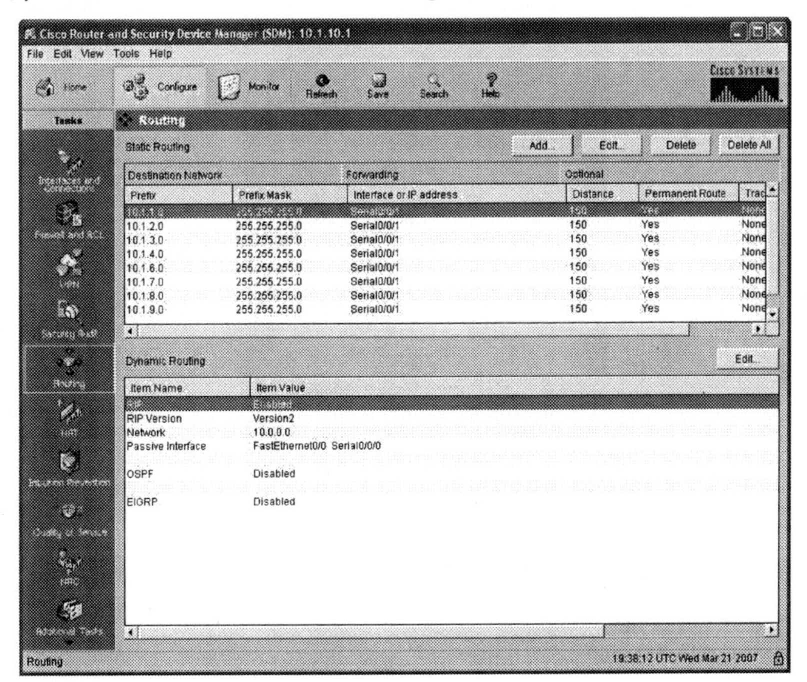

That's it, done.

The configuration seems pretty solid, but remember—only EIGRP routes are going to wind up in the routing table because EIGRP has the lowest AD. So by having RIP running in the background, we're not only using more memory and CPU cycles on the router, but we're sucking up precious bandwidth across every one of our links! This is definitely not good, and it's something you'll really want to keep in mind.

Configuring OSPF with the SDM

For the R3 router, you need to turn off RIP and EIGRP, although RIP won't bother OSPF since OSPF has a lower AD. But you should turn it off anyway.

This screen shows RIP disabled.

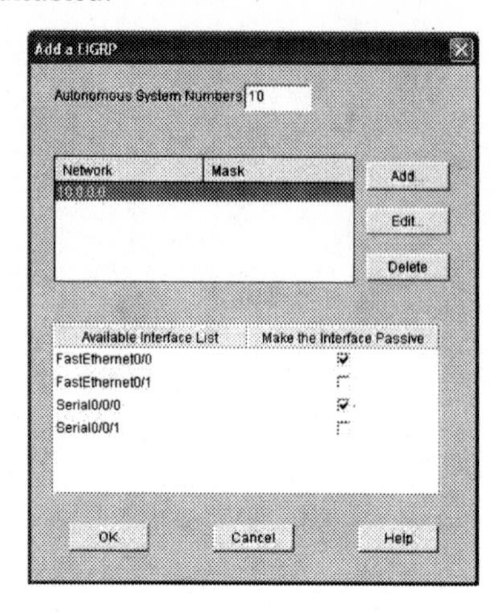

The next Graphic shows EIGRP being disabled. (I just clicked the Delete button.)

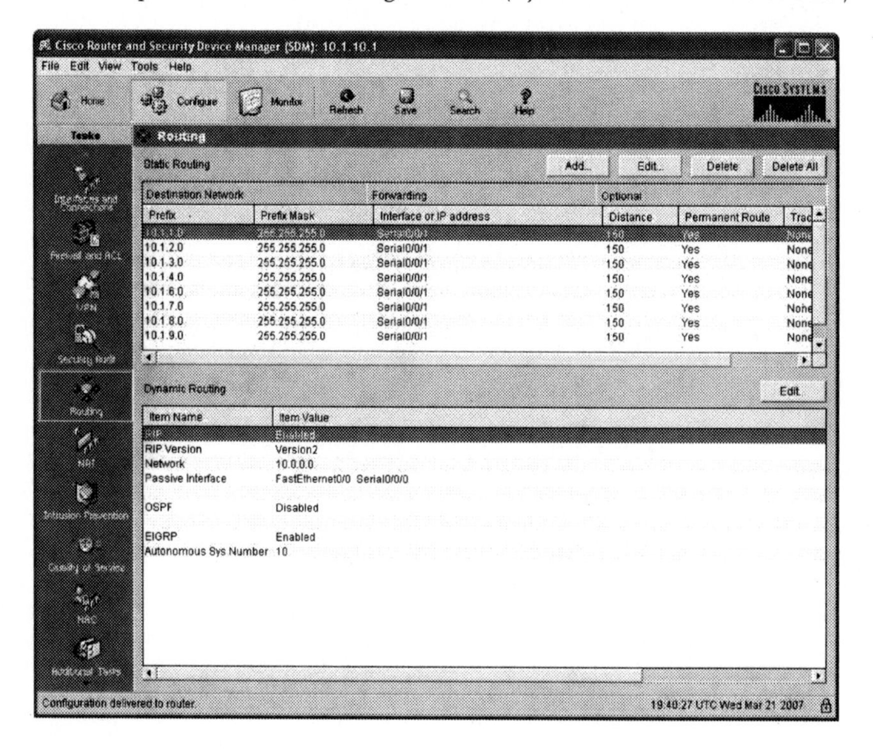

After clicking the OSPF tab, I clicked Add Network and added my OSPF information.

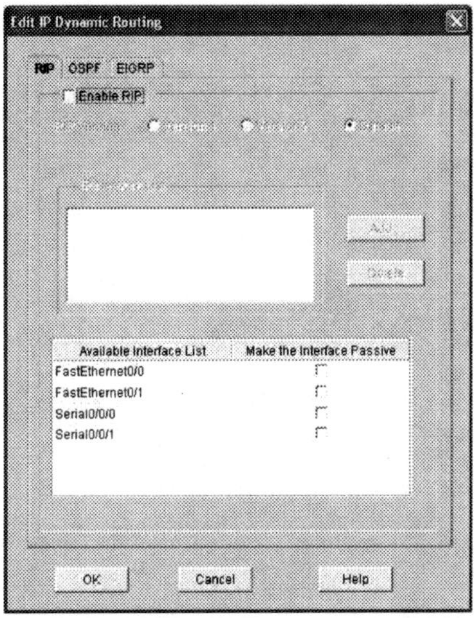

I then clicked OK, chose my passive interfaces, and clicked OK again.

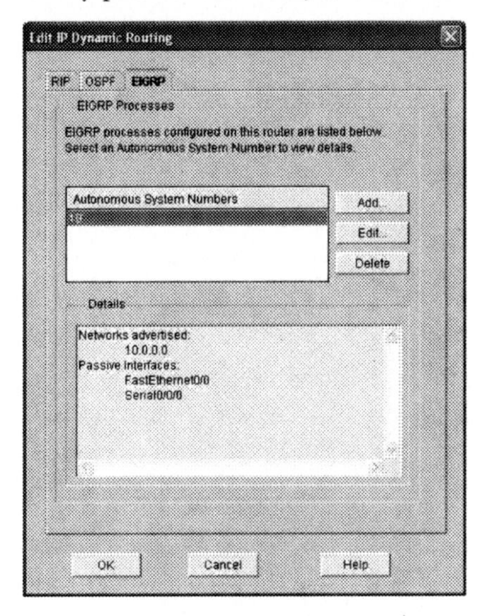

We're good—you can see that we have only OSPF running on the R3 router.

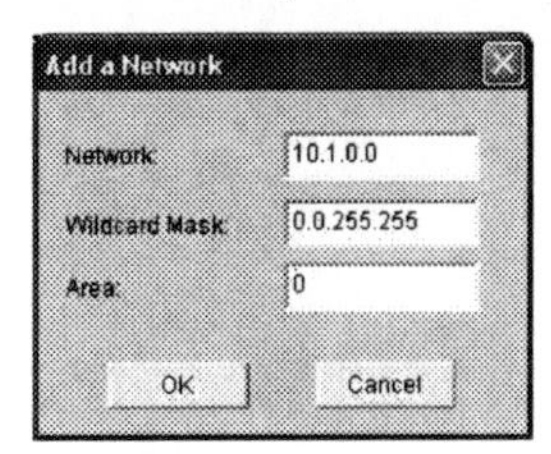

Index

Note to the Reader: Throughout this index **boldfaced** page numbers indicate primary discussions of a topic. *Italicized* page numbers indicate illustrations.

C

D

E

I

J

K

L

M

N

O

P

Q

R

S

T

U

V

W

SERIOUS SKILLS.

The complete CCNA® study solution from Sybex®

CCNA: Cisco® Certified Network Associate Study Guide, Sixth Edition, Exam 640-802

978-0-470-11008-9 • US $49.99

- In-depth coverage of every exam objective, expanded coverage on key topics in the current version of the exam, plus updates that reflect technology developments over the past year
- Enhanced CD contains over an hour of useful video and audio files, as well as the Sybex Test Engine, flashcards, and entire book in PDF format

CCNA: Cisco® Certified Network Associate Study Guide Deluxe, Fifth Edition, Exam 640-802

978-0-470-11009-6 • US $99.99

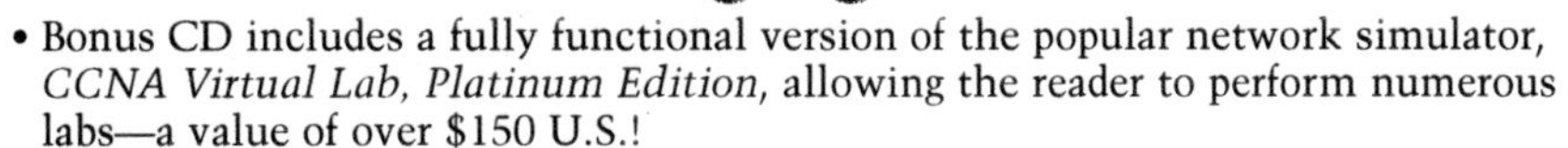

- Bonus CD includes a fully functional version of the popular network simulator, *CCNA Virtual Lab, Platinum Edition*, allowing the reader to perform numerous labs—a value of over $150 U.S.!
- Contains over an hour of video instruction from the author, as well as 30 minutes of audio, in addition to the Sybex Test Engine and flashcards

CCNA: Cisco Certified Network Associate Fast Pass, Third Edition

978-0-470-18571-1 • US $29.99

- Organized by objectives for quick review and reinforcement of key topics
- CD contains two bonus exams, handy flashcard questions, and a searchable PDF of Glossary of Terms

Todd Lammle's CCNA IOS Commands Survival Guide

978-0-470-17560-6 • US $29.99

- Highlights the hundreds of IOS commands needed to pass the exam and that Cisco networking professionals need to know to perform their jobs
- Detailed examples of how to use these commands provide a quick reference guide for CCNA candidates

Visit www.sybex.com

Printed in the United States of America
ED-08-11-11